POTS OF GOLD

David Hendon

POTS OF GOLD

SWIFT PRESS

First published in Great Britain by Swift Press 2025

1 3 5 7 9 8 6 4 2

Copyright © David Hendon, 2025

All rights reserved

The right of David Hendon to be identified as the Author of this Work has been asserted in accordance with the Copyright, Designs and Patents Act 1988

A CIP catalogue record for this book is available from the British Library

We make every effort to make sure our products are safe for the purpose for which they are intended. Our authorised representative in the EU for product safety is Easy Access System Europe, Mustamäe tee 50, 10621 Tallinn, Estonia gpsr.requests@easproject.com

ISBN: 9781800756564
eISBN: 9781800753532

For June and Alan Hendon

CONTENTS

Acknowledgements	ix
Introduction	1
1 Singin' in the Rain	5
2 The Man Comes Around	16
3 Here Comes the Sun	32
4 Clubland	48
5 Like a Hurricane	57
6 The Modern World	74
7 Brothers in Arms	86
8 Back to Black	105
9 This Town Ain't Big Enough for the Both of Us	122
10 My Generation	139
11 All Around the World	158
12 Read All About It	181
13 Common People	196
14 Girls Just Want to Have Fun	216
15 Rocket Man	228
16 For Tomorrow	249
Bibliography	267
Notes	269
Index	272

ACKNOWLEDGEMENTS

Pots of Gold contains interviews I have conducted with the following: Peter Ainsworth, Stuart Bingham, Steve Davis, Ding Junhui, Ken Doherty, Trevor East, Peter Ebdon, Reanne Evans, Clive Everton, Neal Foulds, Barry Hearn, Stephen Hendry, John Higgins, Hazel Irvine, Joe Johnson, Alan McManus, Shaun Murphy, Ronnie O'Sullivan, John Parrott, Ray Reardon, Neil Robertson, Mark Selby, Dennis Taylor, Cliff Thorburn, Judd Trump, John Virgo, Mark Watterson, Mark Williams and Phil Yates.

My thanks to them all for their time and insight. Thanks also to Ivan Hirschowitz, head of media at World Snooker Tour, for his assistance in setting up several of the interviews.

I would like to thank the Swift Team – Diana Broccardo, Mark Richards, Lucie Ewin, Rachel Nobilo, Kathryn Jarvis, Jess Gulliver, Ian Bahrami and Liz Hudson – for their enthusiasm, support and professionalism, and also George Owers, who originally commissioned this book.

'Let's to billiards.'
   Cleopatra to Charmian, Act II, Scene V,
   Antony and Cleopatra by William Shakespeare (1623)

'Pot as many balls as you can.'
   John Virgo, *Big Break* (BBC TV, 1991–2002)

INTRODUCTION

It is September 1987, and I'm eleven years old, standing in front of my new classmates on the first day of 'big' school. We have been asked to introduce ourselves by talking about our favourite hobbies. I have chosen snooker.

1987. The year President Reagan told the USSR's Mikhail Gorbachev to 'tear down this wall' in Berlin. The year Margaret Thatcher's imperious reign as prime minister continued with a third general election triumph. The year of a terrible ferry disaster in Zeebrugge, a deadly hurricane British weather forecasters failed to predict, a shocking fire at King's Cross Station, the debut of *The Simpsons* on Tracey Ullman's comedy show and the stock market crash of Black Monday.

That is the outside world, but my world is snooker. Steve Davis is the reigning world champion. Alex Higgins cannot play in a ranking event for another two months after being banned for assaulting an official the previous year. Stephen Hendry, at eighteen, is a month away from winning his first major title. Ronnie O'Sullivan is an eleven-year-old prospect who regularly beats adults. And here's me, shuffling to the front of the classroom, clutching a few notes and hoping not to stumble over my words.

As I shyly begin to speak, I detect no scorn or even surprise in the eyes of those staring back at me. To be British and interested in snooker in 1987 is nothing out of the ordinary, whatever your age. The game is prominent on all four television channels, enjoying an unlikely honeymoon with the public, having emerged from obscurity to become the biggest sport on TV. Its leading players are household names, regular fixtures on newspaper front pages and in demand for chat shows, entertainment and children's programmes, endorsements and personal appearances.

It's a far cry from the first flowerings of the professional game in the 1920s, when snooker appeared likely to be nothing more than a sideshow, a curiosity with its own distinct subculture and no threat to the established sports, many hewn from public schools. But that was before television, before everything.

This book is a look back at the first hundred years of professional snooker and something of a love letter to a sport which has continued to fascinate me long into adulthood. A British game, exported to the wider world over time, it has survived and adapted to changes in society and its attitudes throughout the past century, retaining a relevance through healthy television audiences and, in its way, revealing something about the national character.

Ten years after that nervous presentation to the class, I began working on the professional circuit, first as junior press officer for the World Professional Billiards and Snooker Association, then as a freelance newspaper and radio journalist, and later as a television commentator for Eurosport and ITV. In almost 30 years spent embedded in the world of professional snooker, I have borne witness to memorable moments, controversies and farcical interludes and got to know many of the biggest names in the sport, a large number of whom kindly gave me their time for this book. *Pots of Gold* is not a Wikipedia-style recitation of who won what and when. I wanted those who were there to tell their personal stories and share their reflections on snooker over the past century.

'The games of a people reveal a great deal about them,' said the Canadian philosopher Marshall McLuhan. For decades, snooker has been full of apparently ordinary characters with extraordinary

INTRODUCTION

stories to tell. It has been a privilege listening to them and to now bring their tales to a wider audience.

Four decades on from that September day in 1987, I feel I am still standing before the class.

So, let me tell you about snooker.

1

SINGIN' IN THE RAIN

For Dennis Taylor, it was a glimpse of colour in a black-and-white world.

Three decades before he potted the most famous ball in snooker history, Taylor was a boy growing up in the 1950s, a time of hardship and struggle as Britain rebuilt after the war. By chance one afternoon as he walked to his home in Coalisland, Northern Ireland, he saw something that changed his life for ever.

'I was eight or nine,' he says. 'There was a club next to the police station. The door happened to be open one day. I saw a snooker table for the first time, and it fascinated me, the colours.'

They have fascinated multitudes ever since. In 1985, 18.5 million people were tuned to BBC2 to watch Taylor pot the last black of the World Championship final and beat Steve Davis 18–17 a few minutes after midnight. By then, snooker had taken a grip on the national consciousness. A sport that had seemed to come from nowhere had become part of the country's collective bloodstream.

Yet it had been a long journey, full of false starts and wayward turns, a very British story of success and failure infused with disputed provenance, organisational chaos, egos, class, eccentricity and ultimate triumph against the odds. A century on from its establishment as a professional sport, it is now played all around the world, while its major competitions draw global audiences in the hundreds of millions.

How did this happen?

• • •

As Samuel Johnson put it, 'When two Englishmen meet, their first talk is of the weather.' For a sport that would become so ingrained in the British national psyche, it is fitting we have the rain to thank for snooker coming into being.

In 1875, the Devonshire Regiment was stationed in Jubbulpore (known today as Jabalpur), an Indian city in the state of Madhya Pradesh. The British Raj had been established 17 years earlier, following a rebellion against the East India Company, the trading group that had taken power across much of the country. Control was transferred to the Crown, and Queen Victoria became the Empress of India.

It was the rainy season, and officers gravitated towards the billiard table in the mess. Billiards has become a catch-all term for cue sports, but at this time English billiards was a well-known game, with a heritage stretching back centuries. Played with three balls, scoring was through a variety of pots and cannons.

There was a romantic theory espoused for a while that it was invented by William Kew, a London pawnbroker, who was said to enjoy taking down the three gold balls that identified his profession and pushing them around his yard with a stick – hence Bill-yard. His surname could explain the name of the equipment used to strike the balls. Clive Everton, the highly respected snooker and billiards journalist and commentator, took a more pragmatic view in his 2012 book *A History of Billiards*. 'This picturesque version of the origins of billiards must be discarded in favour of a series of more fragmentary clues,' he wrote. Everton contended that the word 'billiards' descends from the Latin and old French words for 'ball' – *billa* and *bille* respectively – and that the game has its roots in croquet, a sport played on lawns, where coloured balls are manoeuvred through hoops with a mallet. Early versions of billiards saw players use a mace – a cue with a flat end rather than a tip – to strike the balls.

Cue sports have a rich history. Louis XI of France had a billiard table in the fifteenth century. Mary, Queen of Scots was a keen player and complained that her captors had kept her from her table. They responded by tearing off its cloth and wrapping her beheaded corpse in it following her execution in 1587. In Act II, Scene V of Shakespeare's *Antony and Cleopatra*, the latter tells her servant, Charmian, 'Let's to billiards.'

The game of billiards began largely as a pursuit for the gentry but would permeate wider society. According to Everton, 'At the turn of the eighteenth century, billiards was still largely the pursuit of the French, English and indeed Americans. The game had almost certainly been exported in the 1600s by the early English colonists – the nobility and well to do – but by 1800 there were enough public tables in French cafés, English ale houses and everywhere in America from private houses to the toughest frontier outposts to justify the claim that it was now a game for all classes.'[1]

Billiards remains a highly skilful game, but in time the best players became too good and a degree of dramatic tension was lost from public matches. The cradle cannon, in which two balls are positioned close to a corner pocket, made scoring easy for the most talented exponents and led to Tom Reece making a break of 499,135 over the course of three weeks in 1907 against Joe Chapman, who did not have a single shot throughout the entire time.

Although cradle cannons were banned a few months later, Reece's marathon break underlined the repetitive nature of billiards at the top level and how this threatened the game's capacity to provide entertainment for the public. Later, billiards came to be regarded as so arcane that it was one of the niche British touchstones the Village Green Preservation Society sought to save in The Kinks' eponymous record of 1968.

In between the Reece break and the Ray Davies ditty, billiards had been thoroughly overtaken by the game fashioned while the Jubbulpore rain hammered on the windows of the officers' mess. A general boredom with billiards had led to the military personnel experimenting with other established games, with interest added by introducing wagering. Pyramids involved 15 reds set up initially in a triangular frame. Each time a player potted a red, his opponent had to pay the pre-agreed stake money for each ball. Life pool saw players designated with a cue ball and an object ball, the latter of which became the next player's cue ball. For instance, player A would use the white ball to try and pot the yellow. The yellow would be player B's cue ball, and he would try to pot the pink. Player C had pink as cue ball and green as object ball, and so on. The object of the game was to pot your own object ball three times. Every time it was potted, the player whose cue ball it was would lose a 'life', until only one player remained. Money changed hands as each ball was potted. Players could buy back in with an extra life in exchange for cash. At the end, the remaining player scooped all the money. Black pool added a black ball to life pool, meaning an additional gambling element because there was another ball to be potted after the initial object ball had been sunk.

The commonly accepted theory is that Neville Chamberlain, just nineteen, a second lieutenant with the Devonshires, mashed the various elements of pyramids and life pool together to forge a new game with scope for a greater variety of bets among the soldiers. He kept the 15 reds of pyramids, added the yellow, green and pink of life pool and the black of black pool. Brown and blue would be added later.

In conversation with a visiting subaltern from the Royal Military Academy in Woolwich, Chamberlain learned that a first-year cadet at the institution was known as a 'snooker', essentially implying that within the rigid hierarchy of the army, they were at the bottom of the pile. So it was that the name of a game that would become a multimillion-pound global sport began as an insult.

The derivation of the word 'snooker' is disputed. The term 'cocking a snook' would logically describe a disdainful relationship between the officer class and young cadets, and this may have been adapted to form the word. Another theory is that 'snooker' was derived from the original name for a cadet, 'neux' (from the French term *les neux*). There was also an 1850s music-hall act called Hooker and Snooker, popular in London, which may have helped the word gain common currency.

Chamberlain was 82 when he wrote to *The Field* magazine in 1938 to claim responsibility for snooker's birth, following speculation that it had actually been invented at the academy in Woolwich and that Lord Kitchener – the veteran military general whose face adorned posters bearing the slogan 'Your Country Needs You' at the outbreak of the First World War – was responsible for handwriting the rules. Chamberlain wrote:

> One day it occurred to me that the game of black pool, which we usually played, would be improved if we put down another coloured ball in addition to the black one. This proved a success and, by degrees, the other coloured balls of higher value followed suit. The term 'snooker' was a new one to me, but I soon had the opportunity of exploiting it when one of our party failed to hole a coloured ball which was close to a corner pocket. I called out to him, 'Why, you're a regular snooker!' I had to explain to the company the definition of the word and to soothe the feelings of the culprit I added that we all were, so to speak, snookers at the game so it would be very

appropriate to call it snooker. The suggestion was adopted with enthusiasm.²

The following year, the famous novelist and essayist Compton Mackenzie wrote an article for *Billiard Player* magazine titled 'Origins of a Great Game', which promised to be 'For the first time, the fully authenticated story of the origin of snooker.' Mackenzie supported Chamberlain's claim with further evidence from other distinguished military figures who served in India which he described as 'incontrovertible'.

Chamberlain left the Devonshires in 1878 to join Central India Horse, a cavalry regiment, and moved to the hill station at Ootacamund, in western India. Its club, known as the Ooty, was where the rules of snooker were formalised. They still hang on the wall of the billiard room to this day.

In 1903, the *Madras Weekly Mail* reported on the grip snooker had taken on members of the army:

> There was a time in Waltair when men played cards till the sun was high in the heavens and their thoughtful wives sent up their solar topees for them. Now we cannot get a game of bridge at all. There has only been one game this month so far and no prospect of better things. Snooker is the rage. If you go into the Club at 8am, you will find two or three men playing and every evening there is one table of snookers going on and often two.

Chamberlain was not related to the British prime minister of the same name but enjoyed a successful military career, becoming a colonel in 1894 and being knighted in 1903, having served as inspector-general for the Royal Irish Constabulary. He left the RIC in 1916, after his warnings about an Irish uprising were ignored.

That he left it until his 80s, with snooker by then established as a professional sport, before claiming the credit for its invention have led some to question the accepted narrative. Peter Ainsworth, a renowned billiards and snooker historian, is of the belief that Chamberlain should be credited with developing snooker but that 'There are two major problems with Chamberlain's description of the birth and development of the game of "snooker". Firstly, there is no single cue ball used, with each player using one of the balls on the table as his own, and secondly, there is no reference to a pack of red balls. It may be assumed that the reds were added later, had not Chamberlain said that the balls added were of a "higher value" and, significantly, the red ball was already established in the sequence, being the very first colour to be used in the standard sequence.'

Ainsworth's argument is that two distinct games were developed, before one was finally established, probably at the Ooty Club. It is not clear whether sole credit for that should go to Chamberlain, but there is no clear evidence that anyone else played a greater role in the birth of the game.

'His description of "snooker" as he invented it at Jubbulpore is not snooker. It bears no relationship to it,' Ainsworth says. 'He was very keen to be associated with the name when he was in India. There are several instances where he's entering gymkhanas with animals called Snooker. In December 1882, he entered the Ooty gymkhana with a bullock doing a chariot race, and he called the bullock Jolly Snookers.'

In 1885, Chamberlain met with S. W. Stanley, the billiards coach to the maharajah of Cooch Behar, in Calcutta. 'He was introduced as the inventor of snooker,' Ainsworth says. 'He was associated with it until he left India. He had other things to think of. He went off to South Africa, and then got appointed as inspector-general of the Royal Irish Constabulary in Dublin. He was there 16 years, coinciding with the Easter Rising. He was busy.'

Meanwhile, Stanley returned to Britain in 1887, where Ainsworth believes he passed on Chamberlain's rules of snooker to the billiard-table manufacturers Burroughes & Watts, who published them in 1889. John Roberts Jr, a leading billiards player of the time, has also been widely credited with exporting the new game to the UK.

Whoever was responsible, when the game first reached Britain, it was widely known as 'snooker pool'. Until the rules were formally understood and accepted, variations of snooker pool abounded, including at the Garrick Club in London. One of the more idiosyncratic conventions of 'Savile and Garrick snooker' stated: 'In the event of the yellow ball being involved in a foul stroke, it is custom for the watchers to cry out the word "bollocks".'[3]

The balls in these early days were made from ivory. In the late nineteenth century, 12,000 elephants were killed each year for their tusks, in order to meet demand in the UK. Thankfully, in time chemical compounds were developed so that balls could be manufactured more humanely. They played an unwitting historic role in 1902, when Harry Jackson stole a set of billiard balls during a burglary in London and became the first person in Britain to be sentenced using new fingerprint evidence.

Meanwhile, snooker, having made its way to British shores, was not immediately adopted by billiard halls. According to Everton, 'Not every hall or every club could afford a set of 22 balls though it was not long before the manufacturers appreciated snooker's superior commercial possibilities.'[4]

Although Chamberlain's version of how snooker came to be may have been neatened up by the time he wrote to *The Field*, it seems largely believable as there is no trace of the melded-together versions of life pool and pyramids before 1875.

'There was a lot of speculation about who had invented it,' Ainsworth says. 'Lots of people were asking the question, and no one was answering, until a series of correspondences came up in *The Field* magazine, which prompted him to come forward. He'd been retired in Ascot prior to that, so why he decided to respond at that time, I don't know. I expect he was encouraged by some of his friends, who were aware of his claim. The Mackenzie connection closed the discussion, and probably correctly. Chamberlain has an excellent claim to have invented snooker.'

So this new game was born, ostensibly to give British Army officers something to do while it rained. Gambling made it interesting, but it was also equal parts fun and challenging, a different game entirely to billiards, with more variation. It remained in its earliest days the province of the upper classes.

'It was played in the officers' messes. That was the only place there was a billiard table,' says Ainsworth. 'It was officer classes, therefore, so that was the class who originally knew it and played it. When it came to England, it was through army servicemen's clubs, so it's that level of people. It wasn't working people, it was officers, gentlemen, high-ranking types like politicians. When Burroughes & Watts put the rules together in 1889 for jolly snookers – that was the name, the same as Chamberlain's bullock – they promoted it as rules for country-house parties. That was the level it was aimed at.'

Indeed, in 1901, *The Field* reported:

> Very few country houses of any size are now without a billiard table. As a consequence, the standard of play all round – especially in the amateur ranks – has become much higher . . .

The Billiards Association, which has been doing good work of late, has given us the rules for billiards, pool, pyramids and snooker pool.

As if to prove that it was a sport for rarefied society, the Dundee *Evening Telegraph* reported in 1902 that 'Two billiard tables and all the fittings for the games of pool, pyramids and snooker pool were purchased by the Shah [of Iran] when he was in London.'

By the following year, 1903, snooker had gained sufficient traction that it had won over Charles Vidal Diehl, winner of a billiards tournament for journalists, who wrote a column in the Liverpool *Evening Express*, stating:

> The game is much superior to pyramids, and in restarting the championship of the potting game among professionals the Billiard Association from my mere personal point of view as to what I should like to have seen played, might very well have gone one step further and made the championship one of the game of snooker.

The rules of snooker had been codified by the Billiards Association in 1901. The concept of break-building developed as the game became more competitive. In 1910, Tom Aitken, Cecil Harverson and Phil Morris made centuries. There were no tournaments until 1916, when the English Amateur Championship was formed.

In 1919, the rules were revised. Drawn frames would from now on be decided by a respotted black. The free ball was introduced, in which a player could nominate a different ball if snookered after a foul. An in-off foul – the cue ball finding a pocket – was worth only one point, however. It would not result in a four-point penalty for several more years.

Snooker was gaining a profile through its inclusion at the end of billiards matches, and it was therefore inevitable that ordinary working people would want to try it. 'It started to become popular at clubs and institutes,' says Ainsworth. 'It was always part of the entertainment with billiards that you'd have a game of pyramids after the main event. Snooker just slotted in and filled that place, as an exhibition of something else.'

Gradually, snooker's popularity led to an increase in the number of places where it could be played. 'The temperance movement was key in starting the clubs around the time of the General Strike in 1926,' says John Virgo, a player and later a popular television commentator. In time, the game would become associated with trades such as mining and steelworking, with organised leagues – a way for men to enjoy their leisure time together after long days at work.

However, between the wars snooker was still very much in the shadow of billiards. What it needed was innovators who could recognise and develop its potential: someone good enough at the game to showcase it, and someone savvy and proactive enough to promote it.

In fact, these two pioneers turned out to be the same man.

2

THE MAN COMES AROUND

John Bright Street in Birmingham is located in the heart of the city centre, a short walk from New Street railway station. Among its attractions are the Alexandra Theatre, the Victoria pub and the Grosvenor casino. At the far end is a craft-ale bar and apartment complex, the exact spot where, a century ago, the first professional snooker champion was crowned.

Without Joe Davis, this moment may have arrived much later than the roaring twenties – or not at all. The foremost player of the first half of the twentieth century, Davis possessed a formidable zeal for promotion, of both himself and snooker, kicking down doors to achieve recognition for a game that was still widely regarded as inferior to billiards. Yet he was also fiercely protective of his own reputation, and his iron grip on the sport, on and off the table, ultimately led to its decline and near extinction.

Davis was born in 1901 in Whitwell, a mining village near Chesterfield, in Derbyshire, to Fred and Elizabeth. Fred chose to end his years at the colliery and move into the pub trade, purchasing the Travellers' Rest and, later, the Queens Hotel in Whittington Moor, a bigger establishment, which boasted a full-size billiard table. The eleven-year-old Davis quickly became fascinated by both billiards and the still new sport of snooker, his natural childhood shortness negated to a degree by the fact that the previous owner had lowered the table below floor level to afford spectators a better view of matches, so young Joe was less reliant on using the rest than in a normal set-up. Thoroughly smitten, he would practise each morning before school and charge home during lunch hour for another knock.

Davis described his father as 'a bit of a character' who opened a cinema, where Davis's sister would accompany silent pictures on the piano. 'My mother looked after the pennies because my father was very capable of spending the money,' he added.[1]

Unlike the champions who followed in his wake and who benefited from being able to watch snooker on television, he had nobody to study or try and emulate, but his natural prowess was clear to his father, who engaged a local coach, Ernest Rudge, to instil the rudiments of technique into his son. 'A great benefactor' was how Davis described Rudge. 'He taught me to play and many other things in life.'

Rudge arranged for professional billiards players to play matches at his club, with the young Davis fetching the balls out of the pockets. By thirteen, he was the local amateur billiards champion, having made his first 100 break at the age of twelve, and turned professional in 1919, aged eighteen. There was no professional game in snooker, but the English Amateur Championship had been inaugurated three years earlier and won by Charles Jacques at Burroughes Hall, in Soho Square.

Davis was heavily left-eye-dominant in terms of sighting, which was considered unorthodox at the time, but increasingly he was gaining a reputation. He was yet to become world billiards champion but saw an opportunity with snooker, the young upstart of the cue-sports family, to make a name for himself and, more widely, for the game. Others had tried, with little success. In 1924, Tom Dennis, a player and billiard-hall owner, wrote to the governing body for billiards, asking them to consider promoting an open snooker tournament. The sniffy response he received read: 'It seems doubtful whether snooker as a spectacular game is sufficiently popular to warrant the successful promotion of such a competition.'

In 1925, Davis made a 96 break at Burroughes Hall, beating the previous record of 86 by Tom Newman, set in 1922. He was improving all the time and was determined to demonstrate his prowess in a proper event. The following year, Davis, supported by the promoter and table-maker Bill Camkin, managed to persuade the authorities to reconsider. Ten players entered the first-ever professional championship – the word 'world' would be added later – and a silver trophy was purchased using half of the entry fees (it is still presented to the world champion to this day).

The tournament's first match began on 29 November 1926, the week after F. Scott Fitzgerald published *The Great Gatsby*. Melbourne Inman lined up against Tom Newman at Thurston's Hall in London's Leicester Square, but the shadow of the three-ball game loomed large as the snooker match was tacked on to a billiards contest between the pair, which was promoted as the primary entertainment. Inman won 8–5, and matches continued over the following months. Davis beat Irishman Joe Brady 8–6 in Liverpool and would play Albert Cope at Camkin's Hall in Birmingham, the co-promoter's own club, in the semis. A local newspaper, the *Daily Gazette*, ran a short preview:

> There will be tremendous interest taken in the semi-final of the professional snooker championship at Camkin's rooms, Birmingham, next week, when Albert Cope, our local 'hope', will oppose Joe Davis, and there is great conflict of opinion regarding the chances of these players, for in snooker, to quote the words of the sage, 'anything might happen'.

What happened was a comfortable win for Davis, 12–4. He advanced to the final, where he would play Tom Dennis, also at Camkin's Hall.

In May 1927, Princess Elizabeth, who would reign as queen for seven decades, had just celebrated her first birthday. The Academy of Motion Picture Arts and Sciences, which would annually bestow Oscars for achievements in cinema, was formed. Charles Lindbergh piloted the *Spirit of St. Louis* from New York to Paris, the world's first transatlantic flight. And in John Bright Street, four days were set aside for snooker's historic first professional championship final. It was a 31-frame match, with all frames to be played, even if one player reached the winning target of 16, such was the desire to maximise gate receipts, which would be divvied up by the players as prize money. Davis dominated, winning the first seven frames and leading 12–4 by the end of the second day. On the third, he pulled away to lead 16–7 and therefore could not be caught. The final score was 20–11.

Davis received £6 10s from his share of ticket sales. He was snooker's first professional champion, but his victory failed to make much of a splash with the public or even the cue-sports cognoscenti. *The Billiard Player*, the game's leading organ of the time, gave the event four paragraphs of coverage.

However, what lent the event credibility was Davis himself. 'He transformed the game from a rather crude potting contest to one of tactics, developing break-building and safety play,' according to Clive Everton, the long-serving journalist and television commentator who edited the game's primary magazine, *Snooker Scene*, for 51 years.

Davis had become snooker's first king, a status in which he revelled, although there was no grand plan. 'We were all scrattin' and scrapin' to make a living,' he said in later life.[2] His title defence in 1928 involved only one match as, part of a field of just seven entrants, he was put straight into the final, beating Fred Lawrence 16–13.

Billiards still dominated as a public entertainment, and when Davis won the three-ball game's 1928 world title, thousands of people lined the streets of Chesterfield on his return home. Proud though he was of this achievement, he was keen to showcase snooker as much as possible. That year, he made his first century break in public, during a match in Manchester. In 1929, entries for the Professional Championship dwindled to just five. Davis beat Tom Dennis 19–14, and then defeated him 25–12 in 1930 to become champion for a fourth successive year.

Despite his best efforts, interest in snooker was not growing at an appreciable rate. In fact, in 1931, only two players entered the championship, Davis beating Dennis 25–21 in the Lounge Club, Nottingham, which was owned by Dennis. The closeness of the scores in some of these finals was perhaps due to the fact that gate money was the primary source of income, so it was to the benefit of Davis to keep the match 'live' for as long as possible to sustain the public's interest. The championship bumped along. Davis won from an entry of four in 1932 and five in 1933.

These were very different times. Davis had never driven a vehicle, but a rail strike in 1934 meant he could not get from Nottingham to Kettering to play Tom Newman, the only other entrant that year. Davis duly purchased a car, was given rough instructions from the salesman on how to drive it and set off for the match. He beat Newman 25–22, and went on to retain the title, his ninth in total, the following year, from five entries, making a record break of 110 in the process.

Davis had established an iron grip on the game, and, as the years passed, it only tightened. Younger players were overawed just by being in his presence, as John Pulman, a future world champion, confirmed: 'He had a tremendous aura about him, he was the complete professional player. Not only had he talent, he had showmanship, personality, business acumen, and he towered above everyone else in the game to such an extent that most of the players were virtually beaten before they started playing. He was so overpowering that he put everybody else in the shade.'[3]

Rex Williams, who became world billiards champion in 1968, concurred: 'Playing against him was very difficult. Joe never seemed to worry about his opponents. This was one of the great things about him, the tremendous confidence he had in his own ability. Players never played as well against Joe as they did against other players.'[4]

On 10 December 1935, snooker made its debut on the radio, as the BBC broadcast a 15-minute running commentary of a match between Davis and Horace Lindrum, nephew of the Australian billiards great Walter Lindrum. The following year saw the establishment of the BBC's television service, and on 14 April 1937, a ten-minute broadcast, *An Exhibition of Play*, featured Lindrum and Willie Smith demonstrating the intricacies of snooker. The programme was the first to be transmitted that day – at 3 p.m. – and it was followed by a ten-minute item on daffodils. It would be another 13 years until snooker troubled the national broadcaster's schedules again.

It was strange that Davis had not been selected for the demonstration programme. He was by then an 11-time world champion, winning again from a record field of 13 in 1936 and beating Lindrum 32–29 in 1937. For that year's tournament, a qualifying match was staged, with the winner to join the main draw. It featured Davis's younger brother, 23-year-old Fred, of whom much was expected after he had won three junior billiards titles, but he was suffering from myopia and was too self-conscious to reveal his condition, especially to his all-powerful brother, whose first comment on watching him knocking balls around as a ten-year-old had been 'take that bloody grin off your face'.

Widely expected to win, it was not a lovely day for Fred when Bill Withers defeated him 17–14. Joe saw it as such an affront to the family name that he hammered Withers 30–1 in the next round – gate money be damned. 'Not being able to see and having to endure Joe's fury afterwards made it all so much worse that I felt more depressed than I ever had before,' wrote Fred in his autobiography, *Talking Snooker*, published in 1979. 'Worst of all, in my own mind, I had virtually written off any future I might have had in the game.'

Embarrassed, he consulted an optician. Wearing glasses, he reached the semi-finals in 1938, but Joe still reigned supreme. In 1939, they met in the semi-finals. Joe won 17–14 and beat Sidney Smith 43–30 in the final at Thurston's Hall.

It was clear that Fred looked up to Joe, not just as a big brother but as the first person to master the intricacies of snooker:

> Joe always had been a very good potter but when he started to utilise his billiards knowledge and skill to work out, on his own, the sort of break-building sequences and techniques which have become part of every leading player's armoury, none of his contemporaries could extend him. As he was in the position of being an excellent player before anyone else had even realised how to play the game properly, that he would win those early championships was really a foregone conclusion.[5]

In 1940, the Davis brothers met head to head in the final. Fred had made a championship-record break of 113 in 1939 and was clearly improving, whereas Joe was now 38 and mindful that his hegemony could not last for ever. The likelihood of a passing of the fraternal baton was increased when Fred won ten frames in succession on the third day of the best-of-73-frames final to lead 20–14, but Joe recovered on day four to draw level at 24–24. 'Away from the table, Joe and I got along well and he was pleased that I had established myself near the top of the profession,' wrote Fred. 'But at the table our rivalry was intense. Having been in his shadow for so long it was my burning ambition to beat him while Joe, who had informed me more than once that I never would, was determined to give me no assistance to do so.'[6]

The match remained close, before, leading 36–35, the elder brother saved his best for last, making a break of 101 in the clinching frame. 'Spectators, crammed into the hall and overflowing lobby, cheered for nearly a minute when Joe put down the blue to make the 112th century of his career and won the final with one game to spare,' was how one news agency reported the moment of victory.

The Second World War had broken out a few months earlier, and Fred joined the British Army as the championship took a pause. London was an obvious target for German bombers. Several months after Joe won his 14th world title, the capital was subjected to a sustained wave of attacks, commonly known as the Blitz, which claimed the lives of more than 40,000 civilians. Thurston's itself was destroyed by a bomb in October 1940, reopening seven years later. The World Championship was not held again until 1946, when Davis made it 15 successive title victories with a 78–67 defeat of Horace Lindrum. He compiled his 200th century break during the match.

There was no elation, only relief. 'I am glad it is over,' Davis was quoted as saying in the London *Weekly Dispatch*. 'This has been a big strain. I feel very pleased with myself at hitting my best form at 45 years of age.'

The 12-day final brought in 22,500 spectators. The promoter,

Bob Jelks, had put up £6,000 to stage the match, with profits estimated at £1,400, the players talking half. Davis was a large part of this success. Through sheer longevity, he had achieved a certain celebrity, even if snooker itself was not yet a mainstream sport. The fact he had never lost a match played on level terms gave him a definite cachet, and with Fred and others snapping at his heels he decided to retire from playing in the championship – though not from the game altogether. Thus, a 20-year unbeaten reign remained unsullied by defeat.

By now, Davis had become sufficiently well known as a personality that he had his own snooker-and-billiards-based music-hall act, touring the country with famous comedians and entertainers, including a spot at the London Palladium, where he met his future wife, June, a dancer. A large mirror was erected on stage so that audience members sat in the stalls could follow the action. In this new world of show business, Davis was at first ill at ease. On opening night, he missed his first three shots, causing comedian Tommy Trinder to run on stage and ask, 'Where can we get hold of your brother, Fred?'

Once he settled into his act, it became popular and enhanced his reputation as a star, with a constituency much wider than snooker itself. He raised well over £100,000 for charity during the war and was awarded the OBE. He was the face of snooker, and remained so long after his retirement, a period in which his dislike of losing remained.

Ray Reardon, who became world champion six times in the 1970s, won a Joe Davis cue at the age of fourteen in a BBC competition, receiving his prize from the man himself. Several years later, he played him in an exhibition and saw his competitiveness at first hand, even in a supposedly friendly environment.

'I'd won the English amateur title and was in the police force,'

Reardon told me shortly before his death in 2024. 'Worcester Conservative Club engaged Joe to play and got in touch with our chief constable for me to go and play him over two frames. We had a couple of safety shots each in the first frame, then I knocked a long red in and made 96. He refused to play the next frame. I said to him, "Mr Davis, I assure you that if you play the next frame, you will win it. They've come here to see you, not me." But he wouldn't play the frame.'

This pride in always being seen to be top dog seemed even more acute in relation to his own brother. In 1946, Fred made a 139 break against Joe at Blackpool Tower Circus, then a record. In a 1990 interview with *The Times*, Fred explained what happened next:

> Joe was adamant that the table was not up to the required standard. An official of the Billiards and Snooker Control Council examined it and said he could not ratify the record because, would you believe, the pockets were too big by the width of a piece of tissue paper. I was speechless. The truth, of course, is that he was frightened to death of Joe and guess who held the record at 138? Joe was the Big I Am in those days and got his way in everything. I had a dreadful time in my early days because I was in Joe's shadow. No matter what I did I had no recognition, but it hardened me.

Fred, in fact, beat Joe four times on level terms in his career, but never in the World Championship. When Joe retired, Fred was the obvious favourite to inherit his mantle as world champion, but was beaten to the punch in 1947 at the newly reopened Thurston's Hall by Walter Donaldson of Coatbridge, Scotland, whose preparation for the tournament involved an intensive period spent practising in a friend's loft. Donaldson, whose father had owned a billiard hall, beat the junior Davis 82–63. He was not a flair player. Everton said he 'inexorably ground out victory', with few risks and excellent safety play, adding, 'It was not artistic, exciting or fluent.'

Even so, he was champion and engaged in a rivalry with Davis that would see them contest a total of eight successive world finals. Davis prevailed in 1948 and 1949, before the final moved in 1950 to Blackpool Tower Circus, where Donaldson was the winner, 51–46. Close it may have been, but this was not a classic. According to Everton, 'There was an inordinate amount of safety. The pockets were brutally tight. Pots along the cushion were impossible. Several sessions each took four hours.' In 97 frames of snooker, the highest break was 80.

Though the championship continued as a duel between Davis and Donaldson, it was the elder Davis who enjoyed most attention and acclaim. As far as the general public were concerned, Joe was still number one, a status he encouraged through exhibition appearances and, in 1950, a televised challenge match on the BBC against Donaldson, which was given 45 minutes of airtime. A spate of further challenge matches followed, amid eclectic TV schedules. Before one such broadcast, 20 minutes were given over to Mrs Dorothy Kiltoey, a farmer's wife from Yorkshire, to extol the virtues of tripe.

Snooker had by now become popular as a leisure pursuit for men employed in manufacturing trades such as mining and steelworking, but the image was still one of upper-class refinement. A typical television appearance saw Davis alongside the plummy-voiced Raymond Glendenning, a doyen among sports broadcasters, demonstrating various billiards and snooker trick shots. Dressed in shirt and tie, the pair appeared to be in the plush billiard room of a stately home, giving the impression of an after-dinner game among members of polite society.

Britain at the time was rebuilding after the war. Rationing continued until the mid-1950s. Television sets were not commonplace in British households until after the coronation of Queen Elizabeth II in 1953, a national event that proved the power of the medium to provide a collective experience. With demand high, two years later the government licensed the first commercial channel, ITV.

The BBC gave some coverage to the *News of the World* tournament and to a few frames of the 1952 Davis vs Donaldson world final, although this year uniquely boasted rival champions, following a dispute over money. The Billiards Association and Council Control (BA&CC), the game's governing body, took the view that being world champion was primarily about honour. The professionals – the clue being in the name – wanted to make a decent living. After Davis had beaten Donaldson in 1951, it was revealed the finalists had shared just £500, so the players decided to boycott the official World Championship and stage their own version, the World Professional Matchplay Championship, in which Davis beat Donaldson 38–35.

As a face-saving measure, the BA&CC put on their own world final between Horace Lindrum and New Zealand's Clark McConachy. Lindrum won 94–48 and therefore has his name engraved on the silver trophy, but his daughter Jan later revealed he had been declared technically blind at the time by a specialist from Harley Street, while McConachy was suffering from Parkinson's disease.

Fred won four more world titles between 1953 and 1957, making it eight in total. Joe had meanwhile compiled the first 147 maximum break in competition in 1955, and his television appearances had increased, confirming him as by far the best known figure in the still-fledgling sport. The fact he was not playing in the World Championship therefore seriously devalued it – like *Hamlet* without the prince – and interest, such as it was, dwindled to the point that by 1957, only four players entered. Even Fred was not among them. The final took place in Jersey, where John Pulman defeated Jackie Rea 39–34, after which there were no takers for hosting the 1958 event.

'No promoter was prepared to stage the World Championship between 1957 and 1964,' said Everton. 'It just wasn't worth it then. There was no television, no sponsorship, and there were only four or five active professionals, who spent their time giving club exhibitions.'

Joe Davis's idea for reigniting enthusiasm for snooker was to introduce two new coloured balls: an orange, worth eight points, and a purple, worth ten. He called the game snooker plus, and the 1959 *News of the World* tournament, featuring Joe, Fred and Pulman, was played under these new rules, but it failed to capture the public imagination and was never heard of again.

And so, as a new decade dawned, an era that ushered in The Beatles, John F. Kennedy and great social change, the game entered uncertain times. The 1960s may have swung, but snooker as a professional sport lay dormant. These were grim times for the players, who retreated back into normal life. Fred Davis ran a hotel in Llandudno, Rex Williams a family printing firm in Staffordshire. Walter Donaldson became so fed up with the lack of opportunities that he smashed up the slates of his snooker table and used them to pave a path outside his house. Players still undertook exhibitions, but making a living was hard, with the sport enjoying very little exposure outside of a few matches on black-and-white television, usually involving Joe and Fred and acting as filler on the BBC's flagship Saturday-afternoon sports programme, *Grandstand*.

'It was very slim pickings,' according to Everton. 'Just club exhibitions and the occasional television gig. *Grandstand* would have snooker as a standby if other events were dependent on the weather, or as a sandwich between race meetings, where frames had to last a certain amount of time.'

ITV offered a lifeline in 1961 by organising an event that pitted four professionals against four amateurs. The amateurs, who were enjoying more competitive opportunities, all won. One, Mark Wildman, made the first televised century break in 1962.

By 1964, Williams, who at seventeen had won the English amateur title, was 30 and restless. This should have been the prime period of his career. He took it upon himself to revive the World Championship on a challenge basis, with the reigning champion – in this case, Pulman – taking on a single opponent. The governing body gave their sanction, and Pulman beat Fred Davis 19–16 in the first World Championship to be staged for seven years. Pulman would win six further world titles on this basis against a series of challengers, Williams included, until 1968.

Britain changed profoundly during this period. The Conservatives had been in power from 1951 to 1964, led first by Winston Churchill, who won a surprise election victory after his career in front-line politics had seemingly been drawing to a close. He was replaced in 1955 by Anthony Eden, who resigned two years later over the Suez Crisis. Harold Macmillan was prime minister from 1957 to 1963, before aristocrat Alec Douglas-Home renounced his place in the House of Lords to preside over the final year of Tory rule.

The new Britain, in which deference for authority was in retreat, was summed up by the satirical BBC programme *That Was the Week That Was*, which poked fun at those in power through monologues, sketches and songs. Presented by David

Frost, it featured the likes of Frankie Howerd, Willie Rushton and Millicent Martin. Audiences enjoyed its mocking of an establishment hitherto considered beyond reproach. The new Labour prime minister was Harold Wilson, whose government oversaw reforms in education, housing and other social areas, abolishing the death penalty, decriminalising homosexuality and abortion and legislating against racial discrimination in the workplace.

As change raged, snooker on television stuttered on in its role as filler material, offering up contests of little meaning or narrative designed purely to plug a hole in the schedules. On 8 September 1968, the *Sunday Times* exposed the truth behind these matches, under the headline 'Great TV Snooker Frame-Up'. Its report began:

> A classic example of the way television can corrupt and harm a game has come to light as a result of inquiries into coverage by independent TV and the BBC of snooker in the past few years. Some players who acted in good faith but with the mistaken idea that they were giving snooker a more favourable image have manipulated matches on television to a point where, according to one player, Ray Edmonds: 'It became virtually the same as professional wrestling – completely fixed. You had to be as smart as some jockeys who lose by a nose and look good.'

Edmonds had taken part in what had been billed in advance as a 'five-frame thriller' against George Humphries. 'It was a five-frame thriller because we wangled it that way,' he said. Having won the first frame, he tried to lose the second, but Humphries was struggling so badly that this proved impossible. Edmonds therefore had to take a dive in frames three and four.

Blame was placed on the shoulders of Harold Phillips, the former BA&CC chairman, but some players also believed television had been directly involved. 'I think Harold had to do this to get the TV people to put the matches on,' said Edmonds.

This unseemly episode underlined the fact that snooker as a professional sport lacked proper organisation and, thus, credibility. Williams attempted to rectify this by setting up the World Professional Billiards and Snooker Association in 1968, but 40 years after the first World Championship, the game was lacking relevance and its future looked bleak.

After a rapid rise and fall, a fresh start was needed. It would materialise thanks to some new faces and advancements in technology. Following decades of struggle, snooker was about to exit the black-and-white era and enter the age of colour.

3

HERE COMES THE SUN

Ray's Bar is a private room at Churston Golf Club in Brixham, Devon. When we met in 2023, the club president, in whose honour it is named, had no problem bounding up the staircase at the age of 90, still sharp as a tack, with the same twinkle in his eye that was so familiar to a generation of snooker fans.

Ray Reardon was born in Tredegar in 1932. He had a clear memory of discovering snooker in childhood, thanks to his Uncle Dan. 'He worked on the railways and came to live with us,' he said. 'He bought me a small billiard table. I was five or six at the time. The pockets were too small for the balls, so I used 15 marbles for the reds, and the colours were various other marbles. On a Thursday, Dan would take me up to the mine welfare institute in Tredegar for a couple of hours, and that's how I became interested in snooker.'

Reardon was also a keen swimmer, but snooker had already taken its grip. By the age of twelve, he was visiting the institute for two hours after school, his father having gained special dispensation to nurture his son's talent. 'I won the local club handicap when I was fifteen,' he said. 'I started entering the various snooker and billiards events. There were six available: boys, junior and senior in each. For three years I never won a game. My father was getting very despondent about it.'

He stuck at it and reached the British Junior Championship final, losing out to another Welsh player, Jack Carney. Reardon was invited on to BBC radio's flagship Saturday-morning sports programme to be interviewed about his run to the final, where his disdainful attitude to those in positions of authority first came to the public's attention. 'The presenter, Angus Mackay, didn't know where Aneurin Bevan was born,' he said. 'I said, "He was born in Tredegar." He thought he was born in Ebbw Vale. We had an argument about it. So this was a bad way to start an interview. I was seventeen.'

A year later, his game solid but not yet spectacular, he saw the light during an exhibition match against A. J. Ford, the Welsh amateur champion. 'I got absolutely slaughtered,' he said. 'It was fantastic. I knew halfway through the first game that I was winning nothing today. I saw a style of play that I hadn't seen much of before, certainly not up close. It was little stun shots around the black. I thought, "I can do that." I was on the bus back with my dad, 11 o'clock at night, and he was silent because I'd been walloped. Suddenly, he said, "Good God, boy, what happened?" And I said, "That's the way to play snooker. I can do that." I said I'd go back home and for a couple of weeks play each day for a couple of hours all by myself, just practising that style of play. I entered the Amateur Championship of Wales, and three months later took his title off him.'

Reardon, like most of the menfolk of Tredegar, became a miner. Snooker was still a hobby, the professional game in abeyance following Joe Davis's retirement. His father got a job at Florence Colliery in Stoke-on-Trent, and Reardon followed him there, but on 30 April 1957, at the age of 24, he was nearly killed in a mine collapse. 'I was helping to enlarge a roadway at the coalface when the top heading caved in and I was trapped by the rubble so that I was unable to move a muscle, feet, fingers or face.'

In the pitch black, barely able to breathe, Reardon attempted to stay calm by imagining countless games of marbles with his younger brother, Ron. The rescuers finally dug him out after three hours. He left mining three years later to become a policeman, but snooker remained his passion.

Reardon won the Welsh title six years running and the English Amateur Championship in 1964. By now, the World Championship had been revived on a challenge basis. The professional game was still a closed shop, but Reardon was inspired to apply for entry thanks to the player who would become his great rival.

John Spencer was born in Radcliffe, Lancashire, in 1935, the youngest of five children. His father had lost an arm during the First World War. The family of seven were packed into a three-bedroom council house, but Spencer remembered a warm sense of community, with neighbours providing Christmas presents due to his father's inability to find a regular job. He got into the local grammar school, and at thirteen was introduced to snooker by his elder brother, Bobby. A year later, their father took Spencer to the local billiard hall, The Grott, situated under the marketplace in what was effectively a cellar, and so close to the River Irwell that it was frequently flooded. At fifteen, he made his first century. The *Bury Times* ran a story on him, with the headline 'Boy Snooker Player with a Big Future'.

'Spencer was very exciting when he first came into the game. He was playing deep screw shots from distance that none of the other players of the time were playing,' Clive Everton told me. The problem was, there was no real future in snooker at this time, the early 1950s. Spencer went off to do his national service and drifted away from the game. For 11 years, he did not play at all. In 1964, an old friend, Les Taylor, came to see him and asked him to join his league team. Spencer agreed, and a love affair was rekindled. He entered the English Amateur Championship and progressed to play Reardon in the final.

Spencer lacked some of Reardon's worldliness. Before the final, *Billiards and Snooker*, the sport's leading magazine of the time, asked each player for a photograph. Reardon sent one of himself in his dress suit, proudly holding the Welsh trophy; Spencer, not understanding the significance of the request, reached for the first one he could find – himself in his swimming trunks, on holiday with his brother and their mother.

Reardon won the final, but Spencer became champion two years later and set his sights on the professional ranks. According to Reardon, the old guard were suspicious of the prospective new arrivals. 'Spencer applied to turn professional in 1966, so I decided to do the same,' he said. 'There were four of us: Spencer, me, Gary Owen and David Taylor. We were called to go to a hotel in Dudley. We arrived, and the other pros of the era were there. There were eight of them. We sat down, and the chairman got up to say, "Welcome, but we have to tell you that we've decided not to accept you." I was gobsmacked. I'd left the police force for this. I was married; we had a son. I could see the expressions on the others' faces. They couldn't believe it. Spencer said to me, "Say something."

'I got up after a couple of minutes and said, "I've got news for you. We're going to form an association against you, and none of you will play in our tournaments." I turned to the others and said, "Let's go." We'd got about ten yards, and Fred Davis got up and said, "Don't be so hasty. We've just decided to accept you." That was our warm welcome to the world of snooker.'

With more professionals on the books, it made sense to restore the World Championship to a knockout event. 'They decided we could all put money in and the winner would take all,' said Reardon. 'The entry fee was £100. That was a sixth of my finances. Spencer won it. The next year, they did the same thing, and it was only £20, because none of the others had won it.'

Spencer defeated Gary Owen 37–24 at the Victoria Hall, London, to become the 1969 world champion. Dead frames were played to give audiences something to watch, so the scoreline eventually read 46–27. There was still little mainstream interest in snooker, but just a few months later a miracle happened. The sport's fortunes were transformed forever, thanks to a decision taken by one of British television's greatest figures.

David Attenborough would become a beloved national treasure, bringing the natural world to millions of living rooms through programmes such as *Life on Earth* and *The Blue Planet*. His distinctive narration and resolute integrity helped him establish an authority on screen rarely rivalled in the history of British broadcasting. In 1969, he was controller of BBC2, which had launched five years earlier to supplement the BBC's main channel. A new colour service had been introduced in 1968, and Attenborough needed programming that would specifically showcase it. Snooker, with its coloured balls and small playing area, was deemed the perfect fit, but there were no tournaments outside of the World Championship, whose long format was unsuitable for broadcast. Philip Lewis, a BBC producer, contacted Ted Lowe, whose whispered commentary had thus far accompanied only black-and-white pictures. Lowe was a close friend of Joe Davis from his days as general manager of Leicester Square Hall (formerly Thurston's Hall) and had got his break in broadcasting when BBC regular Raymond Glendenning was struck down by laryngitis. He had long lobbied for snooker to be given a proper chance on television and helped devise the basic one-frame playing format and arranged the eight players. The half-hour programme would be called *Pot Black*.

So it was that Spencer, the new world champion, Reardon and Gary Owen, twice a world amateur champion, were called up to compete against former world champions John Pulman and Fred

Davis, as well as Irish champion Jackie Rea, Rex Williams and Kingsley Kennerley. Three days after Neil Armstrong set foot on the moon, one giant leap for the future of snooker was taken in a television studio in Birmingham.

The first edition of *Pot Black* was broadcast on 23 July 1969. 'Black and White Rag', performed by Winifred Atwell, was chosen as the theme music. The initial programme was a 15-minute introduction to the series, giving viewers unfamiliar with the game some rudimentary pointers. A week later, the first match was shown, between Spencer and Rea. 'The world champion with the eight-bob cue takes on the man who has monopolised the Irish table for the past two decades,' was how the *Radio Times* billed it. Reardon beat Spencer 88 points to 29 in the final broadcast on 10 September. He was presented with the trophy by David Nixon, a popular television magician.

Most of the country could not yet receive the new colour service, but within a couple of years it was more widely available, and *Pot Black*, with a growing audience, became an established favourite, claiming second place in the BBC2 ratings. Snooker suddenly had a national shop window. The players began to gain a profile and, now that they appeared on a hit TV show, could start charging more for exhibition work and stints at holiday camps. Aspiring players also now had a weekly source of inspiration.

'*Pot Black* was on a Tuesday night, and you were glued to the TV,' says John Parrott, who made his breakthrough by winning *Junior Pot Black* in 1982. 'This was in the days when you couldn't record things. You think now how they managed to make a frame last half an hour, but I always watched it and tried to soak as much of it up as possible.'

Dennis Taylor, who made his *Pot Black* debut in 1975, remembers the contrived nature of the format. 'They'd tell you beforehand to try and get it over with in 22 minutes,' he says. 'Back in those days, it wasn't easy to edit it. I remember [Australian] Eddie Charlton saying, "22 minutes? You think I'm coming 12,000 miles to finish a match in 22 minutes? If it takes an hour, it takes an hour."'

Many viewers watched despite not investing in colour televisions, leading to the legend, possibly apocryphal, of Lowe uttering a line that has been quoted with various combinations of colours, without a definitive version ever quite being nailed down: 'For those of you watching in black and white, the yellow is next to the pink.'

Britain in the mid-1970s was a time of constant industrial strife, with strikes leading to regular power cuts. In 1973, Prime Minister Edward Heath instituted a three-day working week to reduce electricity consumption. In the general election of February 1974, Harold Wilson's Labour Party won 301 seats to the Conservatives' 297. Heath's attempt at forming a coalition with the Liberal Party failed and he resigned. Wilson went to the country again in October and gained a majority of three. Eighteen months later, by now convinced of establishment plots to remove him, he surprised the political world by quitting. James Callaghan, who had already served as chancellor, home secretary and foreign secretary, replaced him. Heath was challenged for his party's leadership by Margaret Thatcher, the former education secretary, who beat him in the first ballot and comfortably won the second after he withdrew.

The Britain of the 1970s saw the emergence of disparate music acts and genres with global appeal: Elton John, David Bowie, glam rock and punk. *The Morecambe and Wise Christmas Show* of 1977 pulled in 27 million viewers. The sitcom *Fawlty Towers*, starring John Cleese as a Torquay hotelier, became an instant classic. Saturday mornings were given over for the first time to children's television, such as *Multi-Coloured Swap Shop*, with Noel Edmonds, on BBC1 and the more anarchic *Tiswas* on ITV.

In these changing times, the establishment was on the run, sometimes literally. In 1974, John Bingham, the 7th Earl of Lucan, fled the scene after his family's nanny, Sandra Rivett, was murdered in his Belgravia home. A few weeks later, John Stonehouse, the Member of Parliament for Walsall North, faked his own death in Australia after experiencing self-inflicted financial troubles. He was found in Melbourne on Christmas Eve and would be sentenced to seven years for fraud.

The IRA killed 21 people when bombs exploded at two pubs in Birmingham in November 1974. A few weeks earlier, five people had died in similar attacks in Guildford, in pubs largely frequented by members of the British Army. In 1975, 67 per cent of the population voted to remain in the European Community, also known as the Common Market. The year before, Swedish pop band ABBA had won the Eurovision Song Contest.

This was the backdrop to snooker's rise, in which *Pot Black*, with its polite, uncomplicated air and cheering, colourful presentation, was a welcome distraction from the tumultuous outside world. The programme proved that there was an audience for snooker, with 4 million regularly tuning in for the weekly series. However, the World Championship was still the tournament the players prized most, and Reardon won it for the first time in 1970, withstanding a recovery from John Pulman, who fought back from 27–14 down to trail only 34–33, before Reardon got over the line at 37–34.

He held the title for less than six months, however, as the following season's event was staged in Australia that November. The early rounds were played in a round-robin format, and Reardon was suspicious that when they were over, he and Spencer were drawn in the same half, leaving two Australians, Eddie Charlton and Warren Simpson, to contest the other semi-final. Spencer beat Reardon 34–15 and then Simpson 37–29 to win his second world title.

By now, a fierce rivalry was developing between the two men, one that at times became personal. Reardon seemed to enjoy riling opponents off the table, a way of gaining the upper hand on it. Spencer, however, found his manner irksome.

'He was the sort of person who could laugh 24 hours a day if it was to his advantage,' said Spencer.

> He always seemed to find someone who would let him stay at their house. After the exhibitions or functions he would not go talking to just anyone but instead always used to find out who organised the snooker bookings and that was who he would be with for the rest of the night . . . As far as Reardon was concerned it was free lodgings.[1]

'We played loads of exhibitions together,' Reardon said. 'We became not friends, because you can't be friends with someone you'll play in a competition, but acquaintances. John was a wonderful player, very much to be admired.'

At a time when the cake was relatively small, the fight was on for every slice. 'I was invited to go to Canada for exhibitions, but it didn't happen,' he said. 'Seven or eight years later, we're in Birmingham doing an exhibition. We were in the hotel having a drink, at one or two in the morning, and Spencer said, "You tried to take Canada from me, didn't you?" He'd been harbouring this inside all those bloody years. I said, "Why, do you own Canada? It's open to whoever wants to go. In any case, I never actually went." We became a little distant after that, but I admired him immensely.'

Animosities aside, there was no doubting Reardon's personal charisma. 'There's only two people in my life where I've walked in a room and thought, "Hang on a minute, there's something special coming off them." One was [Spanish golfer] Seve Ballesteros, and the other was Ray Reardon,' says John Parrott. 'He'd walk into a room, and there'd be an aura around him, like in the Ready Brek advert. He was the guv'nor. He was in charge. He was a big presence. He commanded respect.'

'He had a superiority complex,' says Steve Davis, who would eventually equal Reardon's tally of six world titles. 'He was an interesting character. He was the special one for me. He was a clever bastard on the table. He had something the others didn't have. He was a true match player and could cope with it all. There was always a part of me that thought he was a strange one. I knew full well that a lot of the players of his era didn't like him. I didn't come in with that baggage. I just thought, "He's a character." He was the guv'nor at that time, so I always put him on a high pedestal.'

Mark Watterson remembers being at the World Championship in the late 1970s, when his uncle Mike promoted it, and learning that Reardon was not universally loved. 'John Pulman was great mates with John Spencer but he didn't like Ray Reardon,' he says. 'One year they decided to sell posters in the foyer. I was in Mike's room having a sandwich, and John Pulman picked up the poster of Reardon, turned to the room and said, "Have you seen this? Ray Reardon: legend in his own mind."'

Yet, to the audience, Reardon always appeared to be immaculately dressed, and his headmasterly demeanour lent an air of respectability to the sport. 'When players advertised themselves for exhibition work, Ray described himself as "the classic professional," and that's exactly what he was,' says John Virgo. 'He believed in what a professional sportsman should be all about. He was a credit to the game.'

Dennis Taylor agrees. 'Ray was incredible,' he says. 'I always thought John Spencer was better because I was biased towards him, but then I realised that Ray was the better match player. John was more flamboyant, but I'd still have Ray in my top six of all time, he was that good. A great ambassador.'

Clive Everton also saw Reardon's qualities with regard to representing snooker professionally. 'He modelled himself on Joe Davis in terms of how he should comport himself in public, and there's no doubt he was a great ambassador of the game,' he said.

Such a status gave Reardon the opportunity to travel to Australia and South Africa on exhibition tours, even if it meant long stretches away from home. 'I did three five-month tours. I got home once and the dog bit me,' he said.

From 1973 to 1976, Reardon was unstoppable, winning four World Championship titles in a row, in a series of substandard venues, where his demands for more professionalism in the sport became louder and louder. The 1973 championship was staged at the City Exhibition Halls, Manchester. The previous year's event had been a year-long slog around the country, but now the tournament would be played over a fortnight, although the set-up was still primitive. A hole in the roof meant that rain stopped play during the quarter-final between Alex Higgins and Fred Davis, the position of the balls having to be marked as a cover was put on the table. This was by no means the last problem the players would encounter.

'The final was over five days,' said Reardon. 'I was 7–0 down, couldn't see the balls. It was the first time they'd used these lights. The light was right down the middle of the ball, and I couldn't see it. It didn't affect [Eddie] Charlton – he had double eyelids.

I complained to Bruce Donkin, the tournament director. I told him that if the lights weren't removed, there'd be no point in continuing. I go 8–1 down. I thought, "I could lose 38–1" – these are the wild things going through your mind. I called a meeting with Donkin, John Mack, the chap from the sponsors and the TV director. Joe Davis was there too. Eddie wouldn't go. The TV guys said nothing could be done. I said, "Mr Mack, whose tournament is this? Is this the BBC TV World Championship or is it Gallaher's World Championship?" He said, "This is Gallaher's World Championship, and the director can take his cameras away." Suddenly, the lights were taken away. This is what we were up against in those days.'

Reardon prevailed 38–32, with the BBC's *Grandstand* showing highlights, and defended his title in 1974 at Belle Vue, in Manchester, beating Graham Miles 22–12 in the final. By the time of the 1975 event, a new tournament had been added to the calendar.

* * *

Clive Everton was a fine billiards player and leading Welsh amateur in snooker, but journalism was his passion, and in 1966 he was appointed editor of *Billiards and Snooker*, the magazine of the BA&CC. Still a young man and an independent thinker, his ideas did not always meet with approval from the powers that be, and in January 1971, he began his own magazine. Originally titled *World Snooker*, the following year it became *Snooker Scene*.

In 1968, he travelled to London to interview the squash player Jonah Barrington, and somehow departed as his manager. Through this venture he got to know Peter West and Patrick Nally, who ran a consultancy specialising in the relatively new world of sports sponsorship. West Nally advised Gallaher, the parent group of tobacco company Benson & Hedges, and Everton suggested a snooker tournament as a fit for their brand. The Benson & Hedges Masters was launched in 1975, a high-prestige invitation event originally for ten players that would in time become one of snooker's majors.

Spencer and Reardon reached the first Masters final at London's West Centre Hotel. It came down to a deciding frame, with Reardon looking the likely winner, before being put off by the noise of the presentation party getting into position backstage. The trophy would go to Spencer, who won on a respotted black. The plush setting for the Masters – 'dinner jacket, champagne and smoked salmon', according to Reardon – was in marked contrast to the down-at-heel feel of the World Championship, which still had no permanent home. In 1975, it was held at the Nunawading Basketball Stadium, Melbourne, where hopes were high of a home victory for Eddie Charlton, who embodied the Australian love of sport, having been a champion surfer, boxer, cricketer and rugby league player in his youth. In 1956, he carried the Olympic torch on a leg of its procession towards Melbourne.

Charlton was known for his stubborn refusal to play with side on the cue ball and his often ponderous pace around the table. A great competitor, he was also a champion swearer, sledging opponents and generally making every match a life-or-death affair. He became familiar to British audiences by winning *Pot Black* three times and made the first century on the programme. 'He was completely without flair,' said Everton. 'If you practised with him, he had all the shots, he just couldn't bring himself to use them during a match. That conservative attitude did cost him. Maybe if he had loosened up a bit, he would've won the World Championship.'

The 1975 tournament, in his own backyard, was his big chance. When the seedings came out, they made no sense, at least on paper. Reardon was no. 1 – fair enough – but Spencer was in eighth place, meaning he was likely to come up against his great rival in the quarter-finals. Alex Higgins was also in their half, whereas Charlton – who just happened to be the promoter of the event – was in the opposite section. Reardon beat Spencer 19–17 and Higgins 19–14, while Charlton duly came through the other half of the draw to reach the final.

At one point, Reardon led 16–8, but Charlton won nine frames in succession to edge 17–16 in front. He increased this to 28–22, needing three more frames for victory, but at 29–25 missed the frame-ball brown, and Reardon won five in a row. Charlton equalised at 30–30 to force a decider, roared on by a large partisan crowd.

Charlton had a chance at a long red after a Reardon foul early in the frame that would decide the title but chose to put his opponent back in rather than play the shot himself. Reardon knocked it in, and as a shocked Charlton tried to take his seat, he missed and fell on the floor. Reardon laughed at the memory: 'I put my cue on the table, went over and helped him up. Then I went back to the table and made the winning break.'

A year later, the championship was back in Britain. Promoter Maurice Hayes was given the contract after securing cigarette brand Embassy as sponsor. The field would be split between two venues, Middlesbrough Town Hall and Wythenshawe Forum. Reardon and Higgins advanced to the final, but what followed laid bare how far snooker still had to come as a professional sport.

Early on, the glare from the lights made it hard for the players to see the balls properly. Reardon was aghast that children were allowed to run around in the arena and distracted by the constant stream of drinkers heading to and from the bar. The referee, Bill Timms, made several calls the players disagreed with and was eventually replaced by John Williams, after Reardon made his views known to the tournament director. However, his main objection was to the playing conditions.

'The table was horrendous,' Reardon said. 'Much tighter than anything you see these days. It was put in by Rapers of Manchester. I complained about it after the first frame. Nobody wanted to know. The next day, I'm having lunch. The waitress told me there were people who had gone to look at the table. So I went in, and there was the table fitter. The fitter says, "It's all level now." I asked him to show me, so he put the spirit level on the table. It still wasn't level. I said I'd get the press involved, and they [the fitters] said they'd sue me.'

As Reardon fumed, Higgins took solace in drink. 'I took the lead, and now Alex is trailing, he becomes unsteady on his feet. He had too much to drink, basically. It was sad to see. He gave up with a session to spare, that's how bad it was.'

Reardon took control, and with Higgins's display 'both wild and demoralised', according to Everton, eased to a 27–16 victory. His frustrations with the amateurish set-up were many, but he was still delighted to win another world title, coverage of which had once again been shown on the BBC's *Grandstand*.

Reardon's profile had grown to such an extent that he was now in demand to appear on mainstream television programmes, which helped spread snooker's appeal further. He was a genial guest on *Parkinson*, the BBC's flagship Saturday-night talk show. He played himself in the sitcom *Sorry!* He appeared on *The Paul Daniels Magic Show*, *Little and Large* and *The Rod Hull and Emu Show* – all proof of not only his burgeoning reputation but that of the game as well.

And he loved it. 'Just to go on television was fantastic,' he said. 'When you become world champion, you take part in everything that's going. It was free publicity. You'd have to pay huge amounts of money for publicity, and I was getting it for nothing. They thought they were using me, but I was using them.'

Reardon, who died in July 2024, aged ninety-one, was the leading player of the 1970s, an ambassador but also the main proponent for change. Time and again, it was he who was railing against playing conditions, scheduling, officials and sundry other imperfections. He was often criticised for his overbearing manner, but without his zeal for improvement, things would surely have carried on as before.

In his time, he set all the standards on the table, and his legend had a far-reaching impact on those who came later. Mark Williams now owns a club in Tredegar. He got the snooker bug at a young age largely because of the legacy established by Reardon and would win the world title three times, and plenty more besides.

'If you're a Welsh rugby or football player, you get more recognition,' Williams says. 'Ray Reardon is one of the best, if not *the* best, sportsman to come out of Wales. If he'd done what he did in rugby, there'd be statues up to him, but snooker doesn't really get that kind of attention.'

It was clear that for all the strides snooker had made in the 1970s, the World Championship needed better promotion, but everyone agreed that *Pot Black* had been a positive development that pushed the sport closer to the centre of British life. With the game now enjoying a considerable profile on television, it was inevitable that members of the watching public would want to have a go themselves, which meant crossing the threshold into the mysterious world of the British snooker club.

4

CLUBLAND

It feels like every UK-based snooker player's journey has followed a similar path. It typically starts with interest in childhood, often passed down from a previous generation, is then nurtured on a small table at home and progresses to the world of the snooker club, with its big tables and even bigger characters. It is here that a player's talent is properly put to the test, and where they also discover a side to life previously hidden in the shadows.

The old-style British billiard hall would later give way to the more modern snooker club, but the connotations never went away. 'Proficiency at billiards is the sign of a misspent youth' was a phrase attributed to the philosopher Herbert Spencer that entered the common lexicon. Snooker clubs became associated, fairly or otherwise, with low-level crime and general misbehaviour. There is something about their dark environs, the tightly shut curtains and subterranean atmosphere, the smell of beer and cigarette smoke that lingers in the memories of a generation who spent their formative years immersed in this slightly dingy world. 'If your mum caught you going in the snooker club, you'd get a clip round the ear,' says Barry Hearn, a chartered accountant who worked in the fashion industry before becoming chairman of the Lucania chain of snooker clubs in the mid-1970s.

John Virgo's early interest in the game also met with classic parental disapproval. 'I was lucky that there was a snooker club just through the back streets,' he says. 'I first went in there because I went to play football, and all the lads had gone to play snooker.

It was a shilling to join, so I took the glass bottles back to the off-licence to get the money for membership. I'd been in there a few times, and one night got back late. My father wasn't happy. He thought snooker clubs were dens of iniquity, that I shouldn't be going in them. He didn't like their reputation. There was no alcohol, but he didn't like the type of characters who frequented the place. So he stopped me going there. For two years I didn't play, until I left school at fifteen.'

Was his father right in his assessment? 'Yes, he probably was,' Virgo says. 'I never played snooker without having a side bet of some kind. That was the environment I was brought up in. If you told someone you'd just bought a new record player, they'd say, "Oh, you should've told me, I'd have got you one for half that price." Where they would've got it from you dread to think.'

It was a netherworld of knocked-off goods and chancers, as Joe Johnson found out as he climbed the ranks in the Yorkshire area. 'In every billiard hall I went in there were people who knew about life,' he says. 'Anything you wanted, you could get. You could order it, and it'd come within 15 minutes. Someone would go and fetch it from somewhere. You learned about the world, including the things not to do. Everybody used to gamble on the horses, but I'd see people skint and think, "I don't want to be like that," and to this day I've never had a bet on the horses. There were so many characters. There was a guy called Fingers, and anything you wanted, he'd get it. There was a guy called X, he was the only guy I've ever met who split a snooker ball in half, he hit them so hard.'

Stories such as these abounded and created an image problem for snooker clubs that persisted for decades, although Hearn argues a large part of that was down to class prejudice. 'In those days, you didn't want to announce to people that you were involved in any way with snooker because it was the misspent-youth era. It was 90 per cent about class. There was 10 per cent where it was actually a gentleman's game. If you look at pictures of Joe and Fred Davis playing, it was middle-class and upper-class people watching. It was a gentleman's game played after dinner with a bottle of port and a large cigar. But if you came down to the 90 per cent of the market, particularly the Lucania chain I was chairman of, they had at one time 130 clubs, predominantly in Wales, in mining villages. It was working-class.'

Now spending all of his time immersed in the club subculture, Hearn loved the world he had entered. 'The first day I walked into a snooker club I felt at home,' he says. 'I remember walking into the club in Romford, and as I went up the stairs and turned right there was a pile of shoeboxes up to the ceiling and a fella standing in front of it, shouting, "Five pound a pair." I asked him what was going on, and he said, "I've just nicked this lot. I'm just knocking them out." I told him it was my snooker hall and he couldn't do that, but he said he was only trying to make a living. "Give me ten minutes." So I gave him ten minutes, and he cleared the lot out. Robbo Brazier – he went on to drive Steve Davis – he bought the last pair because they were only two quid. They were a size seven, and he was a size eleven. I asked him why he was buying shoes the wrong size, and he goes, "Well, it's a bargain, Baz."'

Clubs were cheap to join. They appealed to a working-class demographic who could never have afforded the membership fees of golf or tennis clubs. Once inside, a constant stream of money matches and side betting sustained the play – the very reason snooker had been invented back in India. The clubs were less rarefied than the Ooty but assumed much the same purpose.

In 1954, Ronnie and Reggie Kray, the infamous twins from London who became feared, mythologised gangsters, bought the

Mile End Billiard Hall, as if to underline the questionable image the game enjoyed. 'Everywhere was money matches and skulduggery and crooked games,' says Hearn, with fondness. 'In those days you could put the table charges up by however much you liked. No one ever cared because for every game the loser paid the table, and everyone always fancied winning. But if you put a penny on a cup of tea, you had a riot on your hands.

'The association was with gangsters, the unemployed, loafers, and this became the image of the game. The first day I walked into the Lucania in Lewisham, there was a shotgun under table one, where four blokes were having a game. I said to the manager he should ask them to leave. He said, "I'd rather not. Why don't you do it?" We ended up having a cup of tea and waited for them to finish. I tried to buy the Stratford Hall once, and the guy that owned it told me that it's a good business, but the Kray brothers were regulars. They wanted four tables, and if the club was full, then those four tables became very, very quickly available. The owner was [singer] Millicent Martin's brother. He was telling me these stories where he'd go up to someone and ask, "You gonna be long?" And they'd reply, "Fuck off, I'll be as long as I want." "Well, Ronnie and Reggie want your table." "I've finished," came the reply. In the end, the Kray brothers were arrested at Mile End [Billiard Hall].'

As *Pot Black* showcased the game on television, demand soared. 'We paid £630,000 for 17 snooker clubs, and they started to make £1 million a year,' says Hearn. 'There was a boom in snooker, fruit machines and video games. These places were packed, and we never spent any money on them. I can't remember ever decorating; we just used to wash the walls every three or four years because of the nicotine stains. They were temperance clubs, so they weren't alcohol-led. The main rival was the local betting shop.'

Neal Foulds, who would follow his father, Geoff, into the professional ranks, remembers the lively world of Ron Gross's club in Neasden. 'It was eight tables, a rough old club. Nothing in there but the tables and the bar,' he says. 'It wasn't particularly well looked after, but what made it good were the people that were in there, like a boxing gym. There were lots of characters in there, and you never really knew their real names. There was a guy, Odds-On Eddie; he'd only play when he was odds-on. There was Fearless Fred and French Frank.

'There was a guy in there they called The Arab, although I think he was actually called John Taylor. He was a fearless gambler. He'd put thousands of pounds on the table. We found out later he used to go in the toilets and shoot up heroin. No one knew at the time. All of a sudden, we hadn't seen him for three months. It turned out he'd killed himself in November, but no one found him until January or February. Snooker clubs were full of these characters. Some were villains, clearly – they'd spent time in Wandsworth jail and so on – but it felt like there was a great atmosphere in these clubs.'

Gross himself was not above taking part in the constant churn of money matches. 'Ron was a straight-laced character, until he'd had a drink,' says Foulds. 'He'd walk in, having gone to the greyhounds at Wembley, and throw all his money on the table, saying, "Match it. I'll play anyone in here, I don't care what for." It was all about money matches. You'd very rarely see anyone play for the love of the game. It was quite a good grounding, I suppose. I didn't have any money really, so if you're playing for your last couple of quid, then you'd be trying hard.'

Steve Davis, who in time would become one of Britain's most recognisable sportspeople, saw the difference between the more relaxed environment of the working men's club and the harder-edged billiard halls. 'The social club and working men's club were non-profits,' he says. 'The fruit machines kept them going. It was for the working man to get cheap beer. The snooker hall was a different environment. The people who went there were a more serious snooker animal, and a certain amount of them were trying to play full-time because they loved the game. That's why there was hustling. How could you make money if you were in a snooker club all day long? The only way would be to play for money.'

Hearn's Romford club became the home of money matches. 'Three hundred people would come into the room. No windows, no fire exit. You wouldn't get permission to stage matches there, but we did,' he says. 'They'd pay a tenner to watch, and 20 to 30 thousand would be staked on a game, and no one ever reneged on a bet. Nothing was written down. It was honesty among working-class thieves. Everyone would smoke, and you couldn't see across the room. A hand would come out of the fog to indicate £500 was on.'

Players would travel the country to undertake exhibition engagements at clubs, never knowing what was awaiting them. Fred Davis turned up at one such establishment and asked to see the table. 'What table?' said his surprised host. 'We thought you'd bring it with you.'

Over time, the new image of snooker being developed on television through *Pot Black* and later the World Championship signalled a change in the environment of clubs. Phil Yates, who would become a journalist and commentator on the sport, noticed the shift as a budding player in the West Midlands. 'When I started playing snooker, clubs weren't what they used to be. They weren't the old billiard halls,' he says. 'They weren't smoke-filled. Most of them were nice. Because the game was expanding and there were a lot of clubs, they were all competing against each other, all trying to outdo each other, so the surrounds were pretty good. You'd get people of all ages and from every socio-economic bracket. Two of the guys I played with in the team, one was a leading court stenographer, and the other was a company director. You ran the whole gamut of people. Everyone felt at home. It was that kind of sport.'

The competition between clubs meant they had to smarten themselves up to attract the new breed of player. 'The first one I went in was called the Steve Davis Snooker Club. It had a painting of him on the wall,' says Alan McManus, who would go on to become one of Scotland's finest players. 'People talk about a misspent youth and dark, smoky halls – this one was anything but. You could order a steak and say how you wanted it done. You'd get the odd character selling knocked-off suits and whatever, but it was a safe environment. There was never any bullying or anything like that.'

One man had the foresight to attempt a change in snooker's image before the television age was established. In 1974, Jim Williamson opened the Northern Snooker Centre in Leeds. More than 50 years on, it is still going while hundreds of clubs that sprang up over the last five decades have closed. 'Everybody told him he was mad to do it,' said Clive Everton. 'In those days, the centre of the game wasn't so much snooker halls but Conservative and Labour clubs. That's where most players had their apprenticeships.'

By the late 1980s, every town in Britain had somewhere to play snooker. Shaun Murphy, who would become world champion in 2005, saw the transition between the old-school club and the more modern establishment while growing up in Northamptonshire, learning the hard way that ingrained attitudes were hard to shift in this very male, very adult world.

'The first snooker club I played at was the Rushden Embassy Club on the high street, above a pharmacy. This would have been the typical snooker club of the day,' Murphy says. 'It had six tables and the characters who sat in the same spot at the bar, the people who were friendly, the people to avoid. They had a monthly handicap tournament, and as a child of ten, I'd won a handful of them. I put my name down for the Christmas handicap, and a load of the club members signed a petition, citing some particular rule which prevented me from playing. They wanted me barred from the club. We sent the petition to the local newspaper, who printed it on the front page. We hung them all out to dry. That was my first introduction to snooker clubs. It was very much a grown-up, adult world. I'm sure there were things going on in there that parents wouldn't want their children exposed to.'

Fortunately, Murphy found a friendlier atmosphere at Raunds, a club owned by former world billiards champion and regular ITV commentator Mark Wildman. 'It was beautiful,' says Murphy. 'I remember the first day I went there and asking my dad if we'd got the right place, because it looked like a hotel. It was still full of wheeler-dealers and dodgy types, but they were great days. All the time I was learning life lessons. I left mainstream education at thirteen, but got enough education in those clubs to last a lifetime.'

Over time, a variety of factors saw a decline in the number of British snooker clubs. For many men, they were havens away from the pressures of home and work life, places to meet up with friends for a pint, a cigarette and a game of snooker. In 2007, the ban on smoking in all indoor venues brought one of these activities to an end and had a dramatic effect on membership figures. Soaring business rates and high-street rents led to club premises being sold off, many of which were turned into offices or apartments. By the 2020s, many clubs boasted more pool than snooker tables as a way of catering for changing tastes, but these potting palaces played their part in the career development of every champion and are remembered with fondness by those who graduated through their doors to greatness.

In 1960s Belfast, there was a club called The Jampot. It was from here that a force of nature was unleashed on the snooker world, sparking excitement and wreaking havoc in equal measure, a hero and anti-hero rolled into one. Snooker in the 1970s was keen to stress a veneer of politeness in the way it presented itself to the television audience, but a hurricane was about to tear through the sport and change it forever.

5

LIKE A HURRICANE

If you travel three miles out of Birmingham city centre, where Joe Davis won the first professional title in 1927, you will find the suburb of Selly Park. The Royal British Legion club on the Pershore Road has long since been knocked down but can lay claim to playing a pivotal role in the development of snooker, acting as host venue for the final of the 1972 World Championship. The professional game was still stuttering along, albeit with increased interest through *Pot Black*, but on a cold February night it received a huge injection of publicity and excitement thanks to its new world champion.

The career of Alexander Gordon Higgins is central to the story of this sport but exists almost in parallel as a fable about the dangers, temptations and limits of fame. While many others who found stardom with snooker have enjoyed happy retirements, Higgins died pitifully at the age of 61, malnourished and alone. Yet he was a central pillar in the construction of the circuit that became a favoured soap opera of the British public in the years that followed, a wild man who dazzled and delighted, aggravated and appalled.

Intoxicating and often intoxicated, he played the game like nobody else. He lived life by his own rules, demonstrating contempt for convention and a frequently cruel lack of regard for the feelings of others. Many disliked him, but far more idolised his rebellious spirit. He was a hero for a swathe of working-class fans who felt overlooked and undermined. He was a gift to snooker.

Born in Belfast in 1949, Higgins lived with his parents and two sisters in a council house in Abingdon Street, Sandy Row. His father was a labourer, working on building sites and the railways. His mother picked potatoes to earn extra money for the household. At eleven, Higgins first entered The Jampot, a billiard hall just off the Donegall Road. 'It was the epitome of every snooker hall you ever imagined in the 40s and 50s,' he wrote in his autobiography, *From the Eye of the Hurricane*. 'Dark and dingy with clouds of cigarette smoke hanging over the tables.'[1]

Higgins was soon playing for money, the adults in the club taking no pity on him, but in the early 1960s there did not seem to be much future in snooker. So, at fifteen, Higgins applied to become a stable boy at a training yard in Oxfordshire and crossed the Irish Sea for a new adventure, becoming an apprentice jockey, before returning to Belfast at eighteen. He entered the 1968 Northern Ireland Amateur Championship and was victorious. Word began to spread about his unorthodox style, the way his body moved and jerked as he played each shot. He was attracting a following, and after almost single-handedly winning the British Team Championship for Belfast YMCA in Bolton was invited to take part in exhibition matches against John Spencer, who had won the revived World Championship. This raised Higgins's profile still further and built a large audience of vociferous fans beguiled by his playing style.

'There were all sorts of stories coming in about this exceptionally fast lad from Northern Ireland who was making centuries in four minutes,' said Clive Everton. In 1971, Higgins applied to become a professional and was accepted, although the tournament circuit consisted of only a handful of events. The 1972 World Championship was played over the course of a year at various venues around Britain. Higgins defeated Ron Gross in Ealing and Maurice Parkin and Jackie Rea in Sheffield. In the quarter-finals, he beat former champion John Pulman in Scotland, before a semi-final against Rex Williams in Bolton, a match that went to a 31st and deciding frame. Williams was 14 in front when he missed a routine blue, letting Higgins in to take the lead, which was never surrendered.

In retrospect, the Williams blue is a shot that helped shape snooker's destiny. Had he potted it and won the match, the old order would have been maintained, with Spencer waiting in the final. As it was, Higgins's journey to the title-deciding match in his first season as a professional caught the public imagination.

The final took place in the concert room of the British Legion. There was no television coverage but significant interest from paying audiences, despite the ramshackle conditions. A miners' strike meant electricity shortages. On the second night, the table lighting cut out and a mobile generator was brought in, but the lights were dull and there was no heating on a chilly winter evening. 'They had a big light shining on the table, and you could see a triangle of smoke,' says journalist Phil Yates, then a nine-year-old attending the final with his father. 'The seats were placed on pallets. It was nothing like it is now. Higgins played so quickly, he was very different from the rest.'

The final was nip and tuck until Higgins won one of the evening sessions 6–0, and he held on to win 37–32. 'To say I was elated would be an understatement. Spencer had played at his best. He'd been determined to win and Alex Higgins had beaten him fair and square.'[2]

Thames Television immediately commissioned a film on Higgins, following him as he waited for trains to take him around the country for exhibitions. John Virgo saw first-hand his mercurial skills and the immediate effect he had on snooker's fortunes. 'There was no feeling whatsoever back then that you could make a living from snooker,' he says. 'Alex Higgins was that little sprinkle of stardust that was needed to really get the public's attention. He had a great talent, an unbelievable talent. I used to drive him to exhibitions because he never drove. He'd be struggling, looking at people in the crowd and insinuating they were putting him off, then all of a sudden he would produce an unbelievable shot, and from that moment on it was just magic, he never missed. He was a genius, there's no doubt about that in my mind.'

Clive Everton believed that Higgins's victory was pivotal to the World Championship gaining wider credibility. 'In those days, each match lasted a week, and the championship lasted the whole season,' he said. 'When Higgins won in '72, it was so well attended that it was clear that snooker was starting to offer the public something new. In 1973, West Nally applied to the WPBSA [World Professional Billiards and Snooker Association] to promote the World Championship and staged it over a fortnight. They got it going again as a proper event.'

Everton recognised Higgins's faults, but also his attraction. 'It's an understatement, but he certainly broke the mould as far as what a professional snooker player looked like,' he said. 'He was anti-establishment, never wanted to be accepted; he just wanted to go his own way. He could be intensely annoying at times, but every Higgins match in the arena was an emotional experience.'

When the 1980s dawned, Higgins served as an unpredictable counterpoint to the reliable Steve Davis, who demolished him 16–6 to win the 1980 UK Championship. Like fire and water, they were opposites, one a thorn in the side of the establishment, the other the epitome of respectability.

The Higgins–Davis rivalry was, in truth, incredibly one-sided. Of the 31 matches played between them, Davis won 25. However, Higgins enjoyed some notable successes against the clean-cut

Londoner, including a 13–9 quarter-final victory in the 1980 World Championship. At the UK Championship in 1983, he fell 7–0 adrift to Davis in the final but, demonstrating the heart for a fight that so thrilled audiences, recovered to snatch a dramatic 16–15 triumph. At the 1985 Masters, he edged Davis 5–4 on the black amid wild scenes, shouting, 'We're fucking back!' into a BBC camera as fans ran onto the arena floor to embrace him.

'I never knew him. I kept away from him. He scared the life out of me,' says Davis. 'I had to do exhibitions with him. I remember going on a plane with him to Canada, and I was in the seat next to him, thinking, "Fucking hell, I've got to sit next to him for eight hours." I was so nervous I tipped a beer over myself and sat in a puddle. We ended up having a great chat. He was a different person because there was no competition to play that day. But he was a turner. The next time he saw you, it was like he didn't even know you. You were the enemy, and he was in nasty mode. I was frightened of him. I didn't socialise with him at all, so I didn't know him. All I knew was what I got when he turned up for an exhibition or a match.'

Davis was a new breed of professional, wedded to technique and practice. The maverick Higgins was the polar opposite, but Davis has no doubt about his intelligence as a player. 'He'd never embraced the modern-day technique of keeping your head still,' he says. 'He was inaccurate, but within that he's second only to Ronnie O'Sullivan, for me, as far as geniuses go, or maybe the same, but with a far poorer technique. What a safety player. Once he got control of the last red and the colours and he was dominating the safety part of it, you felt like at some stage you would lose. That's the biggest accolade I could give him. If he'd had a better technique and a better application in tournaments, he'd have been a multiple winner.'

Davis would dominate the 1980s on the table, but Higgins transcended the sport, becoming a tabloid-newspaper staple due to a chaotic personal life. Boozy nights out, fights, womanising, drug-taking . . . It was a heady cocktail of excess played out as a form of public entertainment, and it became a self-fulfilling existence. Higgins was pegged as a troublemaker, which in turn meant he attracted trouble, as he explained in a 1994 interview with the *Observer*:

> On the train, I can get buttonholed by anybody, and I have to sit and suffer it. There are always people walking up and down the corridor, looking in the compartment. Out of 50 passengers there will be, say, 47 nice people. Out of 500,000 people, that's I don't know how many assholes. Divide that by 365. That's a lot of terrible days.³

Provoked at times he might have been, but Higgins was no innocent. Joe Johnson, who became world champion in 1986, witnessed his erratic behaviour close-up. 'I saw him once in the toilet at Pontins, where he was playing Terry Griffiths,' he says. 'I said to him, "Go on, big A." He looked at me and said, "Don't call me a bighead!" He stormed out and didn't speak to me for two years. Alex could be one of the nicest guys you'd ever meet, but could change in an instant. We toured the Middle East together. It was a great time, but there were some volatile nights, which put me off him a bit, although I admired him as a snooker player.'

Higgins's unstable nature unnerved many on the circuit. 'I avoided him like the plague,' says Trevor East, executive producer of snooker on ITV in the 1980s. 'I thought he was a Jekyll and Hyde, a pretty horrible individual. He was fine when he wasn't pissed or had stuff up his nose. You got to know well enough when to avoid him. A fantastic player, a genius, but a flawed individual.'

Cliff Thorburn beat Higgins 18–16 in the 1980 World Championship final. He needed little motivation to win. The pair had got off on the wrong foot, and the relationship never recovered. 'The first day I met him, we were going to have lunch,' Thorburn says. 'He was out riding horses with his girlfriend. I thought, "That's a little different to my lifestyle." We ended up going to play snooker for £5 a game. He wanted to give me 40 start. Being the gentleman I am, I only took 28. I won some money and walked down the stairs. As I closed the door I heard a snooker ball ringing off it. I thought, "That was a lucky escape." From the first time I met him we had a problem, and after that it just became worse. Alex had this unbelievable energy. No one wanted to win as much as him. He was desperate to win. It just wasn't fun being around him. He had a big chip on his shoulder. You couldn't help but be amazed by his talents, but he got people so upset. He went to the limits. He'd say things and expect nothing to happen. I'm surprised he wasn't killed by somebody.'

A decade after his 1972 victory, when no television cameras were present, Higgins arrived at the 1982 World Championship, which was now afforded blanket coverage by the BBC. Ranked 11th in the world, he was certainly a contender, but behind Davis, Griffiths, Thorburn and several others in the list of likely winners. Davis and Griffiths had contested five finals that season but were each beaten in the first round. Higgins defeated Jim Meadowcroft 10–5, won a decider against Doug Mountjoy and held off Willie Thorne 13–10 to reach the semi-finals, where he faced a 20-year-old Londoner, Jimmy White, who played the game in a similarly natural, exciting manner.

At 15–14, White needed one more frame to advance to the final and threaten to take Higgins's record as youngest world champion. On a break of 41, and playing to bring more reds into the open, White missed a pot on the black. He got in again but, using the rest, missed a red while leading 59–0, with a possible 75 remaining. Higgins stepped forward, and what followed would enter snooker folklore. His back to the wall, this was a case of kill or be killed, the sort of situation in which he felt most alive. He potted the first red but was left in no-man's-land when it came to position. However, he sank a long green and freed a red from the left-hand side cushion. Continuing to chase position, the cue ball roamed around the table, leaving him eminently missable pots, which he nevertheless made. On 13, hampered by a red, he potted a blue with so much spin on the white that it fizzed off the side cushion and back down the table, leaving him awkward on the next ball. On and on it went, the pressure growing, the anticipation inside the arena palpable. This was Higgins at his heroic best, and he would go on to make a courageous, spellbinding clearance to keep the match alive, before dominating the decider to prevail 16–15.

Mark Watterson, then fourteen, and the nephew of the tournament promoter, recalls the excitement of the afternoon. 'Life wasn't like it is today with social media. A live football match on TV was a major talking point,' he says. 'The advantage snooker had was that it was on a lot. No other sport had as much coverage. I sat in the press seats. Terry Griffiths was sat behind me. I was like a kid at Christmas. I was always excited watching Alex. There was just something about him. I can still feel myself sat there now. My biggest memory is Alex putting Jimmy's head on his shoulder at the end.'

Waiting in the final was Ray Reardon, the dominant player of the 1970s, who had already beaten Higgins in the 1976 world final. At 49, time was running out for the Welshman to add to his collection of six world titles, but he was by no means a spent force. 'I knew I could beat Higgins. He never beat me in tournaments or exhibitions,' Reardon said, four decades on, although in fact Higgins had beaten him in both the Masters and the UK Championship in 1980.

Reardon made the early running, building a 5–2 lead, before Higgins hit his stride, winning eight of the next ten frames to lead 10–7. Reardon could not get level, until, 15–12 down, he won three in a row, but thereafter he scored only nine further points as Higgins dominated frame 31, made a 79 break and then one of 135 to become champion again.

Reardon remained convinced Higgins had taken drugs during the final. 'He was 15–12 up. I won the next three to make it 15–15. The guy who left that arena was a loser. The guy who came back in had been on everything. They lost the drugs sample, threw it away. The board did nothing about it. Unbelievable. Snooker was the first sport to bring in drug testing, yet they didn't support the players. They only wanted to go so far.'

In fact, mandatory drug testing at tournaments was not introduced until 1985. This does not rule out Higgins playing under the influence, but he was not tested during the final, so Reardon's conspiracy theory about a cover-up is unlikely.

What is not in doubt is the emotion of the moment. As Higgins was handed the trophy, he spotted his wife, Lynn, in the arena, holding their baby daughter, Lauren, and beckoned to her to join him. Tears streaming down his face, this is the image indelibly associated with his second world title: Alex, Lynn and Lauren Higgins, embracing in his time of triumph, the people's champion once again the world champion. 'The three of us hugged as if we were the only ones in the auditorium,' he reflected later.[4]

Of all the iconic moments in televised snooker, Higgins tearfully cradling baby Lauren endures as much as any. It demonstrated a vulnerability to his character, a sensitivity more relatable to many than the boozy bust-ups, the braggadocio and the trash-talking. In this moment, he was a proud father. Even those turned off by Higgins's antics were warmed by his simple act of humanity.

The various fragments of his world had come together, but they would not stay complete for long. Higgins was not made that way. And as his life retreated into tumultuous waters, his game suffered. His 1983 UK Championship victory did not herald a general resurgence in form. He had appeared in the World Championship semi-finals earlier that year but did not even reach another quarter-final in the game's showpiece event for the rest of his career. From 1985 to 1987, he lost three years running in the last 16 to Griffiths. He still had his moments, reaching the finals of the 1984 UK Championship, the 1988 Grand Prix and the 1990 British Open. In 1989, he broke an ankle after falling from the second-floor window of his Manchester apartment following an altercation. He played in two tournaments while literally hopping around the table and, still hobbling, managed to beat Stephen Hendry 9–8 in the Irish Masters final at Goffs, County Kildare.

This was Higgins at his daring best, but notorious incidents either side of what proved to be his last hurrah illustrated him at his unpleasant worst. At the 1986 UK Championship, he defeated Mike Hallett 9–7 in the last 16, before launching an attack on the size of the pockets, but this was not the story the assembled media would write. On leaving the press conference, Higgins was informed he must give a urine sample as part of the recently introduced WPBSA drug-testing requirements. He immediately flew into a rage, which ended with him headbutting Paul Hatherell, the WPBSA tournament director.

He was allowed to continue in the tournament but was referred to the disciplinary committee. Such was the media interest that camera crews camped outside his house. He emerged wearing a fur hat and ankle-length coat and cradling an early mobile phone the size of a house brick. With a ban very likely, a reporter asked him, 'Can you survive without snooker?' Higgins, quick-witted, if lacking humility, replied, 'Can snooker survive without me?'

He was subsequently banned for six tournaments. Many felt he had got off lightly, but Higgins nursed a sense of resentment that continued to exhibit itself in outbursts and often random bouts of rude behaviour, as witnessed by Phil Yates. 'I started covering the game in September 1988, and he was beginning his decline,' says Yates. 'When he was at a tournament, you'd be secretly hoping he lost because the atmosphere was so hostile. Everyone was on edge. If he knew you had a particular weakness, he'd zero in on you and be horrible about it. One of the journalists in the 1970s had mental health problems because he'd witnessed so much football violence, and Higgins started on about that in one argument. I spoke to him on two or three occasions when he wasn't drunk, and he was a joy. He was very clever. He had a good vocabulary and could hold a really interesting conversation. The problem was that on the vast majority of occasions, he was drunk. It was toxic around him.'

The six-tournament ban led to a decline in his world ranking, and in 1988 Higgins dropped out of the top 16, which meant he had to pre-qualify for the following year's World Championship. His match was scheduled for the day after the Irish Masters final, where he had beaten Hendry. He lost 10–8 to Darren Morgan. A year later, he did qualify, but even before a ball was potted a dark cloud hung over him, following an incident at the World Team Cup a few weeks earlier.

Higgins was competing for Northern Ireland alongside Tommy Murphy and Dennis Taylor, who, as the highest-ranked player in the side, was captain. Higgins and Taylor went way back but were chalk and cheese in terms of personality. While Higgins was not interested in acceptability, Taylor was renowned as a thorough professional. He had helped his compatriot set himself up in a flat when he moved to Blackburn in the late 1960s, donating a television set from the shop where he worked. 'I had some wonderful matches against Alex,' he says. 'There was always a bit of needle, but he had that with most players.'

This needle would resurface, with unpalatable results. As World Cup captain, it was Taylor who determined the team's playing order, but Higgins, who was struggling, was insistent he should stay on after his two frames. Taylor disagreed – in any case, the format would not permit it – and was subjected to a furious, highly personal rant in which Higgins made hurtful comments about his mother and told him, 'You come from Coalisland, I come from the Shankhill. Next time you're in Northern Ireland I'll have you shot.' The diatribe was witnessed by John Spencer, the former world champion, who at the time was WPBSA chairman. 'He lost his head,' says Taylor. 'He didn't want to come off, but that was the format.'

By chance, the two would meet in the first round of the Irish Masters later that month – 'the greatest grudge match of all time,' as it was billed by an eager media. ITN's *News at Ten* sent a camera crew, and Goffs resold ticket stubs to pack in fans, with standing room only due to the demand. Taylor set aside personal enmity and focused on the match. He won 5–2.

A few weeks later, Higgins was beaten 10–5 in the first round of the World Championship by Steve James. With a disciplinary cloud hanging over him, and clearly the worse for drink, he remained in his seat long after the match ended. When he finally did leave the arena, he was asked to attend the customary press conference and, for no discernible reason, punched the press officer, Colin Randle, in the stomach, before launching into a surreal, rambling diatribe, during which he announced his retirement.

'You can shove snooker up your jacksie, I'm not playing no more,' he said, slurring his words. 'I was supposed to be the stalwart of the game, the kid who took all the brunt. Well, the kid who took all the brunt is absolutely sick up to here of taking all the shit.'

For threatening Taylor and punching Randle, Higgins was banned for a year. It meant his world ranking plummeted and he was now required to compete in qualifying rounds, from where younger, hungrier players were emerging. In a profile for the *Sunday Times*, Clive Everton perfectly encapsulated his character:

> Alex Higgins has reached the age of 41 with a set of emotional needs scarcely modified since infancy: an insatiable lust for the limelight, an imperious wish to have his own way and a yearning for unconditional love expressed as an assumption that he will be forgiven no matter what he does. He claims a child's licence to say the most hurtful things he can think of and seeks adult refuge in alcohol and denial of unpalatable realities.[5]

Trouble was a constant companion. At the 1991 UK Championship, he invited Stephen Hendry, who had superseded him as the youngest-ever world champion the previous year, to 'shake hands with the Devil' before their match. After Hendry beat him, there was a disagreement about what had been said at the post-match handshake. Higgins claimed it had been, 'Well done, Stephen, you were a little bit lucky.' In Hendry's telling, he had been told, 'Up your arse, you cunt.'

Ian Doyle, Hendry's manager, was clear in his view of Higgins following this incident: 'He's a demented, raving lunatic. Snooker is bigger than Higgins. He has to be removed from the game. He's a menace to himself and everyone around him.'

In 1994, Higgins appeared for the last time in the televised stage of the World Championship. He had trailed Tony Knowles 6–3 at the halfway point of their final qualifying-round match at the Norbreck Castle Hotel in Blackpool and repaired to a nearby pub, the Mariners, for some refreshments. As he headed back to the hotel, he tripped on a low wall and cut his arm. As the match resumed, Higgins bled on the baize but turned the contest around and prevailed 10–9.

His opponent in round one was Ken Doherty, a Dubliner who had broken through the previous year by winning his maiden ranking title, the Welsh Open. Doherty had grown up idolising Higgins, watching his 1982 triumph as an awestruck twelve-year-old with dreams of becoming a player himself. 'He was my inspiration,' Doherty says. 'When he won the World Championship, it was one of the most iconic moments in our sport, with the tears and the baby coming out. He inspired so many people at that time. He had an electricity, an unpredictability, a charisma that we hadn't seen before in our sport. He came along and sparked it into life. He made it more showbiz. That's why snooker exploded from then on. Clubs were opening up everywhere in the 1980s. We had three snooker clubs just in our little village at one stage. The game just went from strength to strength.'

Their match included a row with the referee, John Williams, whom Higgins asked to move, complaining he was in his line of sight. Williams, one of the game's most experienced officials, refused. (Bizarrely, in a qualifying match the following year, Higgins again asked Williams to move, stating he was 'in my line of thought'.)

Doherty won 10–6 but could not take much pleasure from the win. 'It was a completely hollow victory,' he says. 'I didn't like the match at all because he was at the end of his career and my hero. It's not something I have happy memories about.'

Higgins was in deep decline, and his television appearances became rarer as he spent most of his time mired in qualifiers. Gradually, he faded from view, dropping off the circuit in 1997. After a lifetime of smoking – often the free cigarettes handed out by tournament sponsors – he developed throat cancer and became frighteningly gaunt. He continued to play in seniors and legends competitions, including an emotional last stand in a seniors event in April 2010, having spent the previous week in hospital. He died three months later.

Many within the game argue his various misdemeanours warranted a permanent ban from snooker, long before the incident with Taylor in 1990. Virgo was chairman of the WPBSA from 1988 to 1991, in charge of player discipline. 'You didn't want to ban him because you knew everyone wanted to see him,' he says. 'The sponsors wanted him in the tournaments, but it was getting to such a degree that he was bringing the game into disrepute. When I look back, I think maybe we should've come down a bit harder on him, because maybe that would have been a help to him. With certain people you let them get away with things, and they go even further and abuse the system. In the end, he did get a ban, but that was always on the cards.'

Reardon believed Higgins received reasonable treatment and would not accept help when it was offered. 'I was very pally with Alex, I supported him more than anybody,' he said. 'But he was a real Jekyll and Hyde who could be a bloody nightmare. I could still admire and like him. I liked the nice Alex Higgins. I think the governing body treated him very fairly, but over a period of several years he must have lost thousands in fines. We had a meeting much later on, when he was struggling, and the board came up with a great suggestion that we name a competition after him in Ireland. We said we'd give him the tournament takings for three years. That'd be a lot of money, at least £50,000. We got in touch with his manager. It was a very generous deal. Word came back that he wanted £5,000 in cash up front. We said, "That's okay, we'll take it out of the gate money." Then his manager wanted £3,000, and if any sponsors were found, they wanted 20 per cent of the gate, and if television came in, he wanted 25 per cent of their fees. So we'd end up with nothing. That wasn't the association being unkind. It was just sad.'

Hendry fondly remembers his early association with Higgins. 'When I turned pro, every tournament he'd come and practise with me,' he says. 'It was unbelievable. He obviously liked something in my game. For a couple of years, it was great between us, but when I started to win regularly I was the enemy, like the reincarnation of Steve.'

And, like Davis, Hendry did not want to be in the Higgins orbit for fear of what could happen. 'You didn't want to be around him,' he says. 'I've never seen anyone walk into a room and change the atmosphere like Alex did. Everyone would be waiting to see what he was going to do. You were walking on eggshells. It's sad, because snooker wouldn't be where it is without him. I don't think he'd live in today's game because he didn't score heavily enough, but he was a genius in the way he played. He'd find a difficult way of playing a simple shot.'

Cliff Thorburn, who had more reason than most to form a dim view of Higgins, remembers his old rival with sadness. 'I played him in the seniors when he was on his deathbed,' he says. 'Oh my God, when he came out, I just couldn't believe how he looked. The first thing I wanted to do was hug him. When he passed away, it was very sad. Nobody asked me for my thoughts. I guess they assumed I hated the guy, but I didn't hate him at all. He was so wonderful for the game.'

One interested spectator at Selly Park back in 1972 had been Mike Watterson, a player himself but also an ambitious businessman who saw potential in snooker. After the shambolic staging of the 1976 World Championship, Watterson won the rights to promote the event in 1977. The question was, where? He wanted a venue that offered more comfort for players and spectators alike. Talking it over with his wife, Carole, she mentioned a theatre she had recently visited. Maybe he should have a look at that.

Watterson was distracted. He had taken on the burden of promoting the championship but was not guaranteed a sponsor after Embassy had left the previous year's event unimpressed with the set-up. The BBC were interested in showing highlights but had been given different dates to those Watterson was planning. The venue, though, was the key part of the jigsaw.

He turned to Carole. What was the name of the theatre she had been to? Her reply?

'The Crucible in Sheffield.'

6

THE MODERN WORLD

The Crucible Theatre opened on 9 November 1971 with a show entitled *Fanfare*, a mixture of children's theatre, a translation of Chekhov's *Swan Song* and music hall. Among the actors taking part was a young Ian McKellen. Theatre magazine *The Stage* described opening night as 'An evening of glitter, excitement, expectation and fulfilment.'[1]

The Crucible cost £1 million to build and operate, with £650,000 coming from Sheffield Corporation and the Arts Council. Colin George, the artistic director, had pushed for a thrust stage, with the audience on three sides rather than the traditional proscenium. 'We did so because we wished to involve the spectator rather than control him.'[2]

He had been influenced by the director Sir Tyrone Guthrie, whose theatre in Minneapolis had a similarly 'open' stage. George visited it in 1967, and the experience of seeing the stage for the first time was transformative: 'Gleaming polished wood, a narrow promontory jutting out into space, inviting the actor to stand on it and "ascend the brightest heaven of invention". It was quite the most exciting modern interior I had ever seen.'[3]

George saw the audience as part of the production, rather than merely observers of it. Intimacy was at the theatre's core. As *The Stage* reported, 'The furthest seat is only 59 feet from the centre point of the stage.'[4] The capacity was just under a thousand seats.

Mike Watterson was not a man of the theatre, but he recognised the potential of the Crucible as a new home for snooker and had the determination to make it happen. His nephew, Mark, remembers him as a single-minded man with personal warmth. 'He was always a very driven man, Uncle Michael,' he says. 'Very strong-willed, knew what he wanted and nothing was going to stand in his way. You have to be that kind of character to be in his shoes. He wasn't star-struck; he was focused on what he wanted to get done.'

After his wife's recommendation, Watterson arranged to meet Arnold Elliman, the manager of the Crucible. In his autobiography, serialised in *Snooker Scene* in 2016, he wrote:

> What I saw bowled me over. It seemed perfect, but the question had to be asked, 'How wide is the stage?' 34 feet, was the reply. I was devastated as I needed 36 minimum. Elliman called on the stage manager for a second opinion and the news came back that the width was, in fact, 36 feet.

The BBC's Nick Hunter was invited to examine the theatre. 'He apparently said to Mike when he came to look at it, "I think it's too nice for snooker,"' says Mark Watterson. His uncle nevertheless formed a favourable opinion of the BBC man, who would pioneer television coverage of snooker as the BBC's executive producer. 'Nick was a good professional who knew his business and was always amenable to sensible suggestions.'[5]

Watterson invited Peter Dyke, representing Embassy, to see the venue but did not tell him it had a no-smoking policy, strategically standing in front of the 'No Smoking' sign on the auditorium's door.

What was the Crucible's response to Watterson's overture? The theatre was struggling and needed the money, according to Tedd George, the son of the first artistic director:

Within a couple of years the Crucible was under severe financial strain as recession bit and public finances dried up. A number of options were considered to boost revenues, but the masterstroke came with the decision to host the 1977 World Snooker Championship in the main auditorium. In truth, my father and many theatre professionals were initially aghast at the idea of the Crucible Theatre being used for snooker. But they soon recognised that snooker put the Crucible on the international map and secured the theatre's financial stability. Over time, my father would come to see snooker as another feather in the Crucible's cap, proving that its unique performing area could be used in ways the designers had never imagined.[6]

Watterson had ensured a new start for the World Championship, but already players were becoming suspicious of him. He had made money through his car business, whereas many of them were scraping by with exhibitions and holiday-camp engagements. Far from hiding his success, he drove a gold Rolls-Royce with the number plate CUE 1, sold to him by Joe Davis.

How would the players greet the new championship venue? 'Ray Reardon's reaction to the Crucible was to ask, "So, where's Sheffield?"' says Mark Watterson. 'Players like Cliff Thorburn and Dennis Taylor really appreciated what he did, but one or two of the old guard didn't.'

Reardon himself remembered it differently. 'Everyone was pleased to get to Sheffield,' he said. 'The Crucible was fantastic, a proper venue. All the others weren't.'

The concern was whether the public would show up. Snooker's broadcast exposure was still limited largely to *Pot Black* and a few outings on commercial television. 'Mike gave my dad a load of stickers to put in his Ford Cortina,' says Mark Watterson. 'We'd drive round with the stickers saying, "World Snooker Championship at the Crucible Theatre." He gave my dad loads of tickets to flog to his workmates – he worked for a big engineering firm. The first day, 18 April, Mike sat there, apprehensive, wondering how many would come in. It was 245 for the first game.'

Audiences built as the event went on and the snooker world got used to a changed environment. Morning play was introduced. Players had hitherto been used to playing in the evenings, with long nights stretching due to socialising afterwards, but this was a new start for the championship. The arena contained two tables, split by a thin dividing wall. The audience were sat very close to the action. It all felt markedly different to what had gone before.

'The main difference was we were starting at eleven in the morning,' says John Virgo. 'We'd never done that before. We were the sort of people who got up at that time. Also, the fact there were two tables next to each other, divided by a flimsy screen, so you could hear the noise from the other table. We all knew it was the way forward, so just had to get used to it.'

This was easier said than done. 'In 1979, I was playing Cliff Thorburn, and on the next table is Terry Griffiths playing Alex Higgins,' Virgo says. 'I'm leaning over to play this very important shot, and all of a sudden Higgins must've done something on the other side of the wall. There was a huge roar from the crowd, and I swear my heart stopped beating. It frightened the life out of me. We'd never had this before, and it took a bit of getting used to. In fact, Fred Davis once said to me that Joe would've refused to play under those conditions. That's maybe why the game didn't move forward at a pace it should have.'

'The Crucible looked like the place, although a lot of players didn't like the two tables because it was very tight,' says Dennis

Taylor, who, like Virgo, was part of the 1977 cohort. 'It didn't seem like they would play it there because it wasn't quite big enough, but they managed to get it to work, and it was the greatest thing that ever happened to the game. The Crucible and the BBC giving it an awful lot of coverage – that's when the game really took off.'

Cliff Thorburn, beaten 25–21 in the 1977 final by John Spencer, agrees. 'It was a perfectly shaped venue,' he says. 'I look at pictures of the set now, and things are cardboard and wooden, but I felt like I was in Heaven on Earth. I was mesmerised to be there. It was just done so well. I became good friends with Mike Watterson. Everybody knew everyone. We'd go out for dinner with the referees. We knew their families. We were all seeing this for the first time. We knew something good was coming.'

As a journalist, Clive Everton had seen snooker's tentative rise and was now convinced something had changed. 'On the very first day [of the World Championship] in 1977, I sat in the arena and thought, "This is different." It was clear that snooker, due to Mike Watterson, had taken a big step forward,' he said.

For Spencer, it was a third World Championship victory. He was especially proud to have launched a new era. 'I would say that the Crucible did more for snooker than any player did,' he wrote in his autobiography.[7]

Watterson also promoted the first UK Championship in 1977, open to players resident in the UK and won by Patsy Fagan, an Irishman based in London. It began in Blackpool but moved in its second year to Preston Guild Hall, where it became established as a major event. The World Team Cup followed in 1979. Watterson was undoubtedly doing a good job at gaining snooker exposure and boosting the earnings of players, but many of them seemed more concerned about how much he was pocketing.

'They thought he was making a lot of money,' says Mark Watterson. 'From the outside, you get that, but what you have to remember is that after 1976, it took someone like Mike, with some drive. Ray Reardon was always winning, and the World Championship had flopped in Australia. Mike told me he drove 80,000 miles one year. He put the work in. He spoke to sponsors on a daily basis.'

Watterson did not always find the players cooperative with his vision for promoting the sport. 'Mike went to a meeting about promoting the UK Championship,' says his nephew. 'He gave some leaflets to John Spencer and others to distribute to get some publicity for the tournament. He went to his car and realised he'd forgotten his coat, so he went back to the room. They'd all gone, and the leaflets were in the bin. He said Spencer had once claimed there was colour TV and *Pot Black*, and everything just happened after that, but everything didn't "just happen". He said the players had no idea how to set up tournaments, no idea how to speak to sponsors, no idea how to get the BBC involved, no idea how to get a venue like the Crucible.'

Matters came to a head in 1983, when Watterson was informed by the WPBSA that his services were no longer required. 'People get jealous, or some people do,' said Everton. 'Some insiders at WPBSA put their heads together and basically robbed him of what he'd built up.' Even so, he had made his mark and set snooker on the way to developing a credible circuit, winning the trust and support of broadcasters and sponsors.

In 1978, Reardon won the second World Championship played at the Crucible, taking his career tally to six. He beat Perrie Mans of South Africa 25–18, but much of the interest centred on 64-year-old Fred Davis, champion eight times in the post-war period before snooker's decline, who reached the semi-finals. Trailing 16–14, Davis missed a straightforward pink when well placed to pull a frame back. His brother Joe was watching intently in the audience and became ill as the tension rose. An ambulance was later called, and Davis, the man who had started snooker's professional story, died three months later, on 10 July, aged 77.

'I don't know how Fred missed that pink to this day,' says John Virgo, beaten in the qualifiers by Davis that year. 'When I went out of the arena, at the top of the stairs was Joe Davis, slumped in his chair, shaking his head. He kept saying, "How did he miss that pink?" Three months later, he died. He was distraught. If there was any question of brotherly love, that told you. He was devastated for Fred.'

Mans won the match 18–16. He was renowned as a fine potter but not a break-builder. When he won the Masters the following year, his highest break in the whole tournament was 48. He could not deny Reardon another World Championship victory, and so the stranglehold the Welshman and Spencer had on the game, interrupted only by Higgins in 1972, continued. Between them they had won nine of the last ten world titles. When the run ended, it did so courtesy of an unheralded newcomer.

Terry Griffiths's professional career had started in unpromising fashion when he lost his first match on tour 9–8 to Rex Williams in the 1978 UK Championship, having been 8–2 up. The only other tournament he could play in during his debut year was the World Championship, winning two matches to qualify.

Griffiths was born in Llanelli in 1947, the youngest of three children. His father, Martin, was employed at the tinplate works in the village of Dafen. He was a bright boy and got into the local grammar school, but missed the friends he had grown up with and was a constant truant, eventually getting expelled. 'I thought the grammar school was too posh and felt horribly out of place there.'[8]

The family had a small snooker table in the house, but Griffiths did not show a serious interest until he was fourteen, finding Hatchers, the local snooker club, the perfect place to spend his lunch hour. He improved steadily but had no thoughts of snooker as a career. Instead, he married Annette, with whom he would have two sons, and became a postman. It was the postal strike of 1971 that was to change his life: 'I was practising a lot, since basically I had nothing to do.'[9] Griffiths made his first century break around this time and a few months later reached the final of the Welsh Amateur Championship, convinced now that snooker was worth pursuing seriously.

He became an insurance salesman and won the Welsh Championship three times before becoming English amateur champion in 1977 and again in 1978. He now had to decide whether to apply for professional status. The English title carried such weight that he would surely be accepted, but Griffiths was torn. 'To earn the right money I would have to be successful. Being successful meant I would be away from home a lot, which really I did not want to happen. If I was not successful, then there was no point in turning professional. It was a Catch-22 situation.'[10]

He took the plunge and arrived at the Crucible in April 1979, unknown outside of snooker circles. That would soon change. The BBC had increased its coverage of the World Championship the previous year, with nightly highlights programmes, and in 1979 introduced *Frame of the Day*, which was broadcast in the early evening. There was live coverage of the final in the afternoons, including on *Grandstand*.

The public naturally warmed to Griffiths, a relatable character steeped in family and the world of work. He spoke with humility and was a new face compared to the by-now well-known players of *Pot Black*. He defeated Mans, shaded Higgins 13–12 in a thriller, making a century in the decider, and outlasted Eddie Charlton 19–17 in the semi-finals, a match that ended at 1.40 a.m.

Afterwards, faced with BBC presenter David Vine's microphone, Griffiths simply said, 'I'm in the final now, you know,' with equal parts delight and disbelief. In it, he faced Dennis Taylor, winning the three-day contest 24–16. He had become world champion on his first attempt. The trophy presentation went by in a haze before Griffiths retreated to the dressing room. 'I could hardly believe what had happened. I just sat there and cried with joy. I could not stop.'[11]

It was a personal triumph for the 31-year-old Welshman, and hugely significant for snooker too, just at the moment that television was taking the sport more seriously. The seemingly endless hegemony of Reardon and Spencer had been emphatically ended, giving hope to amateurs everywhere and inspiring them to consider the professional game.

'It was phenomenal because it showed what you could do if you came through the amateur game,' says journalist and broadcaster Phil Yates. 'Before Terry won the World Championship, he was hardly known. I went to an early session of the final. He made so many pressure clearances, it was ridiculous.'

'It was really an extraordinarily quick rise from anonymity to fame,' said Everton. 'A year previously, he'd been selling insurance. Everybody knew he was a good player, but Reardon, Spencer and Higgins were kings then. When he got to the Crucible, he showed very quickly he had something that the older players didn't suspect he had.'

The Griffiths story caught a national mood and proved inspiring to those first becoming aware of snooker. 'My earliest memories were watching Terry destroy everyone in the 1979 World Championship,' says Peter Ebdon, eight years old at the time of the tournament and a future world champion. 'He had a great temperament, wonderful cue action and a great safety game.'

For Griffiths himself, the change was immediate. Suddenly, his diary was full and his time no longer his own. 'Winning it set me on the road. It also turned me into a nervous wreck,' he said on the 30th anniversary of his victory in 2009. 'My ambition had been to get exhibition work through appearing in the championship but it sort of backfired because I hardly had a day off for a year, or so it seemed. I was always going up to London to do TV and various things. Clubs were after me for shows as well. It was all very strange to me, from humble beginnings to all of that.'[12]

The World Championship had by now become firmly established in Sheffield. Following the 1979 event, a letter from Keith Rogers to the local newspaper summed up what snooker had come to mean to the city:

> We don't really have much going for us at present. Two football teams who are a total embarrassment, no permanent first class cricket ground, no racecourse and boxing, which is hardly worth mentioning. Therefore it is extremely gratifying to see that given the best, the public of Sheffield are prepared to turn out, which they did for the snooker in their droves.

The sport had gained cultural cut-through. Clive James, the Australian writer and TV critic for the *Observer*, became a fan, writing of Griffiths:

> While his opponents were plying the cue, he was always to be seen sucking an Embassy. He puffed and dragged. He ashed and stubbed. In the Embassy boardroom they must have been

cheering with bated breath – not an easy trick, but presumably they have time on their hands.[13]

The UK Championship later that year also received BBC coverage, although this very fact almost denied John Virgo his career highlight as he faced off against Griffiths. 'We were finishing the final on *Grandstand* on Saturday afternoon,' he says. 'I was 11–7 in front. The start time had been 2 p.m. all week, but we hadn't realised that for *Grandstand* they wanted it to be 1 p.m. I got a phone call at five to one, asking where I was. I dashed down to the Guild Hall. By the time I got there, I'd had two frames deducted for being late. So now it's 11–9. I played two frames, lost them, so now it's 11–11. I went to my dressing room, and Terry knocked on the door. He said, "You know this isn't my idea. Shall we share the money?" I wasn't interested in the money, I just wanted to win. I managed to win the next frame, but I looked round and the cameras were there, with nobody operating them. It was a bit like *Doctor Who* with the Daleks. There was an industrial dispute. Terry went 13–12 in front, and I sat there, thinking, "This is the story of my life. I've thrown it away." All of a sudden, the thoughts went out of my head, and I won the last two frames. I have no record of it. A year later, the BBC took some footage of me holding up the trophy, but it was staged. It was the worst and best day of my life.'

Snooker was clearly not yet the polished final product, and the players had much to adjust to, but it had taken huge steps forward, thanks in no small part to Mike Watterson. He died in 2019, but his legacy in the sport is assured. Over time, the Crucible became snooker's Mecca, for players and fans alike, a venue that enjoyed the same resonance as Lord's in cricket, Wembley in football and St Andrews in golf. It helped frame snooker as a sport played in comfortable surroundings, not the back rooms of old, and gave the players the best conditions in which to shine.

A few weeks after Griffiths became world champion, Margaret Thatcher's Conservatives won the general election, ensuring Britain had its first female prime minister. A new age was coming, for the country and for snooker, and two men who met by chance one summer afternoon were perfectly positioned to take the game to new heights.

7

BROTHERS IN ARMS

Mascalls is the house that snooker built, or at least paid for. Standing in a secluded lane on the outskirts of Brentwood, in Essex, the Grade II-listed mansion was the Hearn family home for a decade, until it was converted into offices to accommodate the various component parts of the burgeoning Matchroom Sport business.

Today, it is a base for Matchroom Boxing, the Professional Darts Corporation (PDC), Matchroom Multi Sport, which oversees nine-ball pool, netball and fishing, and the World Snooker Tour. Its founder, Barry Hearn, who nominally retired in 2021, becoming 'president' of the group, is the first face you can see through the window as you walk up to the entrance, in his element in the middle of meetings, deal-making and the constant quest to increase profits.

Hearn, who in childhood shared a bedroom with his sister in their cramped council house in Dagenham, is rightly proud of his empire, although he had to overcome some initial familial scepticism. 'When I sold Lucania in 1982, I bought Mascalls, and I brought my mother round to see it,' Hearn says. 'With the connotations of where I'd been spending my time, she asked me a question on the patio: "This is all very nice, but are you doing anything illegal?"'

What Hearn had actually been doing was cashing in on the sudden potential of snooker. He was not responsible for the extraordinary boom that played out in the 1980s but did more than anyone to exploit the game commercially, demonstrating the worth of a sport long considered a working-class pastime with little mainstream appeal or opportunity for profit.

Hearn's philosophical journey was from council-estate socialist to fully paid-up Thatcherite. 'I studied economics at school,' he says. 'We are all influenced by key people growing up, particularly our parents. My father was a staunch Conservative for absolutely no reason whatsoever. He never earned more than £20 a week most of his life, but he believed that certain people were born to lead, and those people were Conservatives. The fact that he had a shit life didn't really come into it.'

A product of his class, Hearn nevertheless refused to be pigeonholed. He saw in Thatcher's encouragement of individual advancement a way to follow his own path. 'A lot of teachers are left-wing, and I had a very radical teacher, a communist almost, who taught us economics. Without doubt he influenced my early thinking about the fairness of society and how we should pool everything. When you have nothing, like we had nothing, that was very appealing. I subsequently found out that it's totally impractical and doesn't work, but when you're sixteen you don't know that. So I joined the Young Socialists. I put a Harold Wilson poster in my window. But then Maggie came in, with a brave new world approach. I was a poster boy for Thatcher because she epitomised everything that I dreamed of – having the shackles taken off us, being able to work. I was paying tax, which was effectively 98 per cent under Labour. I couldn't see how that generated enthusiasm for me to make something of myself. It actually encouraged the black economy, cash jobs and all of that. Thatcher said, "It's out there, and if you want to put the work in, then we'll let you keep a good part of it." That stimulated us. There's a lot of people very anti-Margaret Thatcher's memory, but for me she was only good.'

It has been suggested that the only person who appeared on British television more than Thatcher in the 1980s was Steve Davis. From Plumstead, south-east London, he has a clear memory of his father taking him to Leigh Green working men's club as a young boy, where he would watch his dad play snooker. 'I jumped up and ran to the table and picked the black ball up because it was close to the cushion,' says Davis, as if this happened yesterday. 'My next memory was *Pot Black* on the television. At fourteen, we went to a holiday camp, and that was my first time on a full-sized table. Myself and my father pretty much spent the whole week in the snooker room. My mother didn't see anything of us. By sixteen or seventeen, I got better the more time I got on the table.'

This was the 1970s. Hearn's Lucania chain of snooker clubs was doing well, but there was a notable drop-off in the summer months, when the weather improved and people preferred to be outside. His solution was to launch an event for club members. 'I had a business which was becoming more and more successful year on year. I thought, as most accountants would, "How can I maximise my earnings?" So I started the Lucania National.'

The qualification to play was membership of one of the Lucania clubs. 'They had to prove they played in one of the clubs twice a week,' Hearn says. 'Word got out that it was a proper event. I was sitting in my office one day when Les Coates, the manager at Romford, rang to say there was a kid playing on table 13 and he's really good, I should come and have a look at him. Steve and his dad wanted him to learn, so they were going round clubs playing people. On this occasion, he was playing Vic Harris, who was the best player in Essex at that time. So I went upstairs, and there was this lanky ginger kid, seventeen or eighteen at the time. I didn't know enough to say that this was a star in the making, but what I saw was someone totally dedicated. He had no personality, never spoke to anybody, was just there to play. He came along because he wanted to qualify for the Lucania National, so that little idea I'd had was not only good for business, but it brought Steve Davis into my life, which changed my life.'

Davis just wanted to play, but accepted Hearn's involvement after losing to Geoff Foulds in the second Lucania final. 'Part of the prize was a tour around the country with Geoff, playing other top amateurs,' he says. 'That was the start of Barry organising things. I remember feeling he was very confident and had a lot about him. He didn't seem like your normal billiard-hall owner. He had ideas.'

Davis acquired the nickname 'Nugget' because he was golden in the money matches Hearn organised in Romford and around the country, although, unlike his manager, he was not motivated by financial gain. 'The buzz in the room, the crowd, the fact they were betting on one player or the other, it made it more exciting for me,' Davis says. 'All Barry paid me was £25 a match. I wasn't on a cut of the gate or anything, but for me it was great exposure. It was in front of a packed crowd, and that's your excitement.'

From then on, Davis and Hearn were, as the title of one of the decade's biggest-selling albums went, brothers in arms. They formed a formidable team, Davis clearing up on the table, and Hearn cleaning up off it.

Everyone in the game recognised that Davis was very different to what had come before. Younger than most of the other top players, he had no vices. His dedication to snooker was absolute. 'It wasn't just the standard of his play, it was the standard of his behaviour, of his attitude and approach,' says Phil Yates. 'There were players going out getting pissed and doing various other things, and he didn't. What he did was apply himself 100 per cent.

His father, Bill, was level-headed. His mother was a schoolteacher. They came from a very stoic, hard-working background, and that rubbed off on Steve.'

There is a thin line between being shy and being aloof. Davis was perhaps both. He had few social skills as a young man and kept himself apart from his fellow professionals as he began to make his way on the circuit. His rivals remember a player who raised the bar, even if he was something of an enigma. 'I can honestly say we had two conversations of five minutes or more in 20 years,' says Cliff Thorburn, the first world champion of the 1980s. 'We ended up in Australia years later, after I'd retired. I'm in a bar, and I hear, "Hey, Cliff!" I turn around, and it's Steve. I wanted to say to him, "What do you want this time?"'

'He was very shy,' remembers Neal Foulds, who reached number three in the world in 1987. 'You couldn't get much out of him; he was frightened of his own shadow. But he had an inner confidence about him. He walked round the table as if he owned the place. He was a very hard practiser and incredibly single-minded in what he wanted to do. He was destined to go to the top.'

'The first time I saw him was at Pontins in Prestatyn,' says Dennis Taylor. 'It was eleven at night, and I walked past when he was playing. I thought, "He looks pretty good." He had long ginger hair, shirtsleeves rolled up. He cleared the table two frames running, and I remember thinking, "I hope I never see him again."'

Davis turned professional in 1978, his breakthrough coming at the end of 1980, when he won the UK Championship. Snooker was still finding its way. Television audiences at the 1979 World Championship had reached 9 million. A year later, the viewing public had been gripped by an epic battle between Thorburn and Alex Higgins. In London, terrorists had laid siege to the Iranian embassy, but when the BBC cut away from the snooker for live updates from the scene, they received angry complaints from viewers immersed in the green-baize stand-off.

The UK Championship was broadcast on the BBC, making it a high-profile success, even if the prize money was yet to match the growing interest in snooker. 'I was besotted with snooker, but there was no real money in it at that time,' says Davis. 'When I won the UK Championship, the first prize was six grand. Barry sold me a car for six grand. The managing director of his fruit-machine company had died and left a Rover, so he sold it to me.'

However, Davis had proven he was a winner, which felt more important than any financial rewards. 'More or less overnight my stock had risen, in my own brain as well,' he says. 'I wasn't just talked about as a future champion, I *was* one, and other players were talking about me. I had a massive injection of confidence into my veins.'

The question was whether Davis could now take over at the top of the sport by becoming world champion. He provided an emphatic answer by beating Doug Mountjoy 18–12 at the Crucible in 1981. If Terry Griffiths had broken the defences of the old order, Davis had shattered them completely. 'I remember Doug said afterwards, "Steve can give any of us 14 points a frame start now,"' said Clive Everton. 'He dragged up the standard. The other players knew they needed to do something to make it competitive.'

In the moments following Davis's victory, a euphoric Hearn barrelled into the arena and nearly knocked him over, raising both fists to the travelling Romford supporters in jubilant triumph. The message was there for all to see. A new era had begun, and this formidable partnership was now truly ready to take on the world.

Davis was 23 years old. Polite, clean-cut, but lacking in personality, he was like a piece of clay, ripe to be moulded for sponsors, broadcasters and the general public. For Hearn, the potential was limitless, and he hit the phones to arrange personal appearances, exhibitions, endorsements, television shows, book deals and overseas trips. They went to Dallas, to Bangkok, to Brazil. No corner of Britain remained unvisited. Davis appeared on the anarchic children's programme *Tiswas*. He joined Britain's best-loved entertainers on *The Morecambe and Wise Show*. He became, very quickly, one of the best-known sportspeople in Britain and would soon be the highest paid.

Television audiences were growing all the time. Highlights of the 1982 Yamaha International final, where Davis beat Griffiths, brought in a peak of 13.3 million viewers on ITV. Earlier that year, Davis had made history by compiling the first televised 147 maximum break at the Lada Classic in Oldham.

On and off the table, he found himself leading the dizzying trajectory snooker was taking, but somehow remained grounded. 'He never saw himself as a star,' Hearn says. 'He saw himself as a good snooker player who wanted to beat everybody. He was very competitive, but he paid a price in terms of sacrifice. He had no social life. He never went out or had girlfriends. He dedicated his whole life to playing snooker. He was never a Flash Harry, which is probably why we got on. I was the mouth, he was the player.'

'It was early days, and we didn't have time to think,' says Davis. 'Everybody was clamouring for snooker. I don't remember ever sitting down in the 1980s and thinking about it. It was just about, "What's happening today?" Just occasionally in the summer months I'd catch myself thinking, "Fucking hell, I'm a world champion! I'm the best player in the whole of the world!" But we were on the crest of a wave and as excited as everyone else that the game had gone overground.'

In 1982, Hearn established Matchroom, a management and

promotions stable that featured Davis, Griffiths and Tony Meo and quickly moved into merchandising, cashing in on snooker's popularity with a range of Matchroom-branded aftershaves, duvet covers and board games. Davis signed a £1 million endorsement deal with the brewers Courage – at the time, the single most lucrative sponsorship in British sport.

The circuit began to expand to meet demand, with new tournaments being added. The BBC could not get enough of snooker. Channel 4, which launched in 1982, shared coverage of tournaments with ITV. It was now on every available channel. Trevor East, a former *Tiswas* presenter, was charged with producing ITV's coverage. 'The big difference in those days was that they were all personalities in their own right because they had to go out and earn a living in working men's clubs, playing snooker but also entertaining,' he says. 'They could all tell a joke, they could all have a laugh, and that was one of the main reasons that snooker took off, apart from it being visually appealing.'

It helped that the national game was struggling. A MORI poll found that by 1980, football had fallen behind swimming, darts, golf and snooker as a participation sport. Live TV matches were a rarity, and by 1985, the BBC and ITV were refusing to pay the asking price for broadcasting the Football League, leading to a virtual blackout outside of the FA Cup and internationals. As football was shunned by television so snooker was warmly embraced. 'Football was in decline at that time and it wasn't on live, so snooker ticked all the boxes and filled loads of airtime,' says East. 'It gripped the nation. There were five tournaments on the BBC and four on ITV. It appealed to all age groups. It was exciting but also relaxing viewing.'

The faces and voices of the TV coverage became as recognisable as the players. On the BBC it was anchored by the avuncular

David Vine, already well known to viewers through fronting *A Question of Sport*, *It's a Knockout* and *Miss World*. David Icke was the number-two presenter, a long time before becoming well known as a conspiracy theorist. Lead commentary came from Ted Lowe, Jack Karnehm and Clive Everton. Players such as Rex Williams, John Spencer, Jim Meadowcroft and John Virgo provided analysis. Much of the evening coverage was recorded highlights, offered piecemeal to audiences before the age of digital and streaming.

Virgo learned from Lowe how much of the commentary would be wasted if the matches were not broadcast live. 'When I first had the opportunity to work with him, I had that enthusiasm that I wanted to explain every single thing that was happening,' he says. 'I kept glancing over to Ted, and it looked like he was asleep. These were the days when there wasn't much live snooker; it was just highlights in the evenings. I went back to the hotel and put it on, wondering what I would sound like, but Ted came alive when they came down to the last red because he knew that was the only bit they were going to show. So all the talking I'd done was never heard by anyone. Ted knew how it would be edited.'

On ITV, Dickie Davies, the well-liked presenter of *World of Sport* on Saturday afternoons, was the front man. Former world champion John Pulman led the commentary team, alongside Williams, after his defection from the BBC, Mark Wildman, Ray Edmonds and Dennis Taylor, who built a broadcasting career while still a top player. Pulman in particular made full use of the hospitality lounge. 'It was like going on holiday,' remembers East. 'We had such fun, some bloody good laughs. The Jameson International was very popular, particularly with Pully. I had to keep them in check in the evenings. In the break between sessions, we'd all go to dinner together, and of course they all had a glass of wine. I drank the same amount as they did, so when I knew I'd had enough, I said, "Right, lads, no more wine, we're back at work now.'"

Jameson was one of a number of alcohol and tobacco sponsors who gravitated towards snooker. Embassy, Benson & Hedges and Rothmans were cigarette brands that enjoyed enormous airtime through sponsoring BBC tournaments in which players could smoke freely in the arena. Guinness and Tennent Caledonian were among the drinks companies that put their names to events. As the 1980s wore on, household names such as Dulux and financial brands like Mercantile Credit and Fidelity Unit Trusts saw snooker as an appealing fit.

The demands on Davis were showing little sign of affecting his game. He won four tournaments in the lead-up to his defence of the world title in 1982. However, a few hours before the first session of his opening-round encounter with Tony Knowles, he was signing books in a nearby newsagent's. Suddenly, he hit a wall. He went 8–1 down overnight and lost 10–1 the next morning, a shocking reverse that opened the door for Alex Higgins to come through the pack and win his second world crown.

If Knowles had felt the pressure of holding an overnight lead, he did not show it, visiting Josephine's nightclub between sessions until the early hours. Tall, good-looking and with a confident air, he became snooker's first pin-up as tabloid newspapers began to register the growing interest their readers had in the private lives of the players. Higgins obliged them by regularly finding trouble, usually involving drink and violence. There was Jimmy White, whose natural charm mitigated a wayward lifestyle. Kirk Stevens of Canada wore a white suit and was another popular figure for snooker's growing female fan base.

Snooker was divided into good boys and bad boys. There were the clean-living, respectable players such as Davis, Griffiths and Taylor, and the more exciting, maybe even dangerous, characters like Higgins, White and Knowles. In this sprawling soap opera, everyone had a favourite. Snooker's appeal cut through all barriers, be they of class, age or gender. Women in particular took an interest.

In 1983, Cathy Booth, of the news agency UPI, summed up this phenomenon as if reviewing a Jilly Cooper novel:

> Women account for 66 percent of snooker's audience in Britain. Lady reporters who examined snooker for the London papers say it has the sexy combination of a gentleman's club snobbery and the low-life appeal of smoky snooker halls. Snooker suggests a wasted youth, making the players seem deliciously wicked, they say. 'I love it when Tony Knowles has to edge his leg up on the table,' sighed an office girl to a reporter who herself was eyeing 6-feet-2 of what she described later in print as 'finely tuned muscle and broad beefy shoulders'.[1]

Snooker players were now household names, front-page news. 'It was amazing, unbelievable,' says John Virgo. 'To say we were living the dream would be an understatement. They were great times. You're playing a game you love and earning a living out of it, but you're also being accepted by the country. You're getting mentioned in places you never thought would mention you. To think that kids like us would walk into a snooker club one day with torn trousers. We never thought we'd make a living from it; we were just happy to be good at it. Being a professional, playing on the TV – never in our wildest dreams, ever.'

For the newer players, such attention could be overwhelming. 'When people were waiting outside the stage door at the Crucible for autographs, I didn't really want to be part of that because I didn't feel I was part of it,' says Neal Foulds. 'I was embarrassed to be thought of like that. It wasn't my thing. I shied away from a lot of that. There were so many big personalities around, and I didn't feel part of it, but I look back and can see that I was.'

The BBC, who gave over most of the BBC2 daytime schedule to the World Championship and would show highlights in prime time on BBC1, were central to maintaining the profile of the sport and therefore its interest, but almost lost the rights to ITV, whose own viewing figures for snooker were the rival of most entertainment programmes.

'The numbers it delivered were astonishing, right across the age demographic. That made it extremely popular with the sales departments up and down the ITV network,' says Trevor East. 'I came very close to getting the World Championship, but I was scuppered by my own colleagues at ITV. There was a lot of politics in the background. I'd set up ITV with the chance to buy the World Championship. I told them, "This event will last forever. It's as big as the Grand National." But because I wasn't at London Weekend Television, which basically ran the majority of ITV Sport, they scuppered my bid by using the money to go and bid for athletics. So it was internal politics, and just to rub it in, one of them planted a story in the *Guardian* saying I'd lost the bid. The BBC have no idea how close they came to losing it.'

With this vast exposure across the airwaves, snooker was now central to popular culture, with film and the non-sport areas of television taking note. In 1983, a BBC comedy drama, *Give Us a Break*, was launched, which followed the fortunes of Micky (Robert Lindsay), who is charged with looking after snooker prodigy Mo (Paul McGann).

A 1984 episode of the sitcom *Ever Decreasing Circles* sees Martin (Richard Briers) hopeful of winning the local snooker tournament. He is drawn in the first round against his suave neighbour,

Paul (Peter Egan), who seems to be good at everything. 'We'll probably find out he coaches Steve Davis,' Martin tells his wife, Ann (Penelope Wilton). Paul turns up in a waistcoat with a cue. 'It's my friend Tony's,' he explains. 'Tony Knowles?' Martin asks mockingly. 'No,' Paul assures him. 'Tony Meo.'

The 1984 film *Number One* starred Bob Geldof, the lead singer of the Boomtown Rats, as a wayward Irish snooker prospect, an Alex Higgins surrogate. It co-starred established British actors Ray Winstone, Alison Steadman, Phil Daniels and Alfred Molina. The following year brought *Billy the Kid and the Green Baize Vampire*, a musical comedy–horror about an intense snooker rivalry, also starring Daniels and featuring Alun Armstrong.

It was inevitable that the music world would be next. Alex Higgins released '147 – That's My Idea of Heaven' to an indifferent record-buying public in 1983. What was needed was something catchy that captured the personalities of the players. Step forward Chas Hodges and Dave Peacock, the popular cockney duo Chas & Dave, who in 1986 penned 'Snooker Loopy', featuring the five members of the Matchroom stable: Davis, Griffiths, Meo, Willie Thorne and Taylor. Each player had their own line to sing, and the lyrics were also helpful explainers for the small minority of people yet to be exposed to snooker.

The record reached number six in the singles chart, sitting above Madonna, Whitney Houston, Billy Ocean, Janet Jackson, Robert Palmer and Simply Red in the top 20. Not to be outdone, Higgins, White, Stevens and Knowles released their own single, a cover of 'The Wanderer', under the name Four Away. It failed to chart. Matchroom's follow-up single, 'The Romford Rap', stalled at number 91, and snooker largely left the pop industry alone thereafter.

By now, snooker had permeated every area of British national life. A waxwork of Davis was introduced to Madame Tussauds. He was lampooned on *Spitting Image*, ITV's satirical comedy show featuring puppets of well-known figures, including a memorable sketch in which he is given the nickname 'Interesting'. On the BBC science programme *QED*, commentary doyen Ted Lowe played snooker against a specially built robot. Players did adverts for a range of everyday products: Jimmy White promoted Trebor Softmints; Terry Griffiths, John Spencer and referee Len Ganley advertised Carling Black Label lager; Davis appeared in commercials for Heinz Baked Beans.

In 1986, the *Sunday Times* reported that Archbishop Luigi Barbarito, the pope's ambassador to Britain, was a snooker fan. Politicians wanted a piece of the action too. Hearn persuaded Davis to make an appearance alongside various other celebrities at an election rally for Margaret Thatcher. The event is best remembered for the DJ and TV personality Kenny Everett wearing a gigantic pair of hands and shouting, 'Let's bomb Russia!' and 'Let's kick [Labour politician] Michael Foot's stick away!' If it was supposed to be ironic, the cheers from the Tory faithful suggested otherwise.

Thatcher was re-elected in 1983 and 1987 with increased majorities. After a shaky start as prime minister, she had grown in stature after authorising a task force to retake the Falkland Islands, in the South Atlantic, after Argentina invaded them in 1982, and for standing up to the IRA, who planted a bomb in the Grand Hotel, Brighton, during the 1984 Conservative Party conference, with the aim of assassinating her. She had faced down the unions, holding firm during the year-long miners' strike of 1984/5, and had become a star on the international stage, the Soviets christening her the 'Iron Lady'.

Thatcher's policy of privatisation saw public utilities such as British Telecom and British Gas sold off, sparking a stock-market frenzy. 'Greed is good' was the mantra of Gordon Gekko, Michael Douglas's character in the 1987 film *Wall Street*. Under the financial deregulation of Thatcher and US President Ronald Reagan, capitalism ran wild. Reagan's thesis of 'trickle-down' economics – empowering the rich so that those lower down the financial chain also benefited – failed to have a positive impact on the have-nots of the decade. In mid-1984, around the time Davis became world champion for the third time, the unemployment rate in Britain stood at 11.9 per cent.

Davis now wishes he had stayed out of politics. 'My biggest regret was getting involved in that,' he says of his attendance at the Thatcher rally. 'I didn't want to go, but I was being led by Barry. He said it'd be good for me. The whole country was going down the Loadsamoney road. Looking back, I not only cringe at that, I think it's an awful world we have now because of that era. To think how bad things were during that period of time – the miners' strike and so on – it feels like that was the start of it. I've gone very much the other way now. While people were struggling to deal with the government, I was appearing all over the country for Courage. I went to areas that were really deprived, where they were all out on strike. I didn't get too much aggravation, but I should have. It was a misstep. That was a cruel world. We're now not as much of a caring nation. There's a better way than the way we've gone.'

Politicians on all sides were surely relieved that Alex Higgins did not offer his services. The undisputed leader of the bad-boy pack, he spent more time on the front pages than in the sports sections at the back, as accusations of drug-taking, womanising and general trouble followed him round. Higgins turned up at the 1986 Mercantile Classic with a black eye, claiming he had been kicked by a horse, Dreadnought. It soon transpired he had sustained it during a fight with another player, Paul Medati.

The interest in Higgins peaked the following year, as he faced disciplinary charges after headbutting Paul Hatherell, the tournament director, at the UK Championship. He revealed his punishment live on the *Wogan* chat show on BBC1, alongside his manager, Howard Kruger. Edwina Currie, the undersecretary of state for public health, was the night's other guest.

Hearn declined the opportunity to manage Higgins. He did not fit into the sanitised world he was selling. 'We needed families to come to snooker and the corporate world,' he says. 'Davis was amenable to doing whatever he was told to do, which gave me the opportunity to build what I think was missing. The misspent-youth era was hanging over the game commercially like a black cloud, and Davis and the other Matchroom players all understood that we could make money from playing, but that the real money was outside of that. The image needed to change. In the early days of *Pot Black*, they all wore dicky bows, so that imagery was there already, but what I did was generate the idea that players could be cleaner than clean. We'd become a soap opera, and any soap opera needs characters. It was a time when football was on the decline, a lot of crowd trouble, and people turned to snooker because they thought they were gentlemen. They weren't – they were just dressed as gentlemen.'

Everybody recognised that Hearn's players were a cut above the rest, with their own tournaments promoted by Matchroom and lucrative endorsement deals. They were making serious money, and so was Hearn, but his brash style and increasing power within the sport often saw him at loggerheads with those in authority.

John Virgo dealt with Hearn extensively after becoming WPBSA chairman in 1988. 'I knew Barry from way back, before he ever met Steve Davis,' he says. 'He had a great interest in the game. He liked it. He used to run tournaments for us to play in. When Steve came along, that gave him more power. He's not my type of person, an entrepreneur with the attitude that if you don't like it, you can lump it. I found him difficult to deal with, but the thing I've always said about him is that at least you knew where you stood with him. Others might say one thing to your face and then do the opposite behind your back.'

Hearn had little time for snooker's establishment of the period. 'Every decision that came out of the WPBSA in those days looked after, protected and rewarded those people who sat on the WPBSA board,' he says. 'They hated us. It was a boys' club and always had been. They built their brand by keeping everything small. Jobs for the boys. They had a tournament every year in Australia which Ted Lowe organised, and he divided the appearance money by nine – eight players and him. It wasn't the shit-or-bust approach I prefer, where losers don't get paid. Exactly the opposite in those days. Then along came Davis, and you could feel the animosity.'

Frustrated by what he saw as the old pals' act of the WPBSA, Hearn went his own way, organising tournaments for his Matchroom players and those specially invited as far afield as China, Thailand, Malaysia, Singapore, Hong Kong and Japan. Hearn's stable went from five to eight, with Foulds, Thorburn and White joining the 'Snooker Loopy' singers.

As the circuit expanded, the prize money grew and grew. The world champion of 1980 received £15,000, from a total prize fund of £60,000. By 1989, the winner's cheque had ballooned to £105,000, from a pot of £525,000.

Davis's dominance came to be resented by those who wanted variety. In 1986, Byron Rogers wrote in the *Sunday Times*:

I have come to dislike snooker very much, largely, I am afraid, because of Mr Steve Davis. As Gide, asked about the greatest French poet, said ruefully, 'Victor Hugo, alas.' If Mr Davis showed any emotion, or could lose, then it would be different, but he seems incapable of either.²

Davis was shamefully booed at times on entering arenas. 'It used to hurt me to see that,' says Phil Yates. 'I was still in my formative years, and I used to think, "This guy has done nothing wrong. He's done everything right in his life. He's someone you'd want your own son or daughter to be like. Why is it that British people want the underdog to win? In America, it's the complete opposite. If you're a winner, they love you."'

The sport owed everything to television, so Michael Grade's announcement in 1988, after becoming chief executive of Channel 4, that he was dropping the sport from the channel was a significant moment. This was a period when the only way to distinguish one channel from another was to not have snooker as part of its output. 'There is a snooker mountain in Europe. There are now far too many tournaments,' said Grade, adding, 'Snooker helps boost our viewing figures but it damages the image of the channel.'³

Channel 4's head of sport, Adrian Metcalfe, was quoted as calling snooker and darts 'Mogadon sports', adding, 'You do not have to exercise your brain very hard to enjoy them and they are heavily slewed to the over-fifties in any case. We do not necessarily want older viewers to watch Channel 4.'⁴ The sharing arrangement between ITV and Channel 4 was abandoned, leaving the former with scheduling problems. In 1989, they reduced their snooker portfolio from four tournaments to three. (Metcalfe later became a board member of World Snooker.)

Yet snooker remains the defining British sporting success story of the 1980s. From its humble beginnings, it became a mainstream entertainment. Clubs thrived and sales of small tables went through the roof. Personalities were established who are still regarded fondly decades on. Collective memories were made through epic battles on the baize, generations gathering around the same TV set, something that would later be lost in the multichannel, multiplatform age.

It was Davis and Hearn who between them conquered a decade in which snooker truly entered the bloodstream of British life. In 1988, Davis was voted the BBC's Sports Personality of the Year. A few months later, he won a sixth world title, ending the 1980s having captured 22 of the 48 ranking events staged. By this time, Hearn was starting to look for ventures away from the game that had launched him into the world of sports promotion, in particular boxing. He would go on to become chairman of Leyton Orient Football Club and take over the PDC, overseeing the rejuvenation of darts.

Looking back on it all, Hearn speaks only of fondness for Davis. 'He never knew what the prize money was and never asked,' he says. 'He wasn't there for the money; he was more interested in making his dad proud. But, at the same time, he wanted to be a winner. He was never late, he signed every autograph, until the last fan had left the venue. He was the ultimate professional. Terry Griffiths was the start of the new era, but Davis was the first properly professional snooker player. He didn't get pissed or chase after women or take drugs or gamble. He just played snooker.'

And yet, for all their success, the most memorable snooker match of the 1980s proved to be a traumatic experience for both, a contest layered in tension and drama, a final that, unthinkably, Davis, the imperious master of all he surveyed during a glorious decade, failed to win.

8

BACK TO BLACK

Coalisland is a small town in County Tyrone. Its name derives from the discovery of coal there in the seventeenth century, after which a canal was dug to transport it to Dublin. A Catholic stronghold, its population numbers a few thousand.

Dennis Taylor's first glimpse of a snooker table in the club by Coalisland police station instilled in him a lifelong love of the game, but the road to the top was a long one, paved with hardship, disappointment and loss. The first step was to actually enter the hallowed room housing the tables.

'I knew my brother sometimes went in,' Taylor says. 'It wasn't a members' club, and there was no alcohol. I asked if he could ask the owner if I could sit in and watch. I was only eight or nine. I was allowed to watch the players, and I'd hold the rest and hand it to them if they needed it. Because I was a good little boy, they eventually let me have a shot on the table, but I had to stand on a lemonade box to reach. There was a little black-and-white television in the club, and occasionally on a Saturday they would show Joe and Fred Davis playing.'

When adulthood approached, a living had to be made, but snooker was still a largely underground sport and therefore an unlikely source of income. When he was seventeen, Taylor moved across the Irish Sea to Lancashire to find work. 'I had four aunts who lived in Darwen, just on the border with Blackburn. I stayed with them, and it was like home from home; otherwise I would've been too homesick to last,' he says.

'I got a job in a paper mill, working 12 hours a day, seven days a week. I wasn't quite eighteen, but I got the men's wages. I did that for nearly two years. I worked from six in the morning until six in the evening, got home around half past six, quick bit of tea, jumped on the bus and went down into Blackburn and practised. My aunt said I was exhausting myself. "What are you doing that for? What will you make from snooker? You're better concentrating on your work."'

Taylor was proficient at billiards, a game yet to be fully overtaken by snooker, and aged nineteen, he won the British junior title. This was a year before the start of *Pot Black*. Snooker was still part of the subculture. His aunt's bemusement was understandable.

Then, in 1969, things started to happen. *Pot Black* gave the game regular television exposure, and the World Championship was re-established as a knockout event. Taylor became manager of a snooker club in Preston, and in 1972 was accepted into the professional ranks, such as they were. This was the year his compatriot, Alex Higgins, picked up only £480 for winning the world title.

'I packed my job in at the snooker club in 1974 and paid my own way to go to Canada for the Masters event there,' Taylor says. 'I had £200 in the bank and two children. I got to the final, beating Alex in the semis, and got invited into *Pot Black* through that. In an exhibition I made 349, without the other guy getting a shot. I got a lot of publicity out of that. We would send something like a thousand letters out to snooker clubs to try and get exhibition work. You'd be getting something like £20 a night. But once you got on *Pot Black* – and I got to the final the first two years – it became a lot easier to get exhibitions.'

There was one glaring problem: his eyesight was not the best. He wore glasses in normal life but struggled to play snooker in them. In 1979, he tried soft contact lenses and began seeing things more clearly, reaching the world final, where he lost to Terry Griffiths.

Jack Karnehm was not only a billiards champion and BBC commentator but also, as luck would have it, a spectacle maker. He manufactured a distinct pair of glasses for Taylor that would become his trademark, with vast lenses that covered half of his forehead. 'My eyes had got a bit sore with the lenses. That was when I looked into getting glasses,' he says. 'People thought they were just upside down, but Jack had put the optical centre where it should be. The first time I wore them was in South Africa. I put them on the table and started feeling round for them, like I couldn't see. The crowd thought they were just a novelty thing.'

Taylor was in his early 30s and had established a reputation as something of a nearly man, not just with his defeat to Griffiths but as runner-up in a dozen tournaments in his first decade as a professional, including a 9–0 hammering at the hands of Steve Davis in the 1981 Jameson International. The new glasses helped his confidence, but fate would intervene at the start of the 1984/5 season. He reached the quarter-finals of the first ranking event, the International in Newcastle, when news came through from home that his mother had passed away. Taylor immediately withdrew and went back to Northern Ireland. He was in no mood to play in the next tournament, the Grand Prix in Reading.

'I was playing the best snooker of my career and then got the devastating news. My mum was only 62,' he says. 'I wasn't interested in snooker, but the family said, "Go and play for your mum," and that's what I did. I beat Neal Foulds 9–3 and Cliff Thorburn 10–2 in the final. I knew I was playing well but never expected to win that easily.'

The bereavement had given Taylor perspective but also focus. Now, there was something to play for, an inspiration beyond the usual concerns about prize money and ranking points. Moreover, now that he was a tournament winner, the other players would take notice as attention began to turn to the World Championship of 1985.

• • •

1985. The BBC launches *EastEnders*, a new soap opera about working-class life in London. Time-travel comedy *Back to the Future* tops the global box office. Hollywood icon Rock Hudson dies from AIDS, the highest-profile casualty yet from this new and frightening disease. Music and conscience coalesce at Live Aid, two star-studded concerts held in London and Philadelphia to raise money for, and awareness of, African famine. Neil Kinnock, the Labour leader, delivers a devastating rebuke to the hard-left Militant Tendency at his party's conference in Bournemouth. The speech would be widely praised as brave and necessary and the start of the long process of modernising Labour and therefore making it electable again, but it paints a picture of the main opposition party in opposition not to Mrs Thatcher's government but to itself.

Division is everywhere. The miners' strike ends, but communities are devastated, and wounds open between those who backed the strike and those who defied it. Decades later, they will still not have healed. In Handsworth, a socially deprived inner-city area of Birmingham, riots break out across three nights. Another riot at Broadwater Farm in London claims the life of police officer Keith Blakelock.

These are febrile times, and the national game provides little succour. A few days after the World Championship, a fire ravages the main stand at Valley Parade, home to Bradford City FC, killing 56 spectators. A few weeks later, a charge by a group of Liverpool fans towards Juventus supporters at the crumbling Heysel stadium in Belgium ahead of the European Cup final leads to the collapse of a wall, killing 39 spectators. The match is still played. English teams are banned from European competitions for five years.

Against this distressing backdrop, the outwardly polite, genteel world of snooker is where the nation turns for comfort. In January, Willie Thorne's victory at the Mercantile Classic records a peak audience of 16.2 million for ITV on a Sunday afternoon. Two months later, Silvino Francisco's capture of the British Open brings in 15.5 million in the same slot.

Snooker is a ratings success, but more than that, an oasis of quiet calm against the raging tumult of the outside world. There are no police sirens disturbing the hushed clicking of the balls, no fighting in the audience. Families come to tournaments. Men need not worry about bringing their wives and children. Nothing bad will happen to them.

More than anyone, Steve Davis represents this essential decency so lacking in other parts of society, and he goes into the annual Crucible marathon as favourite again. In the preceding months of the season, he has won two of the five ranking events, most notably a third UK Championship title and three invitation tournaments. In Sheffield this year, he is looking for a fourth world title and third in succession.

'Nineteen eighty-five felt like business as usual,' says Barry Hearn. 'We're sat there at the Crucible, round after round, thinking, "This is what we do." We turn up, we alienate ourselves from the other players by turning up in a stretch limo while they're getting off a bus. We book suites, they share rooms – everything to give you a psychological edge. It was all to get in the other players' heads, to get them thinking they can't live with this bloke.'

After a first-round scare against Neal Foulds – Davis prevailing 10–8 – the reigning champion loses only 15 more frames in three rounds, easily dispatching David Taylor, Terry Griffiths and Ray Reardon to coast into the final. In the other half of the draw, Dennis Taylor has also barely broken sweat. His first-round opponent, Francisco, is on the front pages after being covertly recorded accusing Kirk Stevens, his opponent in the recent British Open final, of being 'high as a kite' on drugs during the match. Taylor beats him 10–2, and loses only 16 further frames in comfortable victories over Eddie Charlton, Cliff Thorburn and Tony Knowles.

'I was confident,' Taylor says. 'I won a couple of matches with a session to spare. I couldn't play much better than that. I was hoping Steve would lose in the other semi-final, but sure enough he got through, so I got myself up for the battle. You had to play well against Steve, otherwise he'd destroy you.'

This feared destruction starts to unfold in the opening session of the final, as Davis wins frame after frame, ending the afternoon 7–0 ahead. Taylor is staring humiliation in the face. 'At the beginning, he wasn't missing anything, so there wasn't much I could do,' he says. 'I was trying not to look at him because if you looked at Steve, it didn't put you in a good frame of mind, watching him clear the table all the time. So I was patient, but when I lost all seven, my heart sank and I wanted the floor to open up.'

Trevor East, a close friend of Taylor, is not at the Crucible to watch the carnage first-hand. 'I was on the board of Derby County at the time, which was only 40 miles down the road,' he says. 'I missed the first session of the final. I came down into the boardroom, switched the TV on, and it was 7–0. I said, "I've got to go." I bombed up the motorway, got into his dressing room, and he was down in the dumps. I said, "You can't cock it up at this stage, what would your mother think?" Which was probably a bit out of order, but he had to snap out of it.'

Davis wins the first frame of the night to make it 8–0. In frame nine, he looks like extending his lead but misses a green with the rest. It's a shot he may not have taken on had he not been so far in front, and one which will haunt him to this day. Taylor eventually clears from green to pink and gets a large round of applause from the audience as he holds up a finger to indicate he now has one frame on the scoreboard. He starts to relax. By the end of the evening, he has made four half-century breaks and is trailing only 9–7. It feels as if he is in front.

'To be only two behind set me up for the final day, and it put Steve in a pretty poor frame of mind because he would've been thinking he should have had it won,' he says. 'I had a bottle of champagne with Trevor, which you'd never normally do while you're playing, but I thought I wasn't going to get to sleep, so let's just have a chat and a relax.'

For Hearn, the satisfaction of a likely landslide victory, increasing Davis's already considerable marketability, is turning into the nightmare of a too-close-to-call finish. 'We came in on the crest of a wave, winning everything, and we go 8–0 up in the final,' he says. 'It was no big surprise. But then there was one complacent moment, where Steve had a tricky green. In a close match, he probably wouldn't have played that shot, but he tried to cut it in, missed, and Taylor won the frame. Next thing you know, it's all square and we're going into a bloodbath.'

On day two, Davis is still widely expected to pull away, but it turns out this determined Northern Irishman, marked as an underachiever, laughed at because of his 'upside-down' glasses, is equal to the fight. They split the third session, to leave Davis 13–11 ahead going into the final night, with only a half-hour turnaround before the denouement.

This Sunday night, the world final takes its place opposite the varying attractions on Britain's other three television channels. BBC1 broadcasts the sitcom *Sorry!*, followed by *Vicious Circle*, a translation of a Jean-Paul Sartre story, in which unsuspecting characters are enclosed in a dark room with no windows and no escape. BBC2 is showing much the same, except one of Davis or Taylor will leave with the trophy. On Channel 4, viewers can watch a documentary about Kilimanjaro and the drama series *Mapp and Lucia*. ITV's main offering is a film about Raoul Wallenberg, a Swedish diplomat who saved thousands from the Holocaust. Later, it's *Tales of the Unexpected*, but most of the viewing nation is tuned not to the Roald Dahl series but to an unlikely real-life drama reaching its crescendo in Sheffield.

A hard-fought evening of snooker is coming down to the crunch. Davis maintains his two-frame advantage at 17–15, leaving him one from the title. Taylor digs deep again to make it 17–17 and take the whole match, the whole 17 days of the tournament, down to one last frame. By now, it is just after 11 p.m. *Bleak House*, the BBC's latest Dickens adaptation, was supposed to start at 10.10. It can wait another week. Nobody is switching off; nobody is going to bed. One more frame . . .

It starts with a prolonged spell of high-quality safety. You can forgive the caution. Everything is on the line. For Davis, his aura of invincibility will just about remain if he can get it won. For Taylor, victory will be vindication for all of his struggles.

'Just before the last frame, he went to the dressing room, and I followed him out, which was caught on camera,' says East. 'Ted Lowe said something like, "And there's Dennis going to compose himself in the dressing room with his good friend . . ." Everyone thought we'd gone for a pep talk. We both had a large brandy.'

This is unconventional, but by now conventions have been set aside. It's a fight for survival. Nerves are obvious, yet this only heightens the drama. Snooker is a sport where if the standard drops, the excitement levels rise. It's the anticipation of what these great talents will do, followed by the shock of them failing to do it. The Crucible rings to oohs and aahs, to gasps of astonishment as balls are missed.

'When I was under pressure, I'd end up going pink, and the more pressure I was under, I'd go red,' Taylor says. 'Steve was going the opposite way – he was becoming whiter by the shot. Under pressure, we were missing the vital balls.'

The audience are both amazed and empathetic. Haven't we all messed up at some point in pursuit of our goals? It's clear that Taylor is getting the majority of the support. The people here have seen Davis win – several times – and have every respect for him, but Britain is full of underdogs who feel trodden down by politicians and economic strife, a fracturing of society, and in Taylor they see a quintessential little guy who might – just might – triumph against the odds.

The previous year, here in South Yorkshire, there was another battle seven miles away at Orgreave, where police and miners clashed violently, but this now is a fair fight: two men, each with a cue, each attempting to master the geometrical challenge of making a ball go down a hole, ad nauseam, until they have enough points to win. It sounds simple, but it's anything but. Even so, there's a prosaic beauty to what is happening, unlike so much else that is being fed to the British public at this time. It's a world away from the glossy prime-time American soaps *Dallas* and *Dynasty*, which rule the airwaves with their lurid, sensational tales of the super-rich. This is unscripted, and it's reaching a climax as the final frame comes down to the colours.

Davis is 15 points ahead on the green. He snookers Taylor, who appears to have got the ball safe with his escape shot, but Davis sends it around three cushions, and it drops into a middle pocket. He now needs just the brown for victory, but it's not potable, so he plays safe, leaving a difficult long pot. Taylor chances his arm and misses but does not leave the brown on.

'Very tense moments now here at the Crucible Theatre,' says Ted Lowe, with some understatement, from the commentary box. A constant murmur accompanies the exchanges on the brown. Taylor overcuts it but gets it safe again. Davis mishits his next shot and inadvertently frees the black – which, with the lead he has, was an insurance ball – from the side cushion. By now, the frame is the longest of the championship. A Taylor safety is met by a Davis attempt at a pot. The brown kisses the black onto the opposite side cushion as it travels towards a corner pocket, stopping several inches short, with the cue ball on the black spot.

Taylor walks around the table to examine the potting angle and then gets down to play the shot. He thunders the brown in at pace, kissing the blue from just off the baulk cushion to leave it potable into the opposite corner. It's a brilliant shot at any time, but under the circumstances seems miraculous. He has his chance to win it. This is someone who was apparently dead and buried 36 hours earlier.

The blue is still an acute angle, but he pots it, jerking his body to will the cue ball away from the side cushion. It stubbornly remains close to the rail, increasing the difficulty of the pot on the pink. 'Can you just quieten down please?' implores referee John Williams, as a hush descends once more.

Taylor pots the pink. 'The final frame, the final black,' proclaims Lowe, as Taylor walks to the trophy and gently kisses the figure at its apex, a shepherdess.

'The brown was the one, the best shot, probably the best shot of my career,' he says. 'If I miss that, I leave it. When I potted the tricky blue, I was near the cushion for the pink. When I took it on, I was always going to leave the double. To this day I don't know why, but as I walked past the trophy I gave the little lady on the top a kiss. I took the double on but was lucky it went safe.'

This is the first salvo in a seven-shot sequence that will enter snooker folklore. Cheers ring out as Taylor's attempted double heads towards the opposite middle pocket, but it catches the jaw and stays out, running safe onto the top cushion as Williams again begs the audience to settle down.

Davis coolly plays a full-length-of-the-table safety. Taylor comes to the table but then goes back to his corner to wipe his hands. He attempts another double at pace, the black again going safe. Lowe chuckles nervously, adding, 'I'm sure Dennis wouldn't mind my saying, he's chanced his arm and it's come out lucky.'

Davis attempts to send the black around the table, but it cannons into the cue ball to leave a pot to the far-corner green pocket. There is plenty of body movement as Taylor, with his best chance yet, misses. 'That was the biggest shot of his life,' says Jim Meadowcroft, Lowe's commentary colleague. Taylor watches in agony as the black comes back up the table towards the opposite corner. The match is surely done.

When he gets to his chair, however, he sees that the black has come away from the pocket and the cue ball is close to the side cushion. It's a cut-back pot, and Davis is favourite to make it, but it's not as easy as it first appeared as Taylor trudged back to his corner believing his race to be run. Even so, he presses his hands to his forehead and, like everyone else, turns his attention to Davis, who recalls of the moment, 'As I'm walking to the table, I'm thinking, "Don't undercut it. Don't hit it thick, don't hit it thick." And I hit it thin.'

He hits it so thin that he overcuts it. The cue ball travels all around the table and leaves Taylor a straightforward pot – if such a thing exists in the circumstances – for the title. 'No!' says Lowe, a short, simple word loaded here with nuance. In that 'no' there is shock, concern, bemusement. Steve Davis doesn't miss match balls. The world has tilted on its axis.

'The pot I was left with was much easier than the one Steve missed,' Taylor says. A deafening cheer rings out as he gets out of his chair and returns to the table. Williams again appeals for calm. 'This is really unbelievable,' says Lowe above the growing hullabaloo. Taylor has a brief look at the potting angle, gets down, concentrates on controlling his cueing and knocks the black in.

'He's done it!' exclaims Lowe, as Taylor raises his cue above his head in celebration. There's a courteous handshake with Davis, and then Taylor stands, almost disbelieving, gripping his cue tightly as if he will need it again, as if he can't quite believe there are no more frames to play.

'I thought Steve would pot the black, Dennis did as well,' says East. 'When the black landed where it did, I thought, "This is in, Davis can't possibly miss this." But when he did, you're stunned. For Dennis to compose himself for that last shot, having seconds before thought he'd lost, was unbelievable.'

It is East's eye Taylor catches in the aftermath of victory, as photographers pour into the arena and the crowd stands and cheers. After laying his cue on the table, he sees his friend in the throng and, wearing a wide grin, wags his finger at him. 'It's him telling me, "I told you I could do it,"' East says. 'I took it as saying, "We've done it." He kindly said I'd helped him and it was a bit of a team effort.'

Meanwhile, Davis's team are distraught. 'The final frame was an hour and five minutes of purgatory,' says Hearn. 'I remember standing behind the curtain, peering round it with my wife and [Davis's driver] Robbo. They got to the final black, and I said to Robbo, "I can't watch. Tell me when he's got it." Then I heard the click of the ball and sigh of the crowd, and I thought, "Bollocks, he's missed it, the useless ginger bastard."'

For Davis, there is no time to calibrate his thoughts. His emotions are shaken by a rare loss from such a commanding position, made all the more traumatic by the manner of the ending. 'At the time, you're living in the moment and the excitement in the room,' he says. 'We didn't have a clue how many people were watching on TV. It gets down to the final ball. You miss it, and the other guy pots it, and then it's over, and you have the shock of it all.'

Enter David Vine, the BBC presenter, who walks onto the Crucible stage to conduct the interviews. He starts with Taylor, who tells him, 'It's a good job the black was over the pocket.' Vine invites Davis to join them. There is another handshake between the two finalists before an awkward exchange between interviewer and beaten man.

'Steve, it's a pretty tough moment this one, isn't it?'

'Yes.'

'Can you believe what's happened here tonight yet?'

'Yeah, it happened in black and white.'

'Has anything like that ever happened before to you in a match? Have you ever gone through that, with the emotions and the tension?'

'No.'

There is some nervous laughter in the audience, but Davis now looks furious. Realisation of the magnitude of what has happened is slowly sinking in. He manages to add that Taylor 'played really well', before Vine returns the microphone to the champion.

Taylor does not wait for a question. 'To beat Cliff Thorburn, who's the hardest player in the world, and then to beat Steve Davis, who's been the best player in the world, there's not a lot more you can say really . . .' He is interrupted by a supporter calling out, reminding him that he has won. Taylor smiles and adds, 'Well, I'm the best this year.'

The BBC director captures the moment perfectly. It is a packed room, but our screens are filled with just two faces: victor and vanquished. Taylor is wearing the broadest smile, his eyes shining with happiness, while the remaining colour drains from Davis. To his credit, he manages the briefest of smiles as Vine brings the interview to an end and the trophy is presented to Taylor.

He takes the acclaim of the audience as Davis retreats to his dressing room. The first person to see him there is John Virgo, who wants to pass on his commiserations. 'He was in floods of tears,' Virgo says. 'It's because of how big a deal the World Championship is and how much effort you put in for those 17 days. What got him was the line from Dennis: "Well, I'm the best this year."'

Such a public reversal leaves Davis feeling, more than anything, confused. How could this have happened? 'For a couple of months afterwards I was in a daze. I couldn't snap myself out of it,' he says. 'I'd go back to shots and replay them. I was in the bath a few weeks afterwards and was replaying shots. The next minute the bath water is cold. I'd gone down a rabbit hole in my brain. It wasn't particularly the black, but other shots. There was the green down the rail, and I couldn't get it out of my brain. I was devastated. Really devastated. I had to wait quite a while for the next tournament, but I was on the road doing exhibitions, where people would ask, "How did you miss that black?" It was good therapy because I wasn't hiding away in a dark room all summer.'

For Taylor, life changes instantly. Everywhere he goes from

now on, for the rest of time, people will want to talk about that black. Indeed, to this day, when club players pot a vital black to win a frame, they still mimic his famous cue-waving, finger-wagging celebration.

He receives a hero's welcome when he returns home the next morning. 'I couldn't believe it when we got back to Blackburn. There was press and TV from all over the place,' he says. 'The two boys had done a banner which read, "Welcome Home Dad." I've heard so many stories. There was one young lad watching it on a black-and-white set in his bedroom. He heard his dad coming up the stairs, so switched it off and pretended he was sleeping. His dad brought him downstairs to watch it on the colour TV.'

For Northern Ireland, riven for nearly two decades by sectarian violence, it is an opportunity for both sides of the divide to unite behind one of their own, as they had when Alex Higgins won three years earlier. The two men are very different, however. Taylor is a fierce competitor, but there is never any fear of trouble when he walks into a room. He becomes one of sport's most marketable, relatable stars.

In fact, Taylor, already a well-known personality, instantly turns into one of Britain's most recognisable faces. His genial manner and quick wit make him a natural for chat shows and personal appearances. He enjoys it all. 'I never refused anything,' he says. 'I went on *The Sooty Show* and potted the black out of Sooty's mouth. Anything I was asked to do, I did. I just embraced it. It was something special.'

Hearn, ever the entrepreneur, is pragmatic: he signs Taylor to his Matchroom stable. Such is the interest, ITV covers the signing live.

Forty years on, Hearn still recognises the pain the defeat caused his great friend at the time. 'Some say it made Davis more than his wins. That's absolute rubbish. It destroyed him,' he says. 'It was the biggest kick in the nuts you could ever have.'

A few days after the final, the viewing figures are confirmed: 18.5 million were watching at the end. This remains the largest ever audience for BBC2 and to this day marks the biggest post-midnight viewership on British television. Snooker has proven beyond doubt its capacity to deliver unforgettable sporting and human drama.

Among those entranced was the celebrated journalist and intellectual, Bernard Levin, who writes:

> I am not interested in snooker, indeed do not even know the rules. What kept me in front of the television set? I was staying with friends in the country, and everybody had gone to bed except my host and I. He rose – he cares for snooker no more than I do – and bade me goodnight; on the way out of the room he paused behind my chair to glance at the screen, and he stood there, unmoving, his body still turned at the angle that was to take him to the door, for the next 45 minutes. We could not know of the amazing finish; but we had both been seized by the realization that we were watching two men approaching very close to perfection; the knowledge was so enthralling that we had to see it out.[1]

The climax of the 1985 final is the moment the stars truly align for snooker. Four decades later, Taylor and Davis still tour the country, doing exhibitions and answering questions about the black-ball finish. There is a magic to it even for those not born when it happened. It serves as proof that life isn't inevitable, that the impossible can happen. In the *Guardian*, sportswriter Frank Keating describes Taylor's victory over an apparently irresistible force as 'Like Sergeant Bilko beating Muhammad Ali over the full 15.'

Davis went on to win three more world titles and remained snooker's pre-eminent force for the rest of the decade, a period of sustained success that has helped him make peace with what happened on that memorable night in 1985. In time, he came to see that he was a part of something special, an almost once-in-a-lifetime event that showcased snooker's appeal and continues to resonate deeply.

'Steve embraces it now,' says John Virgo. 'He gets plenty of enjoyment out of it – although maybe not as much as Dennis.'

9

THIS TOWN AIN'T BIG ENOUGH FOR THE BOTH OF US

Throughout the 1980s, the fortunes of Steve Davis and Margaret Thatcher felt intertwined. At times seeming imperious, they both saw off various setbacks and challengers to spend a decade on top. Indeed, it was starting to feel as if they could, in Thatcher's own words, go 'on and on'. Yet, by the end of 1990, they were each dethroned.

When the end came, it was brutal for both. Thatcher had introduced the community charge, better known as the 'poll tax', to replace local government rates, but the policy was so unpopular it led to riots in Trafalgar Square. Support for the Conservatives plummeted. It was felt the Iron Lady was now so drunk on power and her own impregnability that she would no longer listen to sage voices on her own side. Michael Heseltine, who had resigned from the Cabinet in 1986, stood against her in a leadership contest. She won the most votes in the first round but not enough to stave off a second ballot. One by one, her Cabinet came to her to advise that she stand down, and just like that, without a public vote being cast, the Thatcher era ended after eleven and a half years.

Sport, like politics, is a results business. For Davis, the view from the mountaintop in 1989 was especially picturesque. He had recovered from the defeats to Dennis Taylor in 1985 and Joe Johnson the following year by winning three world titles in succession, taking his career tally to six. 'I went through a phase thinking, "No one can do what I'm doing,"' he says. 'There were people in the 1980s with poor cue actions. The standard wasn't that good at the time, and I thought, "Who is going to come along to outplay me?" 1987–9 was my purple patch. I felt totally unbeatable. It's amazing how quickly the bubble burst.'

The seeds of his destruction were planted at Christmastime in 1981. Davis had won his first World Championship earlier that year and had just defended the UK Championship title. Irene Hendry was walking along Dunfermline High Street with her twelve-year-old son, Stephen. He had no particular interest in snooker. He had no particular interest in anything, which made present-buying a problem. They came alongside the window of the newsagent's John Menzies and saw a six-foot snooker table inside.

'What do you think of that, Stephen?'

'Yeah, it looks interesting.'

Perhaps he was just placating his mother, but the table was purchased. Four years later, Hendry turned professional.

He was not the first shy boy to find shelter from the outside world at the snooker table. Tellingly, he would call his autobiography *Me and the Table*. It was where he was happiest, where he was not expected to mix with others or be outgoing. His attachment became more acute when his parents got divorced. A present bought as a whim became an obsession.

In 1983, barely a year after he first started playing, he won the Scottish under-16 title. The following year, he became Scottish amateur champion. His sudden, rapid rise caught the attention of Stirling businessman Ian Doyle, who offered to manage him. Hendry was only a teenager, but the meticulous Doyle did not treat him with kid gloves. 'Ian never let me rest,' Hendry says. 'When he started managing me, it was all about being world champion and world number one. It wasn't about just having a career and winning a tournament, it was about being the best. That was drummed into me. It was the mantra.'

This disciplinarian approach applied to every part of Hendry's life. 'Ian put the fear of God into me that if I stepped off this line, my career would be over. We clashed quite a lot. Having a girlfriend was difficult. She lived in Blackpool, and I'd ask if I could go down to see her for the weekend, and he'd say no. I was eighteen and a man. There were times I'd sneak behind his back and do it anyway, but then I'd go to a tournament and feel guilty, thinking if I didn't win, that would be why. Maybe it wasn't the healthiest relationship with Ian at times, but he's the biggest influence on my life. I wouldn't have achieved what I did without that direction.'

Under Doyle's strict control, Hendry turned professional in 1985. He was sixteen. From the outset, it was apparent he was a different type of player. The percentage game long favoured by established professionals and taken to new levels by Davis was jettisoned in favour of all-out attack. Allied to his game was careful study of the man ruling snooker. Hendry observed Davis's aloofness, how he set himself apart, his professionalism in terms of preparation. Their games were different, but Hendry had a living, breathing blueprint of how to be a champion to learn from. 'I looked at Steve Davis and thought, "That's where I want to be,"' he says. 'Nothing less would be good enough.'

Hendry qualified for the Crucible at his first attempt in 1986, giving Willie Thorne a scare, before losing 10–8. Thorne applauded him off the stage, a mix of graciousness and relief. In the BBC studio afterwards, Hendry told presenter David Vine he thought he would win the world title 'within the next five years'. It sounded more like a statement of fact than the arrogance of youth.

He won his first ranking title at the 1987 Grand Prix while still only eighteen, and then swiftly began the process of becoming the sport's major force, winning the Masters and UK Championship in 1989. He had, in a short space of time, become the new face of snooker.

How did it make Davis feel? 'Fucking horrible,' he says. 'All of a sudden, nobody's talking about you, it's all Stephen. It was awful. I blamed my technique. I should've realised it was the circle of life and tried to enjoy it, but I didn't. Me and my father beat ourselves up over small adjustments in cueing and grip. Then we started trying everything to change it, and then you're in the wrong frame of mind, you're on the back foot. You think you've rectified it in practice, but it doesn't work in the match and you're back to square one. When Stephen jumped up two levels, it must've done something to my confidence. I didn't become a bad player overnight, but I couldn't beat him.'

The changing of the guard was a shot in the arm for Scottish snooker, whose modern professionals had hitherto not been world-beaters. Suddenly, youngsters flocked to clubs, inspired by a hero not much older than them. Alan McManus, who would go on to beat Hendry in the 1994 Masters final, ending his five-year unbeaten run in the event, was one such starry-eyed fan. 'Stephen was a bit of a mythical figure to me,' he says. 'He was from a different part of Scotland. He did an exhibition in the club when he was seventeen. I was fifteen and got his autograph. He was just fantastic. I'd never seen a player like it. I could play a bit, but he was on a completely different level. I thought, "Okay, this is the benchmark."'

A shot of adrenalin had been injected into the snooker scene north of the border. 'The older Scottish players had jobs, they were working men. They weren't nine-to-five snooker players,' McManus explains. 'Until Stephen came along, Scotland was a backwater in terms of standard. He blew the roof off the whole thing. We saw the Hendry effect: 80–100 boys of around fifteen at junior events talking about him, what he's doing, winning tournaments. Everyone jumped on the bandwagon.'

Despite his shyness, Hendry coped well with the attention he was now under. Snooker is a sport where you can show personality, but it isn't compulsory. Hendry took success in his stride. When he won a tournament, he would be back in the club the following day, practising for the next one. He started to enjoy material things, but it was never about the money. He had a focus on winning. No amount of winning would ever be enough.

Hendry's fellow players during his peak years talk about him with an almost chilling clarity, as if they are victims rather than rivals. 'Stephen was like a serial killer. He was cold,' says McManus. 'He was like the Terminator: you hit him with a metal bar, and it bounces off him; you try and melt him, and he comes back to life.'

Peter Ebdon, beaten by Hendry in the 1996 World Championship final, concurs. 'He was an absolute, ultimate killing machine, like the biggest, baddest great white shark you've ever seen,' he says. 'He was a fearsome competitor. He would blank you if he saw you in a hotel lobby, but he had this aura, he had an edge to him. He understood that it was important not to give anything away. He wanted to batter people. Once he got them down, he wanted to keep them there. The fiercest competitor I ever came across.'

'He was an animal of a competitor,' says John Parrott. 'I thought Steve was bad, but this lad was worse. He was greedy, and that combination made him very, very good. He became the benchmark quite quickly. His break-building was fantastic; we hadn't seen the like of it. It was a totally different game of snooker. His long game was ridiculous. He didn't have a safety game because he didn't need one. He just knocked balls in from everywhere.'

Journalist and commentator Phil Yates covered Hendry's rise, the glory years and his decline. He saw close-up what motivated him. 'He hated losing,' Yates says. 'His primary motivation was to avoid losing. Yes, he wanted to win, but he hated the feeling of defeat. It'd stick with him for weeks, whereas the euphoria of success would only stay with him for an hour or two.'

Mark Williams, who went on to win three world titles, agrees. 'When Stephen used to lose, you couldn't talk to him for two hours,' he says. 'It was like someone had cut his arm off. I couldn't be like that. You try your best, and that's it.'

Hendry reached his first World Championship final in 1990. His opponent was a similarly attacking player but a different kind of character. Their rivalry would define an entire era, as the 1990s became a tale of glory for one, heartbreak for the other.

Anyone who saw Jimmy White as a teenager came to the same conclusion: that he was special. There was something magnetic about his appeal, the apparent ease with which he guided the cue ball around the table. In addition, he had a natural way about him. A Londoner, he was worldly-wise. There was genuine charm. He was irrepressible, kind, cheeky and gregarious, a world away from the cold, laser-focused world of Davis and Hendry.

'I saw him in an exhibition just after he won the world amateur title, and I was 100 per cent convinced he would be world champion, not just once but on multiple occasions,' says Yates. 'The only other player I've thought that about was watching Ronnie O'Sullivan as a youngster. It was a given, to me. He had so much talent. His best was incredibly good.'

Neal Foulds can vividly recall the first time he played White. 'I thought I wasn't a bad player, and then Jimmy turned up one day,' he says. 'My dad had seen him and said maybe I should have a game with him. He was so much better than me. I had no chance. It was a different league. I was nearly thirteen, and Jimmy around a year older. He was the most grown-up thirteen-year-old I'd ever seen, smoking and having a little drink, playing cards. He was incredibly streetwise. He knew everybody.'

This wise-beyond-his-years quality was part of White's appeal. As a boy he would regularly bunk off school to go to Zan's, a snooker club in Tooting. In the end, he made a deal with the headteacher: his absence was condoned as long as he was in the club rather than some other nefarious locale.

Joe Johnson remembers being Yorkshire champion and travelling to London with another player, Ian Williamson, to play against White and Tony Meo. 'Jimmy was fourteen or fifteen and he knocked in a 136 against Ian, beat him 3–0. Afterwards, Jimmy says to me – he's fifteen, I'm 25 – "Do you want to go for a drink, Joe?" I'm thinking, "You're not old enough." He says, "Do you fancy going into the West End?" So we did. Jimmy took us there, and in every place we went, everyone knew him and liked him. It was incredible. It was like going out with the Artful Dodger.'

As White built a public profile in his early 20s, there were few vices and temptations he could resist. He never failed a tournament drugs test but openly admits to having regularly taken cocaine on nights out. On one of them, the Canadian, Kirk Stevens, smoked crack cocaine, and White followed suit, later writing, 'If using cocaine is snorting the Devil's dandruff, then smoking crack cocaine is sucking the Devil's dick.' Stevens's flat turned into a crack den. He had one cassette – Bruce Springsteen's 'Dancing in the Dark' – which would be the backdrop for their slide into oblivion. 'Three months of our lives were lost doing that – lying there, glassy-eyed, spoons, tinfoil and rocks lying everywhere,' wrote White. 'We were two mad kids doing our best to kill ourselves.'[1]

It must have affected his game, but White still had his share of success. Stevens made a dashing 147 against him at the 1984 Masters at Wembley, but White won the match and beat Terry Griffiths in the final. He won four ranking titles and 13 non-ranking events during the 1980s, finishing runner-up to Davis in the 1984 World Championship. His lifestyle was chaotic, but he could still dazzle on the table.

Hendry and White had first met professionally at the 1986 Scottish Masters, White winning 5–1. From the off there was healthy respect. Hendry had looked up to White for his flair, while the 'Whirlwind' found the young Scot's attacking zeal a refreshing change to some of the older sloggers he was playing in most tournaments.

'Jimmy was my hero,' Hendry says. 'You'd be hard pressed to find someone with a bad word to say about him. We didn't mix socially because I wouldn't have kept up, but we did get on. It wasn't a rivalry like that.'

White had beaten Hendry 13–12 in a thrilling second-round match at the Crucible in 1988. It was such a departure from the careful, safety-first approach the public had become accustomed to that the BBC gave over the entirety of its annual snooker review programme to revisit it. Two years on, a Hendry vs White final promised much. With an average frame time of 12 minutes, it delivered. This was a final for a new decade, a festival of potting, with Hendry utterly concentrated on getting to 18 frames first and showing no signs of being overawed. 'I was determined to win and confident I could do it,' he said afterwards, betraying little emotion or exhilaration. It was merely a task he had set himself, which he fully expected to complete.

At 21, Hendry had beaten Alex Higgins's record as youngest

world champion and replaced Davis as world number one. 'Heavy hangs the head that wears a crown' was not a phrase that could be applied to him. He won the first four ranking events of the following season and finished runner-up in the fifth. He arrived back in Sheffield having retained his UK Championship and Masters titles, the latter with an extraordinary comeback from 7–0 and 8–2 down to Mike Hallett, Hendry winning 9–8 to underline his ruthless efficiency on the big occasions.

However, he was beaten by Steve James in the quarter-finals at the Crucible, clearing White's path to a maiden world title. It was not to be. John Parrott won the first seven frames of their final and beat him 18–11. Three world finals, three defeats. White's reputation as a World Championship nearly man was already in place before the two losses that would define his rivalry with Hendry.

There was a rematch between the two in 1992. Coming into the event, White was playing perhaps the best snooker of his whole career, with victory at the European and British Opens. 'I'll have to go sick not to win it,' he told the press. Overconfidence was certainly part of White's make-up, perhaps because he was so naturally gifted that the game came easily to him. The previous season, he had won three tournaments in a row and remarked, 'Somebody is going to have to play very well to beat me now. I hope to win four or five World Championships before I'm finished.'

First, he had to win one. The opening day of the final ended with White leading 10–6. A man unable to sit still at the best of times, the celebrations began that night: 'Every day of the World Championship was a holiday, a party, a day of freedom for me. When you're surrounded by mates and card games and more booze than you can drink then it catches up with you.'[2]

Hendry wouldn't know. He was in bed preparing for a comeback. Even so, at 12–6 it seemed as if White's coronation as world champion was guaranteed. At 14–8, more so. Hendry won the next, before the key last frame of the session, which he claimed with arguably the shot of his career, a tough brown with the cue ball close to a side cushion. Had he missed, to recover from 15–9 down would surely have been too great an ask. As it was, a fight-back from 14–10 adrift in a final that had seemed to be petering out felt more achievable.

White started to make mistakes in the final session. Having sat in his chair at one point in the afternoon thinking who to thank in his victory speech and who to leave out, he was now watching Hendry rack up frame after frame. He levelled at 14–14 before the last interval and completed a ten-frame winning streak with two closing centuries, to win 18–14. The White dream was over for another year.

Viewing figures for the final peaked at 11.6 million on the BBC, proof that snooker was still a huge draw and that the Hendry–White dynamic was capturing the imagination. Twelve months on, there was little drama. Hendry beat White 18–5, with a session to spare, to win his third world title. White had enjoyed several high-profile victories over the Scot – 18–9 in the 1990 World Matchplay final, 10–4 in the 1991 Mercantile Classic final, 9–2 in the semis of the UK Championship later that year – but the Crucible, with its intimacy, scrutiny and importance, added extra layers of pressure, as did the fact that with each passing year, he had not fulfilled his promise by becoming world champion.

They met again in the 1994 final, their rivalry a psychodrama now gripping the British sporting public. It was impossible not to pick a side. White's popularity if anything grew year after year due to his failure to clinch victory, while Hendry's achievements were taken for granted. The championship came down to a deciding frame, the first in a world final since the 1985 black-ball finish.

The black again played its part. White was leading by 13 points, with the remaining five reds perfectly spread. He needed to stay in control for a few more minutes and he would be champion at last, but he snatched at a routine black and missed it. The clearance still had to be made, but nobody doubted that Hendry would complete it.

'Stephen was like the iceman. You knew he wasn't going to miss,' says McManus. 'He did it as if it was like jumping on and off the bus. I find it incredible because I know I wouldn't be able to feel my legs in that situation.'

Four finals, four victories for Hendry over White. The Crucible crowd, who had started to believe it would finally happen for the Londoner, were subdued in their applause. Even Hendry didn't particularly celebrate. It seemed everyone in the room was devastated. Apart from the man who should have been.

'He's beginning to annoy me,' said a beaming White into David Vine's BBC microphone, a quip that goes a long way to defining his essential character. White's philosophy is that the past is gone and tomorrow is yet to come; it's all about the present. Was he disappointed in the moment? Sure, but then it's on to the next adventure.

For Hendry, sentiment never came into it. 'People would say, "Would you give away one world title to be more popular?" No, not at all. I was just there to do a job,' he says. 'It's very cold, for me. Two or three months are building up to it, and for 17 days my job is to go there and win the World Championship. At the end, it's job done. I'm not emotionally built like a lot of people.'

White never again appeared in a World Championship final. Hendry beat him in the semi-finals in 1995. The Londoner and his vast army of supporters kept the belief, but it dwindled as his game deteriorated and new players raised the bar.

Three decades on, Hendry does not feel sorry for White but appreciates the pressure of expectation he must have faced as a crowd favourite. 'There was unbelievable expectation on Jimmy, from himself, from his supporters,' he says. 'I never had 95 per cent of the crowd wanting me to win, so I wouldn't know how to deal with it. I don't know what that pressure is, but he's been in six finals and hasn't won one, so there's obviously something missing. He threw away a 14–8 lead against me; he missed a black off the spot against me. There's definitely a weakness there, but our games were very compatible. I didn't dread playing Jimmy ever because I knew I'd get chances. It was about who would score, because we'd both go for our shots.'

A teenage Mark Williams was one of many White fans left devastated by his failure to land the big one. 'I was on Jimmy's side. He was my hero growing up,' he says. 'The black he missed at 17–17, he bottled it. We've all done it. That was his time to win it. He twitched up. It's pressure. He couldn't get over the line.'

For White, talent alone was not sufficient to land the game's most prized trophy. 'Maybe Jimmy didn't love the war,' says McManus. 'He wasn't a serial killer. Davis was. Hendry was. Jimmy was unbelievably good, but sometimes that isn't enough.'

'Jimmy likes to go out,' is how John Virgo puts it. 'For those 17 days you can curb that, but it's the months before that have got into your system. Stephen's temperament was something else.'

'Jimmy liked life,' says John Parrott. 'He could've been more professional. He enjoyed going out, but he still won 33 events. What a record – six finals. It's an unbelievable Crucible record.'

Neal Foulds agrees and points out that White's good nature may have cost him in the big moments, when he should have been focused only on playing. 'He has a huge amount of friends,' Foulds says. 'In all those finals he was chasing round, trying to get tickets for everyone, which is the worst thing to be doing. It takes you away from your routine. It added lots of pressure on him that so many people wanted to see him win. He was a soft touch with people. He had friends, but there were also people who were like hangers-on. If he was playing a big match, there were so many people who would want to come who didn't want to come to all the other matches. He was swamped by all that. It must have taken its toll on him, but he never complained about it. It's very unfair to just say he was a perennial runner-up. He won everything else.'

'One of the greatest underachievers who still achieved,' is how Davis sees White. 'Technique-wise, a little bit suspect, but talent got over that. You needed him after Alex Higgins. He was so close to being world champion. It took a player like Stephen Hendry to clear up, when a lot of players wouldn't have been able to do that. The unfair thing is, we're judged by World Championships. Most other sports have majors. We're lumbered with just that one that's considered to be the yardstick, and it only comes round once a year.'

Shaun Murphy was entranced as a boy by the Hendry–White battles and would become world champion himself in the following decade. He concurs with Davis's view that snooker's blue-riband event casts a long shadow. 'Have I had a better career than Jimmy White? I don't think so. Am I a better snooker player than him? I don't think so. But I've won the World Championship, and for a lot of people that's what matters,' Murphy says.

Tellingly, though, Murphy grew up using Hendry as a template for how to be successful. 'I always supported Stephen,' he says. 'That was the way I was brought up. I found myself much more affiliated with what I perceived to be the ultimate pro, that professional approach. I had it drilled into me about the late-night lifestyle and how it would affect your snooker. It wasn't allowed in our household. When my father was teaching me, he'd use Davis and Hendry as examples, not Jimmy White. But to me he's still one of the all-time legends.'

John Major, the unassuming successor to Thatcher, was soon fading as prime minister, after a surprise election victory against the odds in 1992, a few weeks before Hendry's own recovery from adversity. Major's majority was only 21, leaving him vulnerable to backbench rebellions, especially over the issue of Europe. He was perceived as weak, and with the new millennium on the horizon, seemed old-fashioned in comparison to the youthful new Labour Party boss, Tony Blair, who became leader of the opposition after the sudden death of Neil Kinnock's successor, John Smith.

As Major faltered, Hendry soared. He won a fifth world title with victory over Nigel Bond in 1995, and a sixth by defeating Peter Ebdon in 1996. Other players simply could not cope with playing him on the biggest stage. 'I wasn't ready for that sort of test, with that sort of pressure, against the person who was then the greatest player of all time. Stephen's mentality as a winner was second to none. He was truly exceptional,' Ebdon says.

Shortly before the 1997 World Championship, Hendry equalled Davis's record tally of 28 ranking titles. What better place than the Crucible to break it? He duly reached the final again, having now won 29 successive matches in the event over a five-year period. He was apparently untouchable. However, he was now not quite as selfishly single-minded as in his younger days. Hendry and his wife, Mandy, had a baby son, Blaine. Before leaving for Sheffield, they received an anonymous letter threatening to throw acid in Blaine's face if Hendry won another world title. It was not the first piece of crank correspondence he had received – far from it, he was once sent a play in which he was killed in the final scene – but was still horrifying to read.

'I didn't have that intensity that I would normally have,' he says. 'Usually, if something went wrong and I lost a frame I should've won, I'd be in the dressing room furious, but I was a lot more casual during that final.' Ken Doherty, appearing in his first world final, beat him 18–12. Hendry compiled five centuries and outscored the Dubliner overall, but the tactically astute Doherty made several key clearances.

'I had the perfect game plan for him,' is how Doherty remembers it. 'He doesn't like the real matchplay stuff, getting drawn in. He made three centuries in the first session and was still 5–3 down. He got more frustrated as the game went on. He was playing shots where you could see he was irritated. I was interacting with the crowd, showing I wasn't nervous. It was like a psychological war, which happens in snooker. I was loving it, and that's what helped me.'

By 1998, White had lost his place in the elite top 16, which meant he had to qualify for the Crucible. In round one, he drew Hendry and beat him 10–4. It was a satisfying win, but no trophies were handed out. For Hendry, it represented a crossroads in his career. He had not lost in the first round at Sheffield since his debut in 1986, had not failed to reach at least the quarter-finals since 1988. The following season saw him suffer a humiliating 9–0 defeat to Marcus Campbell in the last 64 of the UK Championship. It had become a crisis. 'When you're used to so much success, there's a depression in your career when all of a sudden you can't buy a win,' he says. 'You go from a high to a complete low. When you're winning, all the talk is positive. Then, if you're struggling, it's "Is Stephen going to win this match? Has he gone?" It's impossible not to let it affect you.'

Hendry sought out help from Frank Callan, a former Blackpool fishmonger who had become a renowned coach, and returned to the winner's circle relatively quickly, winning the Scottish Open and Irish Masters in early 1999, but the true test always comes at the Crucible. He was still stuck on six titles, alongside Ray Reardon and Steve Davis. 'I went into that tournament with the least self-belief,' he says. 'When I was winning year after year, I just expected to win. I would have a jacket brought down for me for after the final. I took winning for granted.'

After an uncertain couple of years, he could no longer do this, especially with the draw he was handed. In every round, there was a viable title contender standing in his way: Paul Hunter, James Wattana and Matthew Stevens just to reach the semi-finals. He nevertheless dispatched them to go through to an encounter with Ronnie O'Sullivan, the best young talent in the game. They entered the third session with Hendry 9–7 in front and ended it level at 12–12. Hendry had made three centuries, and O'Sullivan two. BBC commentator Clive Everton called it 'snooker from the gods'.

For years, Hendry had held back the tide of younger players coming through in his wake, but this was now a major challenge against a significant talent. One factor that could never be questioned, though, was his temperament when everything was on the line. 'All players have ability. They can pot balls and play safe and all that stuff, but what set Stephen apart is that he was the greatest pressure player of all time,' says Phil Yates. 'Under pressure he was extraordinary. For me, he remains, under the cosh, out on his own.'

Hendry beat O'Sullivan 17–13 and defeated Williams 18–11 in the final. He was a seven-time world champion, the setter of a modern-day record. More importantly, he had proven to the snooker world, and himself, that he was not a spent force. Even this iceman of the baize had to acknowledge the enormity of the moment.

'I was able to block out the talk about the seventh until I finally won it,' he says. 'That was the most emotion I showed after a final. I said afterwards if I never won another match in my career, I'd achieved everything I wanted.'

As the 1990s drew to a close, Hendry had dominated the decade even more ruthlessly than Davis had the 1980s. His rivalry with White had captivated the viewing audience and kept snooker centre stage. He was still only 30, but the new millennium was approaching, and with it the triple threat of three outstanding younger players who would each usurp him at the top of the sport and cement lasting legacies of their own.

10

MY GENERATION

The 1980s snooker boom was also a television success story. A 1990 survey of viewing habits by Sportscan found that snooker accounted for 20 of the 100 most-watched sports programmes of the previous decade.[1] Such exposure inevitably led to a huge increase in participation levels. When Britons were not watching snooker, they were playing it.

The 1986 General Household Study found that snooker and athletics enjoyed the greatest participation increases of any sport in the previous three years, interest in track and field fuelled by the success of long-distance runners Seb Coe, Steve Ovett and Steve Cram, decathlete Daley Thompson and javelin throwers Tessa Sanderson and Fatima Whitbread.[2]

For youngsters around the UK, snooker had become the latest craze, with many clubs oversubscribed. 'There was a waiting list to get in,' says Alan McManus. 'This was 1984, the height of the boom. My club was open until 1 or 2 a.m. Most nights of the week there was a wait to get a table. There were 14 tables. You had two hours and then had to come off. There could be 20 or 30 people waiting to play.'

In Wishaw, North Lanarkshire, nine-year-old John Higgins was one of them. He had just watched Steve Davis defeat Jimmy White to win his third World Championship title and was taken by his father, John senior, an oil-rig worker, to see what the game was about for himself. He remembers an almost religious introduction to this previously closed-off world.

'I'll never forget walking in the club, up a couple of flights of stairs,' Higgins says. 'We get to a little reception desk, and me and my brother say, "That must be Jim Donnelly." He was a snooker professional, and his picture was up on the wall. And then, within about five seconds, Jim Donnelly came out of a private room at the back. My dad introduced us and said we were joining the club, and Jim says, "Great, fantastic," and gave us a tour. I'll never forget seeing his picture and then he's walking towards me.'

Snooker was not an expensive game to play, but money in the Higgins household was tight. 'We were just a normal working-class family,' he says. 'My dad worked two weeks on, two weeks off. My mum was bringing up three kids with what my dad could provide. There were some nights where she couldn't afford to give us three or four pounds to pay for the light, which was two pounds an hour at the time. She says to this day that I was adamant, standing there in my coat with my cue, saying, "You must have four pounds – we're wanting to go and play."'

In 1986, shortly after losing to Joe Johnson in the world final, Steve Davis was enjoying a Chinese meal with friends in Gants Hill, Ilford. 'This guy walked in out of the blue and went, "Steve, that green you potted . . ." I'm thinking, "Who's this bloke? He must know snooker if he remembers a green I potted." He says, "My boy's outside." This kid walks in with a cue case taller than him. Little did I know that a few years later I'd be playing him, watching him turn into the machine he became.'

This was the ten-year-old Ronnie O'Sullivan, who had been playing since the age of seven. His father, Ronnie senior, ran a series of sex shops in Soho. They lived with O'Sullivan's mother, Maria, and his younger sister, Danielle, in a large house in Chigwell. Ronnie senior made plenty of money. Recognising his boy's natural aptitude for snooker, he installed a full-size table in the family home.

Commentator Phil Yates, himself a decent club player, recalls his introduction to O'Sullivan at around this time. 'His grandparents were ice-cream sellers and lived a couple of miles from me,' he says. 'He came to the club where I practised, On Cue, in Old Hill, and the owner rang me and asked me to go and play him. So I went up there, walk in, and there's Ronnie O'Sullivan. We went onto the main match table, and I'm thinking, "He's ten, I'm playing well, and this is basically my own table," so I smashed the balls up from the back with my break-off shot. He could hardly see over the table but made a 50-odd break first shot. I'm thinking, "I can't believe this." He was like the chosen one.'

Tales of O'Sullivan's prodigious talent soon permeated through the bush telegraph of the still quite insular snooker world. He made his first century at ten, a maximum in competition at fifteen. 'When I first saw him, we were fifteen, at Pontins,' Higgins recalls. 'I watched him hit a snooker ball and thought, "This guy is incredible." He hit the ball differently to anyone else. He just had something about him.' But Higgins also saw that while Ronnie senior had a brash, confident air about him, his son could be sensitive. 'In one of our first junior tournaments, when I beat him, he started crying with his dad. I was thinking, "What are you doing? You're fifteen."'

Dilwyn Williams worked at the Marine Colliery, in Cwm, from 1967 to 1989, following in his own father's footsteps. The generational pattern could have continued but for the deindustrialisation of the 1980s and his son Mark's own growing obsession with snooker, which led to him bunking off school to hone his skills.

Dilwyn, recognising his boy's talent and seeing at first hand the rapidly approaching death of the mining industry, became an accomplice, picking Williams up from school shortly after he had arrived there, depositing him in the club in Bargoed and then fetching him again in the evening after his shift down the mine ended. Williams's mother had no knowledge of the subterfuge, but, unsurprisingly, the school noticed. However, its hostile response to this family-endorsed truancy waned somewhat when photographic evidence was produced of Williams with a Welsh junior trophy.

'I would go to school, they'd call the register, and my father would wait for me outside and take me to the snooker club,' Williams says. 'My mother and nan thought I was in school all day. We were threatened with a fine. I didn't turn up for any GCSEs. They said they would fine us for each one I missed, but it never materialised. In the end, they gave me Friday off school officially.'

If mining was a dying industry, maybe snooker could become a career. To hammer home the point, Dilwyn took his son into a mine to show him what life down there was like – an experience seared into Williams's memory. 'I went down a working mine on a proper shift,' he says. 'My father snuck me in with ten men; I was stuck in the middle. Down we went for what seemed like for ever. We were crawling through crap. It was horrible. I was down there hours, on my hands and knees. My father did this for 25 years. My grandfather did it for 40 years. What a tough job. I hated every minute of it. If I didn't make it at snooker, that's where I'd be, down there. There was nothing else to do where I was from.'

Change was coming to snooker. In 1986, Rex Williams had become the oldest player to reach a ranking final when he contested the title-deciding match at the Grand Prix at 53, losing 10–6 to Jimmy White. Two years later, Doug Mountjoy achieved a heart-warming victory at the UK Championship, ten years after first winning it. Out of the top 16, his career apparently in free fall, Mountjoy had painstakingly rebuilt his game with the help of coach Frank Callan. Remarkably, he followed up his 16–12 victory over Hendry at Preston Guild Hall by capturing the circuit's next ranking event, the Mercantile Classic. Mountjoy was 46, but this proved to be a last stand for the veteran contingent who had been mainstays of television snooker in the 1980s. Hendry's ascension to the world title at 21 had ushered in a new era, in which young players thrived.

One by one, the stars of the boom period exited the stage they had so memorably illuminated. By the end of the 1990s, Terry Griffiths, Alex Higgins, Cliff Thorburn, Ray Reardon, John Spencer, Eddie Charlton, Tony Meo, Kirk Stevens and Mountjoy were among a swathe of household names no longer on the tour. Dennis Taylor clung on for a few months into the new millennium before he too was relegated. Willie Thorne departed a year later, and Joe Johnson in 2003.

Davis chugged along as a member of the top 16, no longer top dog but still competitive, his 28th and final victory in a ranking event coming at the 1995 Welsh Open. Two years later, aged 39 and seemingly in terminal decline, he won the Masters for a third time. 'It was sweeter than anything. By that time, I'd gone full circle and people were hoping I'd win. I cherish that, more so than the times when I was expected to win,' he says.

The future belonged to a new generation. Hendry's World Championship success in 1990 lit the blue touchpaper for a revolution. He was only six years older than O'Sullivan, Higgins and Williams. While the champions of the past felt like old men, here was a standard-bearer they could relate to. His attacking game was an inspiration, his fearlessness a quality they all aspired to.

All three outstanding prospects continued to enhance their growing reputations. As Williams impressed in Wales, Higgins became Scottish under-16 and under-18 champion. O'Sullivan won the World Under-21 title in India. But who was really the best? They would come face to face in Birmingham in January 1991, an early staging post in what would become a decades-long battle for supremacy.

The World Masters was a Barry Hearn idea, essentially the Wimbledon of snooker. There were men's and women's singles and doubles events, a mixed doubles and a junior competition for sixteen-year-olds and under. For Higgins, it was a big chance on a national stage. He just needed his school to see it in those terms. 'I asked the headmistress if I could go, but she wouldn't give me the time off, so my mum said, "You're not going, son." My dad said, "No, he's going."'

It proved an inspired decision. Higgins defeated O'Sullivan, the pre-tournament favourite, in the quarter-finals and Williams in the final. 'I went down there and ended up winning the event,' he says. 'Quickly from there it became a whirlwind. Ian Doyle became interested in me. I didn't want to go, but my mum and dad forced it on me, in a way, saying I couldn't give up the opportunity because Ian Doyle was Stephen Hendry's manager and I had a chance of playing Stephen.'

Higgins would therefore fall under the same disciplinarian eye as Hendry had when he was starting out, but he found the strict regime harder to accept. 'Ian wanted me to go to Stirling every day,' he says. 'There were some tough moments when I left the house crying, running round to my Auntie Margaret and telling her to tell my parents that I didn't want to leave the environment that I was in.'

Hendry was impressed by what he saw in his young compatriot during their daily practice sessions. 'You could see the hunger in John,' he says. 'He wasn't just there to practise and have a game; you could see that when he was practising, he was doing it properly.

I've played with so many players who just go through the motions. He had ambition. You could sense it, and that's everything.'

For Williams, turning professional was more of a necessity than an immediate ambition. 'At the time, they made the Welsh junior tournaments sixteen and under, and the senior tournaments eighteen and over. I was seventeen, so I couldn't play in anything. I didn't really have much choice but to turn pro,' he says.

The three young men exhibited differing personalities and appearances. Higgins had the pasty-faced pallor of someone who had spent long periods of his teenage years inside a snooker club. Williams was gangly, cheeky, unafraid to throw himself into the world of adult banter. O'Sullivan was blessed with dark good looks, inherited from his mother's Italian side of the family. His big saucer eyes suggested mischief, excitement.

Snooker's closed-shop approach, limiting the professional circuit to 128 players, had been jettisoned in 1991, when the WPBSA threw the game open to anyone who could afford the entry fees. Hundreds of hopefuls gladly paid their money, swelling the association's coffers and necessitating long periods of qualifying for the main events. In 1992, the Norbreck Castle Hotel on Blackpool seafront was selected due to its vast ballroom, which could accommodate the requisite number of tables. 'They had 24 tables in operation at one time. It was a great festival of the game, balls constantly being potted,' recalls Phil Yates, adding, 'Blackpool at night was like the Wild West. You had 200 to 300 young guys there in a party town.'

Let off the parental leash, several young prospects went down the Jimmy White route of playing harder than they worked, turning up for matches worse for wear. O'Sullivan, Higgins and Williams were notable abstainers from the drinking subculture that grew up around the qualifiers. O'Sullivan would go for long runs along the beach, a way to let off nervous energy and clear his mind. Williams had a simple set-up with his friend, and fellow player, Ian Sargeant, and their minder, Les Griffiths: 'We had a one-bedroom flat. Les would sleep on the sofa, and I'd sleep in a double bed with Sargy. I was young, playing every day for months. It was brilliant.' Higgins was simply obsessed with the game itself. 'I was seventeen, and snooker was all I was interested in,' he says. 'I wasn't wanting to go out for a few drinks. I was lucky in a way because if I'd been a few years older, I could have been lost to the game. Snooker could have become secondary.'

It became immediately apparent that O'Sullivan was far too good for almost everyone. Day after day, he swatted away opponents, young and old, winning his first 38 matches and 74 of the 76 he played in Blackpool during the summer of 1992. The World Championship qualifiers were staged that September, seven months before the Crucible phase would begin. O'Sullivan qualified while still a sixteen-year-old. Interviewed at the time, he said: 'I've got no idea of statistics or records when I'm out there playing, but I must admit I can't believe how well I've done here. I've potted so well for so long. It's all about the will to win. Now I know I've got a definite psychological advantage over my opponents.'[3]

He joined Hearn's Matchroom stable, another indicator that the big league was where he belonged. Young, engaging and playing an exciting brand of the game, O'Sullivan had the snooker world at his feet, but then his own world came crashing down around him. In September 1992, he was playing in the World Amateur Championship in Thailand, when he received a call from his mother: 'Daddy's been arrested. He's in police custody. He's been involved in a fight and someone's been killed.'[4]

Ronnie senior had been in a nightclub in Chelsea, when an altercation ended in him fatally stabbing Bruce Bryan, a driver for

Charlie Kray, brother of the infamous Kray twins. He had been well regarded within the game. He liked people to know he had money but would often step in to buy food for less-well-off players. His devotion to Ronnie junior was unquestioned. As Clive Everton wrote in the *Guardian*, 'The snooker world's perception of Ronnie senior was of a rough diamond with a heart of gold, devoted and close to his son, financially generous to other young players. He had separated his private life from his business, which was hard, mean, criminal and violent.'[5]

Ronnie senior was sentenced to life, with a minimum recommendation of 18 years, and so began a separation that would define his son's outlook for many years, in particular an antipathy towards authority. He had lost his rock just as he was emerging as a public figure.

It felt as if the secure world he had always known had fallen apart, but at the 1993 UK Championship it came back together on the snooker table. It was O'Sullivan's last week as a seventeen-year-old. He was a boy among snooker men, still in only his second season on tour, but he had just won the qualifying event for the Masters and arrived in Preston on a high. He beat Alan McManus, Ken Doherty, Steve Davis and Darren Morgan to reach the final, a chance to test himself against Hendry in one of the biggest occasions in the game, possibly a match too far, but all good experience. That was the theory. The reality was quite different. O'Sullivan made two centuries and raced 6–2 in front by the end of the afternoon session, the final having been reduced to a single-day affair, after years as a best-of-31-frames, two-day contest.

For once, a Hendry recovery did not materialise. O'Sullivan won 10–6 to become the youngest-ever ranking-event winner. He was greeted by a giant roar from the watching spectators, aware they had seen something special. His mother, who had never watched him live before, surprised him by running into the arena in the aftermath of victory, enveloping him in a hug.

'I was just looking forward to playing out there. I didn't really imagine winning the tournament,' said O'Sullivan afterwards in the BBC studio. 'Everything went so quick, it was rush-rush, everyone shouting and screaming. They gave me the trophy and the cash. The cash was nice.' The next day, he took the trophy to HMP Gartree to show his father. Overnight, his star had rocketed. He was box-office, his family story now a national fascination.

A year later, the pressures of fame were weighing on him so heavily that O'Sullivan wanted out. His UK title defence ended in a 9–7 quarter-final defeat to Doherty, after which he said he was considering retirement. He was eighteen. 'If I don't think I'm going to be the best at something, I don't want to do it. I think this might be my last season as a professional. I'll be giving it a couple of days' thought to see where I'm going,' O'Sullivan told the assembled press. Doherty immediately poured cold water on the idea: 'If Ronnie wastes his talent he's a silly boy, because he's a potential world champion.'[6]

Opinion was split between those who thought O'Sullivan a classical spoilt rich kid showing petulance because he had lost and others who wondered if the mental demands on him, living in the spotlight while trying to master this most difficult of games, were causing him to go down a dark path.

Higgins was still with Doyle, but the relationship was an uneasy one. Just as Hearn had prioritised Davis, so Doyle's golden boy would always be Hendry. Matters came to a head at the Dubai Classic in October 1994. A resurgence in fortunes saw Davis challenging Hendry for the provisional number-one ranking. Higgins beat Davis in the first round and is adamant that Doyle saw it only through the prism of Hendry: 'Well done, John, that's a great result for Stephen.'

Higgins left the stable and, freed from shackles that had always been too tight for his liking, went to the Grand Prix in Derby a fortnight later and beat Dave Harold 9–6 to win his first ranking title. He triumphed in two more before the season was out: the International Open, in which he beat Davis in the final; and the British Open, where he saw off O'Sullivan to win the title. Still only nineteen, he had become the first teenager to win three ranking events in a single season.

O'Sullivan had beaten Higgins in the Masters final, but this was his only success of the 1994/5 campaign. Hendry was still to be convinced that the gifted but erratic rising star would pose him persistent problems. 'You could see the talent, it was obvious,' he says. 'As well as Ronnie played, I never thought he was going to be a threat to me because I thought he would be another Jimmy – in and out, and maybe go off the rails.'

For Williams, progress was slower. By the end of the 1994/5 season, O'Sullivan was stationed third in the world rankings, and Higgins 11th. Williams, meanwhile, lagged behind in 39th. When the breakthrough came, it happened on home soil, in Newport. He beat established players such as Willie Thorne, Doherty, Peter Ebdon and Harold to reach the 1996 Welsh Open final, where he comfortably accounted for John Parrott 9–3 to secure his first ranking title. 'I'd been dreaming of winning a tournament, so when it came true, it gave me a lot of belief. If I could win one, surely I was good enough to win another one,' he says.

The mid-1990s, with the new millennium approaching, were a time of optimism, if you were young. Britpop, bringing British guitar music to the fore, had exploded across the culture, reaching its zenith when rival bands Blur and Oasis went head to head in a battle for the singles chart number one. Danny Boyle's *Trainspotting* represented a fresh confidence in British cinema. Chris Evans became a figurehead for the new wave of home-grown entertainers, fronting the anarchic *Big Breakfast* on Channel 4, then the Radio 1 *Breakfast Show* and the live-music and chat show *TFI Friday*. Football, cool again after the Italia '90 World Cup and the formation of the Premier League in 1992, came home to England for Euro '96, and John Major left Downing Street as a Labour landslide ushered in Tony Blair. Technology was developing at a rapid rate. The British public were slowly getting their heads around the concept of sending mail electronically. Online chatrooms and message boards gave enthusiasts of any given subject the opportunity to converse. As boy band Take That split up, the Spice Girls brought pop back into the mainstream and championed 'Girl Power'.

The 1980s boom had passed, but snooker was still occupying a considerable space in British life, thanks in part to a game show. Just as *Pot Black* had been a hit throughout the 1970s and into the 1980s, *Big Break* was a popular staple of the BBC schedules for the whole of the 1990s, finally being axed in 2002. Presented by stand-up comedian Jim Davidson and John Virgo, it showcased a fun side of snooker to mainstream audiences and foregrounded players in a more relaxed setting than the intense environs of major tournaments.

Each edition brought together three players with three members of the public. General-knowledge questions answered correctly by the contestants bought the players time in the first round to, in the words of Virgo, 'pot as many balls as you can'. Two players advanced to round two, where balls potted had a monetary value. The winning pair then went through to the final, with a chance to win a holiday if the player could clear the table in whatever time was left after the contestant had answered five questions.

For Virgo, it was a career lifeline. 'I was towards the end of my playing career, missing blacks off the spot. Then I got the phone call: would I like to do a television quiz show with Jim Davidson?' he says. 'I didn't think it would work, but we did an initial run of eight shows, they put us in the time slot *A Question of Sport* had been in, and we got more viewers than them. Then they put us on prime-time Saturday night, and we were getting 14 million viewers.'

With the sport still centre stage on television, the star pupils of the Class of '92 were becoming clear contenders for the World Championship title. In this three-way arms race, it was a question of who could get there first.

In 1998, Higgins supplied the answer, becoming, at 22, the second-youngest champion with an 18–12 victory over Doherty, who had triumphed a year earlier. 'I could see my mum walking down the stairs as I was clearing the colours up, and I'm thinking, "Don't fall over,"' Higgins says. 'I could see she was crying her eyes out, so I was trying to clear the colours up as quickly as I could. Afterwards, my dad gave me a big hug, and all the emotions came out, thinking, "You've done it," but it doesn't sink in at that moment. I can't really say when it does.'

Certainly, there was little ceremony on the return home. 'Ken won the world title, went back to Ireland, and they had an open-top bus parade through Dublin. I won it a year later and drove back to Wishaw, where a couple of my neighbours said, "Well done,"' he says. 'It's difficult following Stephen Hendry. He'd achieved so much and was still winning so much. You were just A. N. Other coming along. Stephen had done it so many times, so I was just another player who'd won it.'

Higgins received another reality check when invited to join Hendry and Davis on an exhibition tour of China later that summer. 'When we got off the plane, everyone ran towards Steve and Stephen, and I was given their bags to carry,' he says. 'I could only laugh. I was out there with two of my heroes, and I was loving it.'

It seemed possible that the dedicated Higgins could supersede Hendry as Scotland's, and snooker's, next dominant force. In his season as world champion, he added the UK Championship and Masters titles to his CV. He advanced to the semi-finals of the World Championship but lost to Williams, who was then beaten 18–11 by Hendry.

By this point, Williams was rapidly catching his two contemporaries up. He won five more ranking titles after his debut success in 1996 and underlined a growing reputation for big-match temperament by edging a thrilling Masters final against Hendry in 1998, 10–9 on a respotted black. In front of almost 3,000 spectators in the notoriously rowdy Wembley Conference Centre, Hendry blinked first, missing a tricky pot to a middle pocket and leaving an easier one for Williams, whose natural calm had, for once, been tested. 'I was bricking it,' he admits. 'We tossed the coin, and I had to play my first shot. It's the only time I've felt my knees shaking while playing. The tension was unbelievable. It's the most nervous I've ever been in a snooker match. I was absolutely cacking it.'

At the end of 1999, Williams won the UK Championship and headed to the Crucible for the first World Championship of the new millennium a few months later, feeling content with his game and the life snooker was now giving him. 'I was starting to get into a rhythm, starting to win a lot of matches and building up confidence. I was enjoying it. I was young, winning matches and the prize money that comes with it,' he says.

Williams was deep in trouble against Higgins in the semi-finals, trailing 14–10 going into the final session. There was no handshake before play began. Williams did not offer one. It confused Higgins, and he lost focus. Williams came back to win 17–15 but insists there was no gamesmanship at play. 'John said I got into his head because I wouldn't shake his hand at the start. I have no recollection of that whatsoever. If I did that, it wasn't to get in his head.'

He faced another Welshman, Carmarthen's Matthew Stevens, two years his junior in the final. Stevens had recently won the Masters but was yet to capture a ranking title and had lost in the UK Championship final in successive years to Higgins and Williams. Talented for sure, he was already, at 22, in danger of developing the tag of nearly man. This looked certain to be dispelled once and for all when he charged 13–7 in front, but Williams produced a fine recovery, winning 11 of the last 14 frames to clinch victory at 18–16.

There was no wild celebration that night. 'I went to the after-party, was there for an hour, had a pint of milk and went back to the hotel,' he says. When the celebrations did happen a week later, Williams managed to mislay the famous silver trophy first purchased by Joe Davis seven decades earlier. 'I took the trophy into Cwm, had a few drinks – more than a few drinks – and woke up the next day without the trophy,' he says. 'I couldn't remember where I'd put it. I phoned the police station to see if anything had been handed in. I phoned World Snooker, and they were panicking. I was thinking, "I'll have to pay for this." Then my next-door neighbour came round with the trophy. He said he'd woken up for work that morning, and it was lying in the garden, so he took it to work with him.'

Hendry marvels at Williams's capacity to remain calm under pressure, to meet victory and defeat with the same equanimity. 'There will never be anyone like him again,' he says. 'People say there will never be another Ronnie, but eventually you think someone will come along who's unbelievably talented. But there'll never be someone with the temperament Mark has. If I had Mark's temperament, I would've won more tournaments.'

O'Sullivan, for so long considered the leading member of this formidable trio, had been left behind. Problems continued to blight his private life. In 2000, he checked into the Priory Clinic, a well-known rehabilitation centre. 'I feel like I've been on a treadmill of turmoil,' he explained when he emerged. He had won nine ranking titles in seven years, a poor return for such an obvious talent. Furthermore, he had seen his two contemporaries triumph on snooker's greatest stage.

'I thought at times he would waste his talent. Maybe he thought that as well, and it was a wake-up call,' says Phil Yates. 'I saw him lose a load of matches in the 1990s and early 2000s to people who shouldn't have been in the same room as him.'

Erratic he may have been, but he was still capable of the extraordinary. At the Crucible in 1997, O'Sullivan made a maximum break in only five minutes and eight seconds, the fastest ever, a spellbinding exhibition of cue-ball control, poise, panache and sheer star quality. He won the UK Championship for a second time later that year but withdrew from the same event 12 months later. His natural vivacity had been replaced by a sourness. He could be rude and arrogant. In 1998, he won the Irish Masters but was stripped of the title after his urine sample found traces of marijuana. His life was threatening to unravel.

Ahead of the 2001 World Championship, O'Sullivan was in an especially bad place. He told his mother he would be quitting after the tournament. Del Hill, a cheerful, gentle giant of a man, was his constant companion on tour, equal parts company and watchman, keeping O'Sullivan out of trouble and focused on playing.

Hill persuaded him to see a doctor, to whom O'Sullivan admitted that he had had thoughts of suicide. He was diagnosed with depression and offered a course of Prozac, the drug that controls serotonin levels in the brain, but it came with possible side effects, including sickness, and O'Sullivan wanted to wait until after the World Championship before taking it.

Snooker at least remained an outlet, a reason for getting out of bed. At the Crucible, he beat Andy Hicks 10–2 in the first round but felt 'a total mess inside'. By the second round, he was taking the Prozac tablets. He won 13–6 against Dave Harold, beat Peter Ebdon by the same score in the quarter-finals and defeated Joe Swail 17–11 to reach the final.

At the age of 25, he had finally made it to the title match in snooker's biggest event. His opponent for the next two days would be Higgins, his rival in the junior ranks, who had already scaled the Crucible heights. O'Sullivan led 10–6 after day one. Higgins had underperformed, but a comeback could not be ruled out. After the third session, the lead was 14–10. Before the evening's conclusion, a parade of former winners took place in the Crucible arena. At the end, Jimmy White was invited out as the 'people's champion'. He got his customary rousing ovation, but O'Sullivan, waiting to play what would either way be the defining session of his career so far, could not countenance being given such a sympathy vote. He wrapped up victory at 18–14, a destiny at long last fulfilled. He had joined Higgins and Williams as world champion. The three rivals would go on to win it 14 times between them. As they enter their 50s, they are still contenders. Williams reached the final again in 2025, beating Higgins 13–12 on the last black in the quarter-finals. O'Sullivan was a semi-finalist.

Williams has always felt like the junior member of the Class of '92, even though for periods he was the most dominant of the three – in the 2002/3 season he won the game's three oldest and most prestigious titles, a feat previously achieved only by Davis and Hendry. 'I hate being put in with those two,' he says. 'If Ronnie plays well, no one can get near him. John is just behind him, and I'm just behind John. I get a bit uncomfortable being put in with them, but maybe I should give myself a bit more credit.'

Neil Robertson has won more than 20 ranking titles during the period in which O'Sullivan, Higgins and Williams have prevented plenty of other players from being successful, so he is well placed to judge their respective merits. 'They all play the game the right way,' he says. 'Maybe John can get a little more bogged down, but he gives you different problems to Ronnie. He can play just as well as Ronnie, but he's a bit more of a percentage player. Ronnie is more aggressive, so you can sometimes get easier openings against him if he's not quite on it, but he has the crowd behind him. Mark is someone who never panics; he's always calm and unflustered. He's very clever. He'll go for a risky long red, and you'll wonder why, but he puts the cue ball in a position where he won't leave you a pot on. He's not as good as Ronnie in terms of going on a scoring rampage, but he's improved as a break-builder. They're all amazing players, and none of us would be as good as we are if it wasn't for them. Davis raised the level, Hendry raised it further, and then those three raised it even more.'

Judd Trump grew up in awe of O'Sullivan, Higgins and Williams, and in 2022 found himself alongside them in the semi-finals of the World Championship, having beaten Higgins in the 2019 final. 'I don't think I've ever seen three people who want to win as much as them,' he says. 'Ronnie and Mark play it down, but they want to win desperately. Those three coming through together at the same time brought something out in all of them that is very hard to be replicated, because a lot of the other players have never had that level of competition every single year. Nowadays, you're kind of an exception if you get to that level. They came through in an era where it was so competitive.'

The trio have coexisted for decades but have never been close friends. The rivalry is full of respect, but they are different people.

'Early on, I thought he was a spoilt brat,' says Higgins of Williams. 'It didn't help that I'd left Ian Doyle's stable and he was still with them. Little things got said, and you always felt there was a bad feeling in the air, or that's what I felt. When we were juniors, we were friendly. We're not really friends now, but we're the same, in a way. We have kids the same age and we just want to embrace and enjoy the time we have left on the circuit. No point squabbling or getting into arguments.'

Asked if he has a relationship with O'Sullivan, Higgins says, 'Not at all. It always feels like, who is going to make the first move to have a conversation? It's more on his end than mine. He wants to keep himself at a distance. I'm not sure he was always like that. Early in his career, he was quite sociable. There's no ill feeling. There's no one who respects him more than I do.'

Williams agrees. 'I get on better with both of them now than I ever did, but I wouldn't go out for a meal with them or anything like that,' he says. 'We have respect, but it's not like we ring each other up for a beer. We're rivals; we're not friends.'

Even so, as the champions of old faded from the scene, the sport now had a crop of highly talented youngsters ready to take it forward, as snooker increasingly looked outwards to the world beyond its British base.

11

ALL AROUND THE WORLD

The story of snooker is largely one of British men, but not entirely. Over the years, players from foreign climes have tried their luck on the circuit, with varying degrees of success. At the same time, the sport itself reached out to different countries, exporting tournaments and the game's star names to expand its global reach.

As it became established in the UK, snooker's footprint slowly began to spread to other areas of the Commonwealth, notably Australia and Canada. In 1965, the World Championship consisted of a series of challenge matches in South Africa, a country that produced leading players such as Perrie Mans, the 1978 World Championship runner-up and 1979 Masters champion; Silvino Francisco, who won the 1985 British Open; and his nephew, Peter, who became a member of the elite top 16.

To break through from another country and become world champion would require more than just talent. Conditions in Britain were second-nature to home-grown players but often challenging for those from abroad. Uprooting and coming to the UK meant personal sacrifice and considerable expense. Only the hardest would survive. In 1980, an authentic tough guy of the sport shattered the seemingly impenetrable wall that had stood between overseas players and the most prized title in the game.

Cliff Thorburn can vividly remember discovering the subterranean world of cue sports in Canada as a boy, in particular the first time he encountered snooker. 'I was twelve and at my cousin's in Vancouver,' he says. 'We played pool for an hour, and I really loved it, and then my father took me bowling just after that. I heard the clicking of balls, went down these stairs, saw the green cloth and money on the table, the cigarette on the rail. It was just such a thrill. I knew that it was a whole new world. I ran upstairs, and I was out of breath trying to explain to my dad exactly what I saw. He said four words: "Don't go down there."'

But Thorburn kept going down there. He left school at sixteen to pursue a career that few thought held any prospects. 'From the start, pool and snooker had a bad vibe from everybody. I played a game that was horrific for young men in general,' he says.

His father had not fought in the Second World War due to health issues. 'He was the black sheep of the family to a certain extent,' says Thorburn, a mantle he seemed keen to assume himself by choosing the unorthodox life of a snooker player. The closeness with Thorburn senior was magnified because he had been told his mother had died. In fact, aged 20, Thorburn discovered she was still alive. Tellingly, of his aspirations in adolescence, he says, 'I just wanted to achieve for my dad and our family.'

This meant long days and nights immersed in the pool and snooker scene of North America, an exotic and often dangerous world where you grew up fast. Money matches and hustling abounded. One time, in Oakland, Thorburn was well ahead when his opponent's backer pulled a gun on him, forcing him to start losing for fear of his life.

He worked various lowly paid jobs, travelling long distances in search of matches. Snooker was still a somewhat remote sport, played somewhere else. Thorburn was only dimly aware of the professional game in Britain. 'It was 1966. I was eighteen and hitchhiking across Canada,' he says. 'I was in a place called Thunderford Bay, way up in the middle of nowhere. I saw this article on the wall from 1955 that said Joe Davis had made a 147 in London. I didn't even know there was a World Championship. Seven years later, I was playing in one.'

The top professionals would visit each year to play in the Canadian Open. Thorburn became friends with John Spencer, who put the Canadian's name forward to turn professional. From early on, his cautious, life-or-death style was evident, a product of his snooker education in North America. 'I'd played for money, I didn't really play tournaments,' he says. 'So when I turned professional, I didn't know about doing things for the crowd in case they got bored. I didn't think about doing it in style; it was life and death, as if I was gambling.'

Thorburn had little money but made the move to the UK, where most tournaments were held, living modestly through the British winters. 'I felt like I was on another planet,' he says. 'I had a rented room in Bolton. I was putting five-pence pieces into the heater, and just to put my feet in the bed was like dipping my toe in ice water. I didn't dare move, because it was absolutely freezing.'

He adjusted, and his natural competitiveness brought about improvements. Thorburn reached the first World Championship final to be held at the Crucible in 1977, losing 25–21 to Spencer. By 1980, though, he was becoming frustrated. 'In 1978, I lost the last five frames to Eddie Charlton to lose 13–12. 1979, I lost to John Virgo, and I was getting fed up,' he says. 'In January 1980, I was at the B&H Masters in London, and we used to go to an Italian restaurant. All the winners would sign these plates, like "Terry Griffiths, world champion 1979". So I said to the owner, "Get me one of those plates." I put "Cliff Thorburn, world champion 1980". This was before the tournament. I just felt I was rising. There was a calmness there. It had to all come together at some point. I quit smoking or having a beer for a couple of weeks.

I was down 5–3 to Doug Mountjoy in the quarter-finals, and I said, "Screw all that," so I started smoking again and I had a couple of drinks. I won 13–10. There was one frame where we were 25 minutes on the brown. There was no way I was going to lose that game. It was a case of "Fuck the crowd."'

In the final, he faced Alex Higgins. The two were far from friends. Higgins enjoyed the majority of the crowd's support and, leading 9–5, it went to his head. He began to showboat, and Thorburn, sensing his chance, took advantage. 'I knew I was going to beat him,' he says. 'I just felt it. I had this thing inside me. The waters parted, the pockets got bigger. I could just see it.'

Thorburn won 18–16, to make history as the first non-British world champion (discounting Horace Lindrum's disputed win in 1952). Three years later, he made history again by compiling a maximum break at the Crucible in his second-round match against Griffiths – the first 147 in the World Championship. It began with a fluked red and took nearly 14 minutes to compile, a slow-burning drama that ended with Thorburn stood over the last black as BBC commentator Jack Karnehm, speaking for the watching audience, said, 'Good luck, mate.' Thorburn sank it and fell to his knees in ecstasy.

'I dreamt of it about two months before the championship,' he says. 'It was a wonderful occasion, not a pressure-packed thing at all for me. I just wanted to make sure the black went in without touching the jaws. I felt terrific. It didn't feel difficult at all.'

Thorburn is aware that the maximum remains seared into the snooker memories of fans of the era. 'Everybody talks about winning the World Championship in Canada,' he says. 'The 147 means nothing. Yet in the UK they don't talk about the world title. The maximum was a special moment for people. They loved that moment, and they haven't forgotten about it.'

In fact, it was almost immediately tinged with sadness. When Thorburn rang his wife Barbara at home in Canada, she told him she had miscarried. The pair had moved to the UK but never really settled there, and the pull of Canada was too strong to resist. Thorburn reached the world final in 1983, but after a series of close matches – the one with Griffiths ended at 3.51 a.m. – was exhausted, and Steve Davis beat him easily, 18–6. He won three Masters titles and remained a top player until the end of the decade.

Now in his late seventies, he has lost none of the charisma that made him a favourite of 1980s audiences, despite his well-earned nickname of 'The Grinder'. Thorburn has one thing in particular he wants to get off his chest about his famous maximum: 'The World Championship was going for 56 years before I made the 147. Now, people say that I made the first 147 at the Crucible – well, I don't care about that. I care that I was the only guy for 56 years to make one in the World Championship. Screw the Crucible!'

From the mid-1970s to the mid-1990s, Canadian faces were regularly seen in televised tournaments, a popular and charismatic bunch with seemingly exotic backstories and character traits that, though sometimes self-destructive, earned them popularity with British audiences.

Kirk Stevens was ten years Thorburn's junior, a younger-brother figure to whom Thorburn is still fiercely loyal. He turned professional in 1978, the year after his fellow Toronto cueist reached the first Crucible final. Young and good-looking, he instantly became a pin-up, a status bolstered by his choice of attire: a white suit that put fans in mind of John Travolta in the film *Saturday Night Fever*.

Away from home, with fame, money and acclaim providing a heady cocktail in his daily life, Stevens went off the rails. Drugs had never been far from the orbit of Canadian cue sports, and Stevens developed a cocaine habit, in the days before drug testing was introduced by snooker's authorities. In 1985, he reached the British Open final, during which his opponent, Silvino Francisco, confronted him in the toilets, accusing him of being high. Francisco was later recorded by a journalist making the same accusation, and the story blew up. Stevens refuted the charge but later admitted to being 'hopelessly addicted'. However, he denied using drugs during tournaments, and a disrepute charge against him was dropped.

Thorburn, who is still in touch with Stevens, remembers him with fondness. 'Kirk was a wonderful player,' he says. 'He was definitely good enough to win the World Championship, but it seemed that he didn't know it. Everybody was on his side; they loved him. He was dynamic. He had the white suit, he played quickly, he was a good-looking kid. He was a God's-gift snooker player, but if you make a mistake in your life, people don't forget it. They're cruel.'

Bill Werbeniuk became another folk hero for British audiences of the 1980s. A large man with a cheerful countenance, he resembled Oliver Hardy but also reflected a widespread hypocrisy surrounding substance abuse. Stevens's cocaine habit drew disapproval, but Werbeniuk was celebrated for being a legendary drinker. He suffered from a tremor in his arm, which he countered by imbibing alcohol in huge quantities. Before a match, he would regularly down several pints of lager, and his intake during play would amount to another pint per frame, leading to lengthy toilet breaks.

Thorburn describes Werbeniuk as 'an unbelievable cueist and a tough player'. He adds: 'I grew up with Bill. We didn't drink before we turned pro. Then you'd see Bill at the Crucible, and he'd be at the hotel at 8 a.m. and he'd have four or five empty pints there. Being overseas players, if we lost, we'd stay up drinking. It'd be breakfast time, and we were still there. We couldn't just go home like the British players. It was more money to buy a new plane ticket – what a great excuse that is!'

This eclectic trio won the World Team Cup for Canada in 1982 and were runners-up on three other occasions. Thorburn eventually retired in 1997. Stevens's drug issues had seen him leave the circuit a few years earlier, although he did attempt a comeback in the late 1990s. Werbeniuk's professional career ended in 1992, after Inderal, the beta blocker he took, became a banned substance. He died in 2003, aged fifty-six.

They inspired several other Canadians to try their hand as professionals. Jim Wych twice reached the World Championship quarter-finals. Alain Robidoux was a semi-finalist in 1997, having made the German Masters final a few months earlier. His career was effectively ended when his cue was deliberately broken into several pieces because its manufacturer was offended by a sponsor's logo being affixed to the butt end. Bob Chaperon came from nowhere to win the 1990 British Open. Shortly afterwards, he, Robidoux and Thorburn won the World Cup for Canada.

Thorburn was the trailblazer for Canadian snooker, but also for the non-British contingent forced to come to the UK to follow their dreams. For Ken Doherty, it was a shorter journey from Ireland but still a sacrifice to move to Ilford, in Essex, as a teenager. There are few more engaging characters in snooker than Doherty, whose machine-gun laugh peppers every anecdote. As a boy, he was allowed to stay up with his father to watch *Pot Black*. His dad loved Ray Reardon, but when Doherty saw Alex Higgins, he became entranced.

His home soon became Jason's, in Ranelagh, where he would stand on a biscuit tin to reach the full-size tables. He began winning the Saturday handicap tournaments and spending more and more time there, much to his mother's disapproval. 'I'd get the bus home from school, pass by the house and go straight to the snooker club,' he says. 'The schoolbag would go under the table. I used to empty the ashtrays and sweep the floor and get an hour of free snooker. My mother would come in around 6 p.m. to tell me my dinner was on the table. She didn't like me being in there. She came in one time with a wooden spoon and waved it in front of the manager, saying, "If he fails his exams, I'm going to hold you responsible."'

He rose quickly through the Irish amateur ranks, and in 1989, aged nineteen, won the World Under-21 title in Reykjavík. A few months later, he triumphed at the World Amateur Championship in Singapore. Doherty was on his way to the top but had become the best player in Ireland and needed to push himself by practising with better-quality opposition.

Eugene Hughes, a senior Irish professional, was based in Turnham Green, West London, and Doherty moved over to join him, after assuring his tearful mother that he'd be back if he could not make a go of snooker. Each day he would get the Underground to Barking and then a bus to Ilford Snooker Centre, where Hughes had arranged free practice.

More young Irish players came over, and they stayed together as a gang in various bed and breakfasts and rented accommodation, one of which almost caused their demise after the owner tried to kill himself following an argument with his wife by turning on the gas in the kitchen. Fortunately, one member of the party had a job working for Ronnie O'Sullivan senior in Soho and came home late. Smelling the gas, he left the lights off and opened all the windows.

Despite this unpromising start, Doherty's formidable competitive spirit and tactical awareness, allied to the scoring game that was becoming the modern way of playing, soon came to the fore, and in 1990 he turned professional. His breakthrough moment came in 1993, when he won the Welsh Open. Various titles and appearances in finals followed, but heading into the 1997 World Championship, the results had dried up. 'I'd had a bad run-in to the tournament. My form was terrible,' he says. 'The first round against Mark Davis was a big match for me, because it guaranteed I'd be in the top 16 if I won it. After I beat him, it released a lot of pressure and tension. I played with such freedom after that.'

Wins over Steve Davis and John Higgins set up a semi-final meeting with Robidoux, whom he comfortably beat 17–7. This meant a final against the great Stephen Hendry, who was aiming for a seventh Crucible title and sixth in a row. Doherty refused to be overawed. 'I was relishing it,' he says. 'I'd beaten Stephen a few times in my career up to that point, so I wasn't afraid of him. I wasn't as intimidated as I might have been. When I went back to the hotel at night, I would visualise myself holding the trophy. It gave me a calmness. I could just see it. This was what I'd grown up watching. They were the moments that were my inspiration. I was just going to enjoy it and play my own game.'

He led 15–7, before a Hendry charge saw the defending champion win five frames in succession. 'At 15–12 I got nervous because he'd made comebacks before which were well documented, ones which I'd watched at the time,' Doherty says. 'I could feel myself in that position, thinking, "Please, not now." He missed one red at 15–12. I jumped out of my chair like a greyhound coming to the table and won that frame, which was a turning point. The nerves went after that.'

One person not watching as Doherty closed out an 18–12 win was his mother, whose nerves were such that she could not endure the tension. 'She went out on her bike for the final session,' he says. 'She couldn't handle all the people coming round to the house and the TV crews. So she went down to Donnybrook church and was lighting candles for me, then she got a puncture and had to walk home with her bike. The first thing I did when I got home was hand her the trophy, and it took pride of place on her television set. She cleaned it every day.'

He reached the final again the following season, losing 18–12 to John Higgins. Another world final followed in 2003, when Mark Williams beat him 18–16. Doherty also appeared in three UK Championship finals and two at the Masters, where in 2000 he missed the last black of what would have been a 147 break, with a sports car worth £80,000 waiting as a prize. The miss would have haunted many players, but Doherty, with his happy-go-lucky approach to life, managed to laugh it off.

These days, he's an established and popular television pundit, much in demand for appearances in the wider media, but the 1997 win remains frozen in time. 'I look back at some of the images and it seems like yesterday. You relive the moments and memories,' he says. 'The years just go so quickly.'

If anything, the years went slowly before another non-British player became world champion. Australia had been represented for two decades primarily by Eddie Charlton, while Warren King reached the 1990 Mercantile Classic final and John Campbell got to number 18 in the world. In the late 1990s, Quinten Hann, a handsome but wayward character, reached the top 16 but was eventually banned after being recorded by a newspaper agreeing to fix a match for £50,000.

Melbourne's Neil Robertson was more level-headed, demonstrating discipline and determination in equal measure to reach the top of the sport. Robertson's parents divorced a few years after he was born. Weekends were spent with his father, playing casual games of snooker and pool, before he and his brother,

Mark, went to the local arcade. His dad then bought a share of the snooker club, and the sport became a more serious commitment. Robertson entered junior events every Sunday morning. At thirteen, he realised he was better than the other juniors and began spending more and more time on the table. Three years later, he turned professional, after reaching the semi-finals of the Oceania Championship at his home club, which earned him a tour card.

Looking back, Robertson is astonished he was allowed to travel to the UK at sixteen. 'It was crazy,' he says. 'I can't believe I did that. I'd never let [his son] Alexander do that by himself. I was nowhere near good enough to make an impact, but my dad thought it'd be a really good experience. I don't know if it was or not. I lost a bit of interest afterwards because I didn't know if I was going to be good enough. There was a lot of self-doubt because I only won a few matches.'

Robertson dropped off the tour after one season, but returned as an eighteen-year-old, still raw as a player and a fish out of water. 'I stayed in Leicester for six months,' he says. 'It was bang in the middle of the English winter, really cold and a completely different lifestyle. I had no contact with family and friends. I knew Mark Selby, and that was it. It wasn't what I thought it would be. It was a half-hour walk to the club, and I didn't have much money. We'd stop off at a BP garage and get microwaved food. The TV had four channels. There was no internet. It was rough.'

He was relegated for a second time on his 20th birthday, after losing 10–9 to James Reynolds in the World Championship qualifiers. Robertson returned home to Australia, believing snooker as a career may not be for him after all. He went to the local job centre without much clue as to what he wanted to do. The queue was so long that it gave him time to think. He resolved to give the game one last go and earned a third crack at the pro tour by winning the 2003 World Under-21 title. 'I felt it was last-chance saloon to really have an impact on the sport.'

Arriving with only £500 to his name, he settled in Cambridge, where Joe Perry, a top-16 player, demonstrated kindness to him and the other young Australian players by allowing them to play on his personal table and practising with them. Robertson's game improved as a result, but he was still homesick, at a time before Skype or Zoom. 'A couple of times a week we'd go to an internet café and send long emails home,' he says. 'Then we'd go back and check the responses. I'd have a phonecard so I could call home. With mobiles back then you could only text, and it was super-expensive to even do that.'

Within a few months, he won the qualifying event for the Masters and played Jimmy White at Wembley Conference Centre. The following year, he qualified for the Crucible for the first time, and in 2006, won his first ranking title, the Grand Prix in Aberdeen. This was the prelude to becoming a regular winner. In fact, from 2006 to 2022 he won at least one title per calendar year, including two triumphs at the Masters and three at the UK Championship.

At the 2010 World Championship, he was facing a seemingly hopeless position, 11–5 down in the second round to Martin Gould, but pulled off a stirring recovery to win 13–12 and went all the way to the title, beating Graeme Dott 18–13 in the final. His mother, Alison, had set off from Australia during the semi-finals and surprised Robertson by being present for the title decider, unfurling the Aussie flag in the moments after his victory.

'It was the first time I'd seen her for ten months, so it was very emotional,' he says. 'When I saw her waving to me at the start of the match, I almost started crying. I had to shake myself out of that.'

Like all world champions, Robertson was swept into an immediate swirl of interviews in the hours after victory, but he recalls a brief moment of solitude as he waited to be introduced at the post-final party when the enormity of the achievement sank in. He spent most of the night on the phone to his father back in Australia.

It was the career highlight for a player with plenty to choose from. Robertson's arrow-straight cue action is swooned over by players, fans and pundits alike. His accurate long potting is a major strength, as are his powers of concentration. In the 2013/14 season, he became the first player to compile a century of centuries in a single campaign, his tally ending at 103. His memory for matches, and shots within matches, is unnervingly clear. Yet, off the table, his preparation has often been sketchy. He once set off to play a qualifying match in the Yorkshire town of Barnsley by driving to a small village in Gloucestershire of the same name. At the Crucible once, he opened his bag to discover he had forgotten to pack his shoes. He dashed to a nearby shop to buy a new pair, but they rubbed his heels so badly that he lost all eight frames of the session.

These mishaps aside, Robertson is the most successful of all the non-British players. His record of success on the table is impressive enough, but taken with the personal sacrifices he has made, the story is one of fortitude against the odds. 'Time stops for you,' he says of the experience of being dislocated from family. 'You go back home, and people's lives have changed. When I went back to Australia for Christmas in 2023, my nephews had forgotten who I was. I struggle to deal with it. It's very difficult.'

The British grip on snooker has been historically so strong that Robertson believes players from other parts of the world who have enjoyed success should be shown more respect. 'Say Australia was the boom country for snooker. If I was playing multiple tournaments there, with home support, I'd have over 30 ranking titles to my name,' he says. 'If the World Championship was played in

Australia, I'd have won it multiple times, no doubt whatsoever. No overseas player has won the world title more than once. It's very hard. You never have any genuine support. You have some neutrals or your core fans, but you don't have that home support. That's very tough. It's a miracle what I've achieved. It's bloody tough. We should celebrate the overseas players more.'

By the time Robertson became world champion, players were used to an increased travel schedule. The 1975 World Championship, held in Australia, was retrospectively awarded points, which went towards forming the first ranking list, but it took until 1988 before another ranking event – that is, a tournament for the whole 128-player tour – was held outside British shores, when Jimmy White defeated Steve Davis to win the Canadian Masters. This was staged in a country that had hosted invitation events since the 1970s, but the next foreign foray saw snooker visiting a nation with no history or, as it turned out, interest in the sport.

The 1989 European Open was originally earmarked for Belgium, but concern from the Belgian authorities over the participation of South African players at the time of apartheid saw the WPBSA instead book the Casino de Deauville, in France. A thriving hub of well-to-do sorts in the summer, it was virtually deserted in late January, when snooker's great and good descended on it.

'It was a disaster, farcical,' says Phil Yates, who covered the event as a journalist. 'In July and August, that's where all of the money, the old money in Europe, goes. There's a big race meeting there in the summer. It's a beautiful place. But in the winter, it's completely out of season. It was a tumbleweed kind of town.'

Snooker had little resonance with the few locals who were in attendance. Yates recalls Irish player Eugene Hughes heading for his dressing room at the interval of his match, dressed in bow tie and waistcoat. 'There was an old lady there in the casino who thought he was a waiter. She asked him to get her a brandy.'

The sense of farce continued in the arena. 'John Parrott was playing a match, and the French MC did all these introductions, even though there were only about four people in there,' says Yates. 'A woman in the front row stood up and said, "Can you do all of that again in English please, we're from Portsmouth?"'

Parrott defeated Terry Griffiths 9–8 to win the title, the first of a series of victories for the Liverpudlian outside the UK. He defended his European crown in Lyon the following year, after which France was jettisoned as the host nation and the tournament staged in the Netherlands, Belgium and Malta, all of which had varying degrees of cue-sports heritage.

Malta was on the snooker map thanks to Tony Drago, an extraordinary talent who played the game at a rapid pace. He won a frame at the 1988 International Open in three minutes – a record. The following year, he joined Silvino Francisco and New Zealand's Dene O'Kane in forming the Rest of the World side at the World Team Cup. They reached the final against England, represented by the top three ranked players in the world – Davis, White and Neal Foulds – and were only beaten 9–8 on a respotted black.

Dubai was another location where snooker planted its flag. Barry Hearn had established an invitation event there, before the WPBSA moved in with a ranking tournament that ran for six years from 1989 to 1994. An Australian Open was announced for 1989, but concerns surrounding the legitimacy of the promoter were heightened when the Melbourne address he had given turned out to be a bus shelter. The event was hastily moved to Hong Kong, where Mike Hallett beat O'Kane 9–8.

A week later, the Asian Open took place in Bangkok, and the success of a local player led to an unexpected snooker boom in

Thailand. James Wattana had first come to prominence as a sixteen-year-old, when he won a Matchroom-promoted invitation event in his home city. Three years on, he had joined the professional ranks, after winning the world amateur title. The Asian Open was only his second event on tour, but he beat established players Hallett, Mountjoy, Francisco and Griffiths to reach the final, where Hendry defeated him 9–6.

The first Asian star of snooker, he quickly became a top player, reaching a high of third in the rankings and winning 11 professional titles. 'For Neil Robertson, it's been a real sacrifice to be away from his family, but at least he could speak the language,' says Phil Yates. 'When Wattana came over, he had to learn, playing Scrabble with the journalist John Dee. He had this extra layer of responsibility every time he played. It got to the point that if he was playing a tournament in Britain, he would expressly tell his manager not to tell him if he was on live TV in Thailand.'

The interest in Wattana led to 12 ranking events being staged in Thailand between 1989 and 2002. Crucially, he won two of them, in 1994 and 1995. Yates remembers the vibrant scene on the streets of Bangkok as snooker gripped the nation. 'They couldn't get live television in what we'd consider prime time, so the evening sessions were really late, 10–10.30 p.m. starts,' he says. 'It meant there were big gaps between afternoon and evening sessions, so one day we went out for a meal. The tournament was very close to one of Bangkok's red-light districts, Soi Cowboy. You had to walk through it to get to the restaurant. We had our meal, and as we walked back to the venue, the match having started, we saw that every television in these bars was tuned to the snooker. The punters were watching it. The girls on the poles were watching it. We realised this was a game that gripped a nation. When James Wattana won his first ranking title in Thailand, 20 million watched it, which was a third of the population.'

Wattana also starred in a heartbreaking human drama at the 1991 British Open. Shortly before his match against Drago, he was informed that his father had been shot in Bangkok. No further information was available as to his condition. Wattana made a 147 break, only the fourth televised maximum, and won the match, but was informed afterwards that his father had died of his injuries.

Snooker was still a British sport in terms of its home base, but the WPBSA recognised that there were new worlds to conquer. As in the UK, television was key. Eurosport launched in 1989 as a partnership between the European Broadcasting Union – a group of free-to-air broadcasters across the continent – and Rupert Murdoch's Sky. Based in Paris, its programming was varied, running the full gamut from football and tennis to arm-wrestling and dog frisbee, the intricacies of which need not bother us here.

Snooker found its way onto Eurosport in dribs and drabs, until a landmark deal was struck in 2003 to broadcast every World Snooker event. This meant that for the first time, viewers in the UK and beyond could watch live coverage of tournaments from outside Britain. It also exposed snooker to new audiences and resulted in millions of new fans being created in the 60 countries where the sport was now available to watch.

Germany developed a particular affinity, having hosted tournaments in the 1990s, before Eurosport's blanket coverage began. The German Masters at the Tempodrom in Berlin was first staged in 2011 and quickly became a favourite with players and fans alike. German Eurosport's commentator Rolf Kalb, who used to send away for videotapes of snooker in the 1980s, became a cult figure, presiding over his own country's boom and educating new viewers as to the nuances of the game.

By 2025, there had been ranking events staged in Austria, Belgium, Latvia, Turkey, Gibraltar and Bulgaria, and other tournaments in Romania, Poland and Portugal, all as a result of Eurosport's evangelistic coverage. The most prominent player to emerge from the continent during this new snooker boom was Luca Brecel of Belgium, a natural talent from a young age who made his Crucible debut at the age of seventeen.

Brecel's breakthrough came in 2017, when he won the China Championship, his first ranking title, and despite some inconsistency he won two more, the 2021 Scottish Open and 2022 Championship League, and appeared in the 2021 UK Championship final, before an unlikely and audacious run to the world title in 2023. In five previous Crucible appearances he had failed to win a match. Another in a long line of snooker-playing introverts, he decided a complete change in outlook was required to remove the pressure of playing on the sport's most famous stage, and so went out partying before the tournament, arriving having undertaken little practice.

He edged Ricky Walden 10–9 in the first round, Mark Williams 13–11 in the second and recovered from 10–6 down to beat Ronnie O'Sullivan 13–10 in the quarter-finals, blitzing through all seven frames of their final session in little more than an hour. He made a terrible start to his semi-final with Si Jiahui, falling 14–5 adrift, but by now inspiration was driving him forward and Brecel fought back to win 17–15 and set up a final against Mark Selby.

At the end of the first day, Brecel held a narrow 9–8 advantage. Selby, a Crucible specialist with four world titles already on his CV, was widely expected to be too strong when it came to the crunch, but Brecel produced a brilliant display on the second afternoon of the final, compiling four centuries to pull away to a 15–10 lead, before winning the first of the evening to be within two frames of the title. Selby, obstinate and determined when in adversity, rallied to 16–15, but Brecel won a scrappy frame before a fifth century of the day carried him across the line an 18–15 winner.

The satisfaction came from the unorthodox approach he had taken to the tournament and also from becoming the first non-British winner in thirteen years, and only the fourth at the Crucible. Thorburn, Doherty, Robertson and Brecel managed to break the UK's stranglehold on the World Championship. The real surprise was that nobody from snooker's modern powerhouse had been able to do so yet. The new millennium contained several challenges for the sport, but one country above all others provided evidence of its future global direction. In China, snooker had become a national obsession, thanks chiefly to a genuine home-grown superstar.

Ding Junhui discovered cue sports at the age of nine, accompanying his father after school to watch him play pool with friends. 'When he wasn't playing, I hit a few shots. I loved the feeling of the balls going in the pockets,' he says.

As he started to hit more shots, his considerable talent became evident. At twelve, his father took him to southern China to get proper coaching. Aged fifteen, Ding won the Asian Under-21 Championship, the Asian Championship, the World Under-21 Championship and gold for China in the Asian Games.

Peter Ebdon saw this emerging prodigy up close. 'I practised with Ding when he was fifteen, when he first came over to the academy in Rushden. Every year, Keith [Warren, Ebdon's manager and head of the academy] would bring players over from China and Thailand to practise with more experienced professionals in the UK, and after a couple of weeks he'd give me a call to ask me what I thought of them. I'd usually say, "He's good, but there's a lot of good players out there." The very first day I practised with Ding, after I finished the session I called Keith and said, "This lad is really special. He is going to be a superstar." I was defending world champion at the time and I couldn't get near him. His cue ball – his positional play – impressed me as much as anything. It was outstanding. He had incredible talent.'

Ding turned professional at sixteen. It meant spending many months in the UK, his first time away from his family, in a country where he spoke virtually no words of the language. Although he impressed on the table, away from it he was deeply isolated. 'I found it hard,' he says. 'I didn't talk much when I was younger. I was scared of living there. I had no friends. I just concentrated on my practice. When I walked to the table, it was a safe time for me. There were a few Chinese players who came over, but we didn't see much of each other because of our different match times, and they would leave if they were out of a tournament. I was homesick at the time, particularly at Chinese New Year. I would be alone, no one to talk to. This was the first time I had experienced this.'

The first ranking event staged in mainland China was the 1990 Asian Open in Guangzhou, won by Stephen Hendry. It took nine years for the second to arrive, the 1999 China International in Shanghai, where John Higgins triumphed. After Mark Williams won the 2002 China Open, with snooker struggling financially following the enforced loss of tobacco sponsorship due to government legislation, it looked as if the sport's flirtation with the Far East may have been over. No further events were staged in China for three years, but Ding's emergence as a rising star was the catalyst for a return in 2005.

This was to be the first ranking tournament staged in Beijing. Ding would ordinarily have had to chance his arm in the qualifiers held in the UK, but to make sure he was present in the final stages, the decision was made to withdraw him from the event and then reinstall him as a wild card, along with 15 other Chinese invitees. The future of snooker in China, and possibly the sport as a whole, was resting on whether this gamble paid off.

Ding came through the wild-card round with a 5–2 victory over Mark Davis, before a 5–0 whitewash of Ebdon, a result that resounded in the Chinese media. By the time he played Stuart Bingham in the last 16, interest was picking up. He scraped through this match 5–4, then beat Marco Fu 5–2 in the quarter-finals and Doherty 6–0 in the semi-finals to face Hendry in the final. During the week, he had turned eighteen.

By now, there was a fervour around this shy and humble teenager. In China, youth is valued highly in sport. Sportspeople often retire at a young age. If Ding could achieve success in a game that was relatively new to much of the population while barely out of school, it would be an inspiration to a new generation. And so it proved.

Hendry led 4–1, before attempting a difficult red that turned the final. He won only one further frame as Ding sprinted to a 9–5 victory. When the viewing figures on Chinese television came through, they were astonishing: 110 million had been watching at the moment of triumph.

A decade later, there were up to five big-money tournaments a year in China, and dozens of young players, inspired by Ding's breakthrough, had emerged. The Chinese state invested in academies. Some schools even put snooker on the curriculum. Cities such as Daqing, Yushan, Wuhan and Haikou bid against each other to stage events, driving up prize funds in the process. Ding had started a revolution.

Hendry, who now visits China regularly for sponsorship work, recognises the importance of Ding's victory. 'People in China still ask me if I let him win. They don't know me at all,' he says. 'I could see the attention he was getting and the talent, but the reaction afterwards told you something big would happen. They see snooker as a gentleman's game, with the bow ties and suits. They love British things. They love individual sports. They don't seem as good at team sports. You have to put work into something and master it. It's natural to work at something for hours and hours and become good at it.'

A few months after his success in Beijing, Ding became the second-youngest winner of the UK Championship. He won the Masters in 2011, and during the 2013/14 season became only the second player to capture five ranking titles in a single campaign. He became established as the figurehead of Chinese snooker and opened his own academy in Sheffield. His legacy in the sport was secure. The final question was, could he complete the fairy tale by becoming world champion?

He got close in 2016, reaching the final but losing 18–14 to Mark Selby. Ding reached the semi-finals the following year, but has struggled in Sheffield since. 'It's so difficult,' he says of the World Championship. 'People think I have the talent to win it, but playing at the Crucible I don't feel like that. It's so tough, much different from other tournaments. There's the most pressure, the hardest matches all season. You have to stay in your form for two weeks. There's the World Championship and then the other tournaments. It's totally different.'

Hendry believes the pressure on Ding to perform for his country has weighed too heavily. 'Ding is the best player not to win the World Championship, but there's too much expectation on him in terms of winning it for China,' he says. 'The two things they really go mad for is Olympic gold and someone to be world champion at their sport. Growing up, Ding would have that attitude. I don't think he's been able to put it in his mind that he's going to win it for himself first. I did. People said, "You won it for Scotland." No, I won it for me. I don't think Ding's been able to do that.'

As Ding's success sparked a boom that helped snooker grow globally, it started to look to new markets, in particular the Middle East. Saudi Arabia, a country governed by strict religious laws, had begun to invest heavily in sport. Its critics claimed this was to cover up human-rights abuses, but football, boxing and golf saw the path to riches, and snooker followed suit. In March 2024, an invitation event was staged with the gimmick of an extra golden ball, which would be potted at the end of a 147 break for an additional £500,000. Nobody did so, and the prize was doubled to £1 million for the next staging. A ranking event in Riyadh later in 2024 carried the same £500,000 first prize as the World Championship.

It would seem surreal to snooker's early professionals that the game ended up being played not just in parts of the world with no previous heritage but for serious money. It had taken several decades, but the sport was finally being shaken out of its British straitjacket and becoming properly international.

In 2025, a Chinese player did become world champion. It was not Ding but one of the many young players he inspired. Yet this was not received with the unalloyed joy such an achievement deserves due to a complicated backstory.

With all the money sloshing around, temptation had for some time been lapping at the feet of the players. Snooker's innocence, if it ever existed, was long in the past as a number of high-profile scandals tarnished its image and threatened its credibility.

12

READ ALL ABOUT IT

When snooker hit the heights on television, money flooded into the sport and with it the many temptations associated with excess. The game was now a national soap opera, its leading players household names, and they were not immune to the various scandals that afflicted the worlds of entertainment, politics and national life in general.

After years in which the sports section would not give snooker any house room, now the gossip columns reflected the sudden public interest in the private lives of the game's stars. Marriage break-ups were analysed; there was a focus on the cars the players drove, the houses they lived in, where they went on holiday. They became a source of fascination and speculation, exacerbated by the newspaper circulation wars of the 1980s. The tabloids signed players up to lucrative ghosted columns, one way of ensuring positive coverage, and in many cases the protagonists encouraged the image they were handed by the press.

Tony Knowles, who reached number two in the rankings, was tall, dark and handsome, and so became one of snooker's first authentic pin-ups. He did little to play down his image as a sexually voracious lothario of the baize, cooperating in a series of articles in the *Sun* in 1984 in which he catalogued various erotic adventures. Dubbed 'a three-part farrago of sexual boasting' by Clive Everton it led to a disrepute charge and £5,000 fine.[1]

Alex Higgins was out on his own as a serial offender, keeping the WPBSA disciplinary committee busy with a steady stream of misbehaviour, usually fuelled by alcohol, ranging from urinating in a plant pot to the physical assault of officials. For a period it was news if Higgins was not in the news, but he could normally be relied upon to find trouble. It cost him the number-one spot in the world rankings in 1982, after he was docked points for misbehaviour.

Barry Hearn labelled 1980s snooker '*Coronation Street* with balls', and the roles for the cast were set. Bill Werbeniuk was a drinker. Willie Thorne was a gambler. Knowles liked the ladies. Higgins liked a fight. Steve Davis had no discernible vices, although even he was eventually caught up in a newspaper 'kiss and tell' story in the 1990s.

Sexual escapades and boozy nights out are good tabloid fodder, but in terms of the integrity of a sport, there are two transgressions that are damaging to its image and potential survival: cheating in order to win dishonestly and deliberately trying to lose for financial gain.

Performance-enhancing drugs are the scourge of athletic sports. Few who saw it will forget the shock of BBC presenter Desmond Lynam being handed a piece of paper during a highlights programme at the 1988 Seoul Olympics informing him, and the viewers, that Canadian sprinter Ben Johnson had tested positive for an anabolic steroid after winning the men's 100 metres gold in world-record time. Lance Armstrong, who won the Tour de France seven times, later admitted to being a serial doper, one of many in elite-level cycling. Football, tennis, baseball and many other sports had to face their own doping scandals, while similar rumours attached themselves to various sportspeople, unfairly or not.

Snooker introduced mandatory drug testing in 1985, after a series of newspaper allegations involving players ingesting recreational substances such as cocaine. Those who later admitted this, such as Jimmy White and Kirk Stevens, never failed a test, although Cliff Thorburn was fined £10,000 after testing positive for cocaine in 1988. A decade later, Ronnie O'Sullivan was stripped of the Irish Masters title, having beaten Ken Doherty 9–3 in the final, after testing positive for marijuana. In 2001, he won the World Championship while taking the antidepressant Prozac, but this was not on the banned list.

There had been a brief furore in the 1980s over the use of beta blockers, which control the heart rate. Players medically prescribed them for health conditions were unfairly maligned, not least by Colin Moynihan, the minister for sport, who described their use as 'tantamount to cheating'.[2] Other players fell foul of the rules by taking cold cures without checking the contents and testing positive for substances on the banned list in the process.

Compared to most sports, drugs have not been a major problem in snooker. Far more serious has been the issue of match fixing. Even in the sport's earliest days, there had been a whiff of manipulation around matches. Reliant on money from ticket sales, Joe Davis was suspected of going easy on opponents in his World Championship contests to make them closer and drive up revenue. He and his brother Fred would magically make their matches on the BBC last as long as was needed before the next horse race, in the days when snooker on television existed mainly as a kind of sandwich filling between other sports.

However, when the professional circuit began to take shape, a more pernicious element came into the sport, keen to cheat the bookmakers by persuading players to lose frames or even matches on purpose. Various approaches were made by shady figures, most of which were shunned – but not all.

Focus fell on the Franciscos, Silvino and Peter, from South Africa. They both became top-16 players but were involved in matches that rang alarm bells with some bookmakers. Silvino was never charged with malpractice, but he was arrested after losing 5–1 to Terry Griffiths at the 1989 Masters, the match having attracted suspicious betting patterns. No firm proof of wrongdoing emerged, and the matter was dropped.

At the 1995 World Championship, an inquiry was launched after bookmakers suspended betting on Jimmy White's match against Peter Francisco. A large amount of bets had been placed on White to win 10–2. In such circumstances, the winner of the match need not be in on the fix. White, in fact, sought out John Spencer, then the WPBSA chairman, between sessions to express his concern that Francisco was not trying.

There is a belief that snooker is easy to fix because players have to miss a pot by only a narrow margin for the ball to stay out. In fact, if they attempt to miss narrowly, they run the risk of potting it, so to make sure the failure has to be glaring, thus raising suspicions. More usually in fixed matches it is shot selection that alerts other players, such as illogical safety play that lets the opponent in or overcomplicated positional shots when easier options exist. On the BBC's commentary for the White vs Francisco match, Dennis Taylor said, 'I can't figure out what's going wrong with Peter. His thinking doesn't seem to be there.'[3]

If a betting coup was to come off, Francisco had to lose 10–2. At 2–2, he had no wriggle room. At the time, White was not in the best of form, and there was the usual pressure associated with the first round at the Crucible. At 4–2, a very scrappy frame was reaching its conclusion, with Francisco, at least on the face of it, in a good position to win it. He was to miss a yellow by such a distance that it did not even hit the jaws of the pocket. White won 10–2. A committee of former players – Geoff Foulds, Mike Watterson and Bill Oliver – reviewed the whole match, and Francisco was banned for five years.

In the years that followed, there were some lower-key matches, early in tournaments and often near the end of the season, when a player's approximate ranking for the following year was already known, that attracted alarm from bookmakers. The decision to make the Grand Prix a round-robin event in 2006 and 2007 also led to suspicions over the integrity of matches, as players could afford to lose and still advance to the knockout phase.

More seriously, there was a police investigation into a match at the 2008 UK Championship between Scottish players Stephen Maguire and Jamie Burnett. A heavy volume of bets had been placed on Maguire winning 9–3. At 8-3, a close frame ensued. With three balls remaining and a chance to clear, Burnett left himself a long blue, potted it and then missed the pink, only to fluke it. He now had the black for 8–4 but missed it by a large margin. Maguire won 9–3. Strathclyde Police interviewed both players, but no charges were brought and there was no sanction from the WPBSA.

These instances of suspicious matches did not help snooker's image but would feel like small beer compared to a sensational story that threatened the career of one of the greats. The night before the 2010 World Championship final between Neil Robertson and Graeme Dott, it emerged that the *News of the World* had a front-page exclusive accusing John Higgins of agreeing to fix matches. It was as if a bomb had exploded at the Crucible. Everyone working there, as well as legions of snooker fans, was stunned and saddened. The game's showpiece match was overshadowed. Higgins, a much-liked and respected champion of the sport, was immediately suspended.

The story was a classic *News of the World* exposé, undertaken by its chief investigative reporter, Mazher Mahmood, widely known as the 'fake sheikh', as many of his stories were derived from him dressing up in traditional Arabian garb while pretending to be a rich and powerful investor looking to put money into ventures involving celebrities. In this way he snared actors, sportspeople and various other hapless high-profile people into dodgy behaviour, which he then gleefully reported.

Higgins had been knocked out of the 2010 World Championship by Steve Davis, an unlikely victory for the old warhorse, then aged 52. Eliminated from the sport's blue-riband event, Higgins travelled to Ukraine with his manager, Pat Mooney, where a meeting had been arranged with a potential investor for their fledgling World Series, an attempt to cash in on the popularity of snooker on Eurosport by staging invitation tournaments across the continent. Unbeknownst to them, the 'investor' was Mahmood. Luridly, a *News of the World* video appeared to show Higgins agreeing to receive €300,000 for throwing frames in future events. No money changed hands on camera, but the damage done to Higgins's reputation and that of the sport was, at first, colossal.

Not everyone was convinced. The investigative journalist Nick Harris had doubts as to the integrity of the *News of the World*'s reporting and undertook audio and video analysis of the footage released by the newspaper, which suggested major inconsistencies. On his Sporting Intelligence website, Harris reported:

> The potential business partners belonged to a company called Alfa Equity, where the senior negotiator was a man called Marcus D'Souza. Except Alfa Equity was a fake company, established as part of the sting, and Marcus D'Souza was actually Mazher Mahmood. The sting had been a long time in the planning and one source suggested the *NOTW* may have spent as much as £200,000 on perpetrating it. It was elaborate

to the extent that when Mooney and Higgins arrived in Kyiv, on separate flights, they were met by limousines on the tarmac and fast-tracked through customs. This gave the impression of local high-level backing for the proposed events.[4]

Higgins and Mooney were wined and dined on their arrival to such a degree that Higgins went back to his room heavily drunk but having said nothing untoward. Harris reported that the newspaper, having already spent a considerable amount on the story, was now getting desperate:

> One well-informed source later alleged to me that late into the night on Thursday 29 April 2010, Mazher Mahmood made a phone call to the *NOTW*'s then editor, Colin Myler, to tell him that they had 'absolutely nothing' on Higgins at that point. There was no hint that he was a match-fixer or would become one, no matter how many leading questions were asked.
>
> So to the morning of Friday 30 April 2010, and one final attempt to get Higgins on camera saying something dodgy. By this point he was massively hungover, suspicious about what was happening and still in the dark about Alfa wanting to know whether exhibitions could be rigged. There were so many gaping holes in the intro claim that Higgins had shaken hands 'on a disgraceful deal to fix a string of high-profile matches after demanding a €300,000 kickback'.
>
> The video purporting to show a handshake was clearly filmed on an entirely separate occasion to footage shown in the same video. This first picture showed Higgins shaking hands and a table set out a certain way. Another scene within seconds showed four people including Higgins toasting something with vodka. The table was set up differently in these two scenes, and Mahmood was wearing different clothes.

What was a reader/viewer supposed to believe from this? That Higgins shakes hand on this match-fix deal, and then four conspirators toast the deal with vodka? That's how it looks. This wasn't even the same meeting.⁵

An investigation was conducted by former Metropolitan Police superintendent David Douglas on behalf of the WPBSA. An independent tribunal chaired by Ian Mill QC did not find Higgins guilty of match fixing – after all, none of the matches mentioned were ever played – but he was found to have breached betting rules by failing to report an approach to manipulate matches.

One of the many myths around the case is that Higgins was not punished. In fact, he was fined £75,000, the biggest financial sanction ever imposed on a snooker player, and suspended for six months from the date of the original story, meaning he could not play in the first few events of the following season.

When his suspension was up, he won his first tournament back, a minor ranking event in Germany. A few weeks later, he recovered from 9–5 down to beat Mark Williams 10–9 and win a third UK Championship. Early in 2011, his father, John senior, died. By now driven by grief and a sense of injustice, Higgins won the Welsh Open and at the Crucible defeated the game's rising star, Judd Trump, 18–15 to become world champion for a fourth time.

'I felt as if I wanted to stick two fingers up to the whole world, but it would've killed me if I'd kept up that sort of intensity. It's not me,' Higgins says now. 'This is why I respect guys like Davis and Hendry. They had that intensity, but that concentration would've killed me. After I won the world title again, it was like my head was going to fall off. Behind closed doors I was still grieving.'

Two months after Higgins triumphed at the World Championship, the *News of the World* was sensationally shut down by its owner, Rupert Murdoch, following revelations that journalists had routinely hacked the voicemail messages of celebrities and members of the public caught up in major news events. The tipping point for the general public was the allegation that a journalist had intercepted a message on the phone of Milly Dowler, a teenage girl who had gone missing and was later found murdered.

Mahmood was jailed in 2016 for conspiring to pervert the course of justice, following the collapse of a trial involving pop star Tulisa Contostavlos, who had been revealed by the 'fake sheikh' to be dealing drugs, after he posed as a film producer offering several million for a part in a 'film', before asking her for drugs – a classic case of entrapment. The judge, Alistair McCreath, questioned Mahmood's truthfulness and dismissed the case.

The match-fixing allegations took an emotional toll on Higgins. He was embraced again by the snooker world but is still, wrongly, identified by some as a cheat. 'I'll never get over that episode in my life,' he says, 'but to the people who know me and love me it's never brought up. It's not a thing to them. Maybe it still is to the outside world.'

* * *

Stephen Lee was a member of the celebrated Class of '92, turning professional as a teenager alongside Ronnie O'Sullivan, Higgins and Williams. Blessed with a silky-smooth cue action, Lee won the British under-16 and under-18 titles and in 1992 became English amateur champion, a few weeks before becoming a pro. In terms of trophies, he did not enjoy the success of his famous contemporaries, but silverware still came his way. He won the 1998 Grand Prix, 2001 LG Cup, 2002 Scottish Open and 2006 Welsh Open. After a spell in the doldrums, he returned to form and secured the 2012 Players Championship. Lee reached a high of fifth in the world rankings and was a semi-finalist in the 2003 World Championship.

However, when snooker was itself struggling for sponsorship and therefore prize money, he found an alternative source of income: he deliberately lost frames and matches while his associates bet on them. A damning report by Sports Resolutions in 2012 found Lee guilty of a catalogue of fixing, including the throwing of frames at the Crucible. His close circle was heavily implicated. The report stated:

> The bets were placed by three groups of people. The first were organised by his then sponsor who opened multiple betting accounts with various associates. These accounts were used to place the bets. The second group were coordinated by his then manager who placed almost identical bets, the third was an individual known to Lee who placed the same bets independently of the other two groups. Lee was in contact with the groups in the lead up to the matches in question and afterwards. In one case the person collected the successful bet and placed the half of the winnings into Lee's wife's bank account.[6]

Condemnation for Lee was widespread but not universal. It was clear he had fallen in with a bad lot, but he himself may not have been significantly enriched by the fixing. Tellingly, the investigation concluded: 'It is not clear how much Lee benefited from their activity or of his motivation to get involved in match fixing.'

To some, Lee's activities represented a wider malaise in British public life. At the time these matches were being manipulated, it came to light through a series of *Daily Telegraph* articles that members of both houses of parliament were abusing the expenses system on an industrial scale. Conservative MP Sir Peter Viggers was revealed to have claimed more than £30,000 for 'gardening expenses', which included a floating duck house for one of his properties. Labour home secretary Jacqui Smith resigned after it emerged her husband had charged pornographic films to the family telephone bill, which the taxpayer was expected to cover.

Trust in politics was already low after the Iraq War of 2003, the justification for which was Iraqi president Saddam Hussein's 'weapons of mass destruction', which imperilled his neighbours and the wider world. Following an invasion led by US and British forces, these arms were never found. Then came the financial crisis of 2007, in which years of excessive lending, particularly in the US subprime mortgage market, began a contagion that left banks in serious danger of collapse. They were bailed out by the taxpayer to the tune of billions, and no one went to jail.

It turned out that snooker players also cheated. Lee was punished heavily, receiving a 12-year ban and ordered to pay £40,000 in legal costs. The World Snooker Tour tightened up its rules on gambling, establishing an integrity unit and banning players from betting on matches, even those in which they were not involved. However, some fell foul of the new regulations, so ingrained was betting in the DNA of the sport. Snooker had begun as a gambling game for British Army officers, and since then many players had never competed in a match without some sort of financial stake to make it meaningful. Side betting had always been part of the culture, so a number of players continued to have wagers on matches they were not competing in and were given various fines and suspensions.

To the outside world, it was a confusing picture. Following the outlawing of tobacco advertising and sponsorship in 2003, betting companies were now the main backers of snooker tournaments, but the sport was also waging war against gambling. Despite the bad publicity, snooker's reputational damage was relatively low, but this was threatened by another betting scandal, this time with troubling cultural undertones.

In 2023, ten Chinese players received bans and suspensions for a litany of match-fixing cases. The players had all moved to the UK to play on the World Snooker Tour and were living in close proximity to each other in Sheffield. Without any real adult supervision, the youngest of the contingent were led astray by more established members of the group. The report into the affair by Sports Resolutions identified senior players Liang Wenbo and Li Hang as the ringleaders, and they were each given lifetime bans from the sport.

Liang had won the 2016 English Open. He was known for being an emotional player, but his reputation was already severely damaged after he was found guilty in 2022 of physically assaulting a woman in Sheffield city centre. The match-fixing report found that

> Liang reached out over time to a large number of Chinese snooker players to solicit or induce them to fix or contrive the result or score of a snooker match, that he had made threats to at least two Chinese snooker players, that he was intimidating and that he was in the habit of putting pressure on young players facing financial difficulties to engage in match fixing activities.[7]

Among those caught up in the scandal were Yan Bingtao and Zhao Xintong, who had each become leading players. Yan had won the 2021 Masters at the age of 20, Zhao the 2021 UK Championship at 24. They should have represented the next generation of Chinese superstars and were both contenders for the World Championship title, but they were given suspensions by the WPBSA – Yan until 2027, and Zhao until 2024. The Chinese Billiards and Snooker Association further banned Yan from playing in China until 2030, and Zhao until 2025.

There was understandable outrage from their fellow players at the reputational damage done to snooker by this affair, but it also exposed some uncomfortable truths about how the professional tour was structured. Qualifiers, even for Chinese ranking events, were held in the UK, therefore anyone hoping to make it in the game had to base themselves there. These young Chinese players barely spoke any English, so understandably they banded together. They were also experiencing a sudden freedom, away from parental control, in a country more liberal than their homeland. The 2020 COVID pandemic further increased their feelings of isolation. The Sports Resolutions report found that

> During the COVID-19 pandemic, the Respondents were not able to return to their native China. Many of them felt lonely, bored and even more isolated during this time. Many of them also suffered on a continuing basis from financial difficulties, exacerbated by the pressures of living costs in the UK, the expenses of travelling to compete in snooker tournaments abroad and ill-judged gambling and betting habits. This set of circumstances made the youngsters among the Respondents particularly susceptible to influence and manipulation from the older Chinese snooker players, who took them under their wing. They were accorded respect by the youngsters, who looked to them for advice and guidance.[8]

There were those within the sport who wondered if the scandal would negatively impact China's relationship with snooker, but in 2023, four years after the last major event staged there before the shutdown for the pandemic, the World Snooker Tour made a triumphant return. If anything, there was even more interest. New Chinese tournaments were added to the schedule, the game's leading stars were in demand for lucrative exhibitions, and the banned players were merely replaced with even more talented youngsters.

And then something incredible happened. Zhao Xintong, despite still being banned in China, was allowed to enter the 2024/25 Q Tour, a series of events played in snooker clubs that serves as a qualifying circuit for the professional game. Zhao had not been charged with fixing matches; in fact, the inquiry found he had attempted to prevent Yan Bingtao from doing so. The official report stated: 'His involvement was limited to placing bets for Yan through Li [Hang], whereby he became liable as a party to two match fixes. He is good friends with Yan, whom he has known since the age of 16. He attempted to dissuade Yan from match fixing on both occasions with no success. He felt he had no other option but to place the bets for Yan, as Yan had requested. He has shown genuine remorse for his actions.'[9]

Zhao won four of the five Q Tour tournaments he entered, which meant he regained his tour card for the 2025/6 season and was eligible to play in the World Championship under amateur status. Starting in the first qualifying round, he won four matches to reach the Crucible, where audiences were treated to his audacious talent for long potting. Seemingly unaffected by the fuss around his return, with opinions split as to whether he should be welcomed back with open arms or not, he just got on with playing and found himself in the semi-finals against his idol, Ronnie O'Sullivan.

Sentiment was set aside as Zhao won all eight frames of their second session to march into a 12–4 lead, later winning 17–7 without the need for a fourth session. In the final, he faced another multiple world champion, Mark Williams, and quickly raced 7–1 in front. 17–8 down going into the last session, Williams rallied briefly, but Zhao got over the line 18–12 to create history for China.

On his eighth birthday, Zhao had watched Ding Junhui win the 2005 China Open on television. Now, the Chinese snooker boom, which began at that moment, had finally produced a world champion. Zhao's victory, which he celebrated by proudly holding his country's flag aloft in the Crucible arena, represented a potential shift in the balance of power within snooker, but more importantly, it was a moment of personal redemption for Zhao himself. Not everyone in the sport agreed, but many felt his victory had wiped the slate clean.

Scandal is part of sport. It is part of life. Snooker was bruised by these instances of shady behaviour but never fatally threatened. Time and again, its popularity meant it was able to negotiate itself out of the quagmire, proving the worth of the game itself. And for a legion of ordinary guys made good, it provided a route out of obscurity and into lifelong stardom.

13

COMMON PEOPLE

Dennis Taylor's victory in 1985 struck a national chord not just because of the dramatic manner in which it was achieved but because Taylor himself was so relatable. Here was a man with a young family who had been steeped in the world of work before turning professional. If Steve Davis could appear cold and robotic, the new champion was very much human. He could have been your neighbour.

He is by no means the exception in snooker's story. So many world champions have been ordinary guys made good, few more so than the man who succeeded Taylor to the Crucible crown in 1986. Joe Johnson found himself catapulted to sudden fame, yet somehow kept his feet on the ground, one of a number of everyday heroes to have shared in snooker's wider success.

NO ORDINARY JOE

Johnson was born in Bradford in 1952, part of the post-war generation who grew up in a Britain that was still rebuilding. His father was from Pakistan but left his English wife when young Joe was four, and his new stepdad, Ken, nurtured the boy's early interest in snooker, which began, not unlike Taylor's own enlightenment, with a first, tantalising glimpse of the table.

'I was six or seven, and there used to be a youth centre near where I lived,' Johnson says. 'You could see a snooker table through the window, and it was all lit up. I thought to myself, "That looks wonderful." I was looking in from the outside, my nose up against the window, and it was hypnotic. I thought, "I want to play that game."'

His father bought him a half-size table at the age of eleven, and four years later he finally got a chance to play on a full-size version, where his natural eye for potting brought him attention. Bradford's economy relied heavily on the wool trade, and Johnson got a job in the office of a firm that transported the material all over Europe. 'It was next door to the local billiard hall, so I used to go there in my hour's lunch break and play,' he says. 'At teatime I'd finish work and go and practise again. It was so handy for me. I got to a decent standard, and they were going to make me transport manager, but it was blocked for some reason, so I decided to leave. A friend of mine who worked on the gas board got me a job. I needed the money because I was a newlywed. All over Yorkshire there were clubs who organised invitation tournaments, 16 players at a time. I earned a good living from that. I used to win loads of them.'

Johnson was starting to do well from amateur snooker while still clinging to the security of full-time employment. A Damascene moment came early one morning when he left home late and had to run to get the bus to work. 'I could see it pulling in, a quarter of a mile away,' he says. 'I started running and realised I wasn't going to make it. I thought, "What the hell am I doing? I'm getting up at seven in the morning, running for the bus to get £25 a week from the gas board, and I'm earning £150 a week in these little tournaments, and I'm only playing part-time." So I stopped running, turned round, went home, took my overalls off and said, "I've finished." That was late 1978, and I turned professional a year later.'

It was hard at first. There were just a few tournaments and not much prize money. His professional status meant he could no longer compete in the amateur events where he had been so successful. 'Suddenly, my kids, the food on the table, the bills depended on me winning matches. I remember thinking, "This is hard. I have to win,"' he says.

Success was slow to materialise, although he did make the last 16 of the 1981 UK Championship. He inched up the rankings thanks to a gradual improvement in fortunes and reached the final of the 1983 Professional Players Tournament, a ranking event, where he lost 9–8 to Tony Knowles. By the start of the 1985/6 season, he had crept into the elite top 16 at 16th, meaning he would be seeded at the Crucible.

It was 33-year-old Johnson's third appearance in Sheffield. Taylor had drubbed him 10–1 on his debut, and he was due to meet the defending champion again in round two, but Taylor lost on the opening day to Mike Hallett. Johnson, who beat Dave Martin 10–3 in the first round, saw off Hallett 13–6 to go through to a quarter-final against Terry Griffiths, who had beaten him in the English amateur final in 1978 and every subsequent time they had played.

'I'd never beaten Terry, but what made it a little bit easier was that I'd already got more money than I'd ever seen in my life,' Johnson says. 'That money bought my house. It was a great feeling, and I was cemented in the top 16. I had no fears now about what would happen. Against Terry, I decided to open the balls and go for my shots and not get involved in his game. I did that and was leading 9–7 going into the final session, and then he won five on the trot. I thought, "He's done me again." Then he missed a straight green off the spot, screwing back for the reds, and I got up from my chair and thought, "He's going to need a couple of chances to win, and he's only going to get them if I miss." I played the snooker I was capable of but very rarely showed in tournaments.'

This was a four-frame blitz that marked Johnson out as a serious title contender. Breaks of 102 and 110 were the highlights of a devastating 52-minute spell that got him over the line 13–12. Griffiths could see what the future held for his still somewhat naive conqueror. 'After I beat him, he took me into the toilets and told me about all the good things that would happen now, told me to be careful about the press, to go on holiday after the tournament,' Johnson says. 'He said some lovely things. For him to do that after he'd just been beaten spoke volumes for him.'

Griffiths was prescient. Enjoying huge support on home ground in Yorkshire, Johnson defeated Knowles 16–8 to face Steve Davis in the final. It was a contrast in personalities. Davis remained laser-focused while Johnson was easy to warm to, with his broad smile and distinct pink shoes. He looked like someone enjoying himself on a day out.

For Davis, this was a chance for redemption after the black-ball defeat of the previous year, but what unfolded was in some ways even more surprising: he was outplayed. Roared on by a delighted partisan crowd, Johnson beat him 18–12, defying pre-tournament odds of 150–1. 'I didn't feel pressure,' he says. 'I had the ranking points, I had the money, I was just playing snooker. Steve was expected to win, I wasn't. I didn't expect to win myself. Even when I was a few frames ahead going into the final session, I didn't expect to win. Even at 17–12 I didn't expect to win. I expected him to come back at me. But it was like because I was prepared for that to happen, it didn't.'

The media hellscape predicted by Griffiths was duly made flesh and, for a quiet family man like Johnson, was hard to deal with, but he also enjoyed himself in the spotlight, even if his game suffered with all the new demands on his time. 'The next morning, we were woken up by flashing cameras,' he says. 'We invited them all in and had a cup of tea with them. Then they started bidding for my story. I ended up getting £50,000 from the *Daily Star*. I couldn't believe it. It was weird and it was hard. I was on the front page of every newspaper. I had to turn Terry Wogan down because I was so fed up of being on TV. I was on everything.'

Doors were suddenly opened, which seemed extraordinary to someone who had been running for the bus a decade earlier. 'I couldn't believe that people knew me and wanted to know me,' Johnson says. 'I was in a long line of people at a charity event being introduced to Princess Diana. She said to me, "I remember your shoes." We got talking, and she invited me and my wife to a tennis match. She said I could pick who I wanted to go with. I was a Cliff Richard fan, so she invited him. I wanted to sit next to Cliff, but I was next to Diana.'

Johnson, like Taylor, always came across well in his media appearances, an everyman embodying the interlocking priorities of working-class life: family, work and leisure. He had seven children, had been a gas fitter and sang in a band, Made in Japan. His local profile was such that he released a charity single in aid of victims of the 1985 Bradford City FC fire. Most bizarrely, he was booked to do an exhibition on the *QE2*. 'I said to the table-fitter, "The table doesn't look level." He said, "It's level, I've put things under the legs to make sure." When I smacked the reds open, all 15 went in one corner. That was the end of the evening.'

Despite a poor season as champion, Johnson made it back to the final again a year later, running Davis close before losing 18–14. He suffered health problems in the years that followed, including several heart attacks, and his form steadily declined, but he was still in demand for exhibitions and coaching and became a commentator for Eurosport.

His exit from the stage was a graceful one, and he looks back with only pride and gratitude for the life snooker gave him. 'It's nice to be remembered,' Johnson says. 'There's a picture taken at the 40th anniversary of the World Championship at the Crucible. Cliff Thorburn is recreating the yellow from his 147, and I'm sat in the front row with the other former champions. I feel a lot of humility to think that I'm part of that. It's so special to have been involved with it.'

THE SCOUSER

Five years after Johnson's triumph, another likeable player reached snooker's zenith. John Parrott was born and raised on Merseyside, the home of two great British exports, The Beatles and Liverpool Football Club, although Parrott is an Evertonian. His introduction to another British obsession came out of the blue, at the age of eleven.

'I was playing crown green bowls in Wavertree Park in Liverpool, and it started raining,' he says. 'My father said, "Come on, we'll go over to the club and see if you like snooker." As soon as I went in, I was hooked. There was smoke hanging over the table. I was fascinated. My dad got his cue out of his case, showed me how to stand and so on, and I remember thinking, "This is for me."'

Health and safety in 1970s Britain was not a major concern. This, after all, was a decade in which John Noakes, presenter of children's TV show *Blue Peter*, climbed to the top of Nelson's Column without a harness. 'It was a funny little club,' Parrott says. 'They had the lead nicked off the roof, so there was a bucket at the black-spot end to catch the rain. We were the only team to be rained off on a Wednesday night because someone forgot to empty the bucket. We had two fires that pumped out carbon monoxide and sent pensioners to the local hospital as a result. There was no fresh air. The windows were never open and they were painted black because the owner wouldn't pay for curtains. There were so many things wrong with it, but I absolutely loved the place.'

The various deathtraps did not impede Parrott's progression on the table, which included an appearance on the junior version of the BBC programme that had given snooker precious oxygen. 'I became all right at it really quickly,' he says. 'I'd only been playing six weeks when I made a 50 break. My father's highest break in all the years he played was 52, so he said, "Right, we need to get you a proper cue." I was entered into the North-West Junior Championship two years later and won that at fourteen. Then, two years after that, I was in national finals and then *Junior Pot Black*.'

Snooker, as for many other future champions, became a haven away from the pressures of home. Parrott's parents split up when he was young, and he lived with an auntie until he was twelve, when he moved back in with his father. Weekends were spent honing his skills on the baize.

Parrott's promise led to him turning professional in 1983. For him, it was like walking onto the set of a soap opera. 'It was the boom,' he says. 'Your TV at home had four buttons on it, and three of them had snooker on. We were all starting to get recognised, and it was good to be on the roller coaster.' The ride was not always comfortable, however. The realities of life on tour and the gap in standard between the amateur and professional ranks soon became apparent. 'It was quite intimidating,' he says. 'You learn very early that your game and your level isn't going to cut the mustard. When I first turned pro, I was playing people who were just tying me up in knots. It made me realise that I'd have to get a lot better, otherwise I'd get left behind.'

In 1989, Parrott made the long-awaited breakthrough, winning the European Open in Deauville, his first ranking title. He went to the Crucible a few weeks later feeling confident, but his entire outlook changed on the opening day of the championship, when a crush at the Hillsborough stadium, a few miles from the theatre, led to the deaths of 97 Liverpool fans attending the FA Cup semi-final against Nottingham Forest. Police at first blamed the spectators, a narrative gleefully taken up by large sections of the British media, before the true story of incompetence and poor safety standards emerged, eventually leading to a verdict of unlawful killing in 2016.

Parrott was at Goodison Park that afternoon, watching Everton play Norwich City in the other semi-final, but he felt the pain of his city deeply. For his first-round match against Steve James the following day, he wore a black armband. He won 10–9, and eventually made it to the final, where Steve Davis, now a five-time world champion, was waiting. What followed was the heaviest defeat ever inflicted at the Crucible, an 18–3 annihilation that finished with a session to spare, leaving Parrott forced to go back out and entertain the fans who had bought tickets for the now-redundant evening.

'I had nothing left to give and just had to take it on the chin. I was absolutely flat out,' he says. 'Steve was relentless, one of the worst you could play against if you didn't have your stuff. It was a bit like a boxing match where one of us wasn't allowed to hit. It wasn't very pleasant.'

It was an embarrassing reverse, but Parrott had arrived at the top of the game. Two years later, he came to Sheffield with renewed vigour. 'I had a new cue, and I knew it was the best one I'd ever had,' he says. 'The week before Sheffield, I went to the club, played eight frames and made seven centuries and a 90. I was hitting the ball as well as ever. All the ducks were in a line. John Spencer was in my camp at the time. Steve was playing Dennis Taylor [in the quarter-finals], who I was beating quite a lot. John said, "I want Steve. I want you to show that it was a fluke two years ago." I beat him 16–10, and it was one of the best matches I ever played.'

The ghosts of 1989 were exorcised by beating Davis in the semis, but Parrott had to face people's favourite Jimmy White in the final. If the crowd were to be a factor, they were silenced early. Parrott produced what remains one of the finest-ever Crucible sessions, storming 7–0 in front in only 72 minutes, with a string of breaks. He kept the lead to win 18–11.

'It was a blur,' he says. 'Players who have won it more than once must've really enjoyed the second or third one, because they could take it in. We went on holiday to Antigua, and I spent three weeks watching the fan go round on the ceiling, thinking, "Jesus, I've won the World Championship." To see my dad come out at the end was great – he was in bits. Liverpool asked me to parade the trophy at Anfield. I got an unbelievable reception. They were special times.'

Parrott remained a top player for another decade, adding the UK Championship title to his CV later in 1991. His easy-going manner and ready supply of wit led to him becoming a captain on the long-running BBC quiz show *A Question of Sport*. He joined the BBC's snooker team in 2001 and also co-presented the corporation's racing coverage.

These days, he enjoys a life of golf, watching football and spending time with family. The stress of winning or losing at snooker is long in the past, but his fondness for the game remains. 'When you think about the places we've been able to travel to, we saw the world. It was very special.'

WINNER, WINNER

For a young boy in Essex in the early 1980s, there wasn't far to look for inspiration. Steve Davis, based in Romford, was becoming the best-known sportsperson in the country. The Davis effect on the next generation cannot be overstated. Stuart Bingham remembers watching the 1985 final as an eight-year-old in Basildon, bereft as Dennis Taylor sank the last black. 'Everyone in my house was cheering, and I was crying because Davis was a winner and the local hero. He was my hero too, the Godfather of the area,' he says.

Even at eight, Bingham was a snooker obsessive. He remembers his parents buying a small table two years earlier and explaining it away by telling him it was a present for someone else. 'Christmas Day I opened the garage, and there it was,' he says, the memory still vivid.

Sport had yet to become just another cog in the wheel of capitalism. This was an era when it wasn't all about generating as much income as possible. Access to sport in the community, the attitude that recreational pastimes were good for local cohesion, exposed Bingham to various activities. 'I played lots of ball sports when I was young,' he says. 'I had tennis lessons, squash . . . My mum and dad backed me whatever I wanted to do. Rugby, basketball, golf. I always had that sporting interest in me.'

A downturn in the British economy under John Major's premiership had an unlikely positive effect on Bingham's progression. 'In 1990, I started properly,' he says. 'My mum and dad went to buy a house during the recession, where interest rates went up. The house fell through, and we moved somewhere different, closer to the senior school where my brother was. In his last year, he got free membership at the club, a five-minute walk from where we were living in Basildon. If we'd gone to the original house, I might never have played snooker.'

But play he did, in the thriving junior scene of the time, when amateurs often looked like world-beaters. 'I was fifteen when I made my first century,' he says. 'The day I left school, I did my last exam, went home, took my uniform off, put on some jeans and a top, went down the club and made my second 100 break.'

Bingham was by now fully in the grip of an addiction. The groundbreaking BBC children's drama series of the time, *Grange Hill*, implored its young viewers to 'Just Say No', after a major character, Zammo, became hooked on heroin. Bingham just said yes to snooker, getting his fix as regularly as he could.

There was no thought of not making it. 'There's a video of me as a fourteen-year-old at Christmas, opening the Matchroom book. The inside cover was the Crucible Theatre, with the likes of Doug Mountjoy, Willie Thorne and those guys. I'm looking at it, and I say in my high-pitched voice, "I'll play there one day." I didn't have a fallback. My mum's wages went on my snooker lessons. My parents backed me fully. She was a cleaner, then she went to manage a discount store. My dad was a welder. When I left school, I got the job of cleaning the tables in the club. I used to get a fiver a day to clean 18 tables. It was £2.32 an hour. They had a match table with a chalkboard next to it, one frame, winner stays on. So if I lost two games, that was me done for the day, but sometimes I'd win ten to 20 matches on the trot, so I'd be there all day.'

Bingham's first significant breakthrough came on the cusp of his 20th birthday, when he won the English Amateur Championship, a title that makes the wider game sit up and take notice. Later that year, he travelled to New Zealand and won the world amateur title, which earned him professional status.

Progress was slow. He had his moments, including an opening-day defeat of Stephen Hendry at the 2000 World Championship, but in his first decade on tour reached no higher than 37th in the world rankings. Within the sport, he was known to be a regular winner, thanks to his hoovering up of pro-am titles around the country. His love of competition ensured no venue was beneath him, but he was yet to do it on a bigger stage. His professional fortunes began to turn when Barry Hearn took the reins at World Snooker in 2010, introducing many more tournaments, big and small. Size mattered little to Bingham. He just wanted to play.

The following year, 2011, he dug for victory in the former gold-mining town of Bendigo and won the Australian Open, his first ranking title. He became a top-16 player in his late 30s and piled up various trophies before reaching the quarter-finals of the 2015 World Championship, where he would face a contemporary from Essex, Ronnie O'Sullivan, for the right to get through to the Crucible's one-table stage.

'I knew my game was there, but it's different against Ronnie. He has 95 per cent of the crowd on his side and just seems to always punish you,' he says. 'I went 9–8 down, and then didn't miss a ball for the next five frames.' He beat O'Sullivan 13–9, and then met the prodigiously talented Judd Trump in the semi-finals. 'I heard his manager at the time said, "This'll be an easy win for Judd." That's the worst thing you can say.' Bingham won a classic contest 17–16.

Those underrating him had one last chance to be proven right when he squared up to Shaun Murphy, the 2005 champion, in the final. For Bingham, who had stared in wonder at that golden Crucible vista in his snooker book as a boy, just playing the title decider was a lifelong dream realised, and the adrenalin kept him up at night. 'I averaged about five hours' sleep a night. I didn't switch off,' he says.

The final ebbed and flowed. Bingham trailed 9–8 going into the crucial last day. 'That's the best night's sleep I had the whole tournament, seven and a half hours. Before the last session, I had a shower, my wife was brushing her teeth, and I said, "I'm done." She said, "What do you mean?" And I said, "I don't want to go out there." That's when it hit me.' It hits him again as he remembers this moment, his eyes watering. 'Little things, like me as a kid, looking back. Emotionally, it means everything.'

Bingham did go out for the last session and won the match 18–15. He was world champion. 'Winner, winner, chicken dinner!' he exclaimed as he was handed the microphone. A decade on, he is still processing what he achieved. 'It took me two weeks to get over it, to start sleeping properly,' he says. 'I still don't think it's sunk in. I remember asking Graeme [Dott, the 2006 champion] when we were on a minibus somewhere in China. He said it'll be for when you retire and you realise what you've done.'

Bingham was another relatable personality who made good through his dedicated attitude and refusal to give up through the bad times. Early in his career, he acquired the nickname 'Ballrun', based on the premise that he enjoyed more than his fair share of luck, yet his story has nothing to do with fortune. He simply loves being at a snooker table.

THE MASTER OF BRINKMANSHIP

Of all the ordinary men who have reached the top of snooker from an unpromising start in life, Mark Selby has risen the highest. In a country of haves and have-nots, he was marked out from a young age to be part of the underclass: broken home, economic deprivation, educational underachiever. The sort of boy who would find trouble. The sort of boy who would not amount to anything.

Between 2014 and 2021, Selby won the World Championship four times. His story sums up the value of sport and its capacity to change lives, and how strength of character can alter an entire life's path.

Selby grew up on a council estate in New Parks, Leicester. His mother departed the family home when he was eight, leaving his father, David, to raise him and his elder brother on his own. Household chores did not come naturally to his dad. Meals were basic. So was leisure time. It was largely about escaping the house and its sadness.

'My dad always went to the pub or social club, where they were all playing pool,' Selby says. 'It wasn't until I went to watch Eddie Manning, an ex-professional, in an exhibition at the social club that I even saw snooker. I played one frame against him, and he said he could see I had a bit of potential and should go to Willie Thorne's club. From then I started playing a lot more.'

This was around the time of his mother's departure from the family scene. A familiar theme of snooker table as refuge emerged. Selby found a new home at Willie Thorne's, a club owned by one of snooker's stars of the 1980s and run by his brother, Malcolm, an evangelist for the junior game, who struck a deal: Selby could practise for free if he helped out with a few necessary chores around the club – brushing tables, cleaning up. For Selby, it became something to focus on rather than begin the long drift into a feckless life of boredom, unemployment, hardship.

'He was like a second father to me. If it wasn't for him, I wouldn't be sat here today,' he says. 'I wasn't brought up with money. My dad didn't have much. We lived on a council estate. Malcolm gave me free practice from the age of ten or eleven, so I was going there every day rather than just one or two days a week. That helped me improve a lot. He would take me around the country to junior tournaments. He'd say, "You're probably going to get bashed up a lot of the time, but you'll learn from it and improve." I was losing but I wasn't getting disheartened – I was enjoying the challenge. I was determined to improve more and more. It kept me off the streets. If I wasn't involved in snooker, I don't know where I would've been. I might have got into trouble or gone down the wrong road. A lot of my friends were just hanging around, probably up to no good. The snooker club was a good place to be.'

What he lacked in raw talent, he more than made up for in sheer determination. From a young age, Selby developed a reputation for a never-say-die attitude, with a tactical game far more mature than his years. Shaun Murphy was a contemporary who went on to become a rival in the professional ranks. As a boy, he saw close up Selby's grit, at an age when trying to pot everything was the norm. 'Of that generation, he wouldn't have been anywhere near the top of the list of people who would go on and have a major career in snooker,' Murphy says. 'He had that same tenacity then but wasn't a great scorer. When he married the two together, he became lethal.'

Selby's resolute approach hardened further when tragedy intervened. At sixteen, he had turned professional. A few months later, his father died. 'He was my stability in life, taking me to comps, cheering me on, and then from nowhere, out of the blue, we lost him,' he says. 'For the first six months afterwards I barely played at all. Snooker was the last thing on my mind. I just wanted to have him back. A guy called Alan Perkins took me in and tried to turn around all my negative thoughts. He would say my dad would want me to try for him. As time went on I decided I was going to do it for him, and that's what's driven me to the success I've had. My father always said to me that in snooker it's never over until it's over. You can be sat in your chair thinking you've lost, but it's a strange game, things can happen. Don't ever give in until the last ball is potted.'

Selby had promised his dad he would never give up, no matter how dire the situation in a match, a vow he stuck to. But home life was challenging and grief at times overwhelmed him. He had dark thoughts of suicide. Snooker pulled him through. 'I didn't know where to turn,' he says. 'There was me and my brother, who's eight years older than me, but it felt at times like I was looking after him. If it wasn't for Alan, I probably wouldn't be here.

'I gave myself a target of 25 or 26, thinking if I could be making a decent living from snooker, then I'd carry on playing. If I was scrimping and scraping, then I'd rather get a full-time job. I left school a year before GCSEs with no qualifications and nothing to fall back on. I'd probably be signing on.'

At eighteen, Selby qualified for the China Open in Shanghai, where his lack of worldliness became clear when he was seen standing in the hotel lobby, in full playing attire, at 1.30 in the morning, cue in hand. A referee enjoying a late-night drink asked him what he was doing. Waiting for a taxi to the venue – he was playing at 2.30, came the reply. In the afternoon, though, the official pointed out. It was pitch black outside, but Selby had not twigged. This was a world that, growing up, he had not been destined to see. The following day, he beat Stephen Hendry. In the next round, he defeated Ronnie O'Sullivan before losing in the semi-finals.

The next year, 2003, he reached a ranking final at the Scottish Open, but the emotional backdrop remained complex. Looking for family, he had married an older woman, becoming a stepfather to her young children, even though he was still really a kid himself. The marriage did not last. On the English pool circuit, he met Vikki Layton. A closeness formed, and they married in 2011.

By now, Selby's target of making it by his mid-20s had come to fruition. He reached the World Championship final as a qualifier at the age of 23 in 2007, losing 18–13 to John Higgins. The following year, he won his first ranking title, with the brinkmanship that would come to define his career, coming from 8–5 down to beat crowd favourite O'Sullivan in the Welsh Open. A few weeks earlier, he had won the Masters, a title he would capture again in 2010 and 2013. He was also UK champion in 2012. What was missing was snooker's greatest prize.

By 2014, he was 30. He reached the semi-finals of the World Championship, where he edged Neil Robertson 17–15 late on the Saturday night. Media commitments awaited, and he finally got to bed in the early hours, shattered, ahead of a final against O'Sullivan, unbeaten at the Crucible in three years. O'Sullivan led 10–5 with two frames to play on the opening day. Sheer willpower helped Selby win them. He slept soundly and came out the next day feeling fresh and ready to take the fight to his opponent, blunting his naturally attacking game and forcing him onto the back foot. The strategy worked perfectly. O'Sullivan was all at sea as Selby took control.

'I saw Ronnie a couple of times between sessions, and he looked at his wits' end,' says commentator Phil Yates. 'For the first time, I think, in his life he'd come up against someone he couldn't work out how to get the better of. Selby can take a more rhythmic player out of that rhythm, but it's not just that, it's the cleverness of his shots and his temperament. If you build a reputation as someone who constantly fights back, it becomes a self-fulfilling prophecy. The guy in the other chair is expecting the comeback, and that puts them under pressure.'

Selby pressed on to a 17–14 lead. The next frame came down to the last red, Selby needing every ball left on the table to become champion. The Crucible is where the strongest snooker legs turn to jelly, but as he set about the winning clearance, a calmness overcame him. 'I felt really relaxed,' he says. 'I was zoned in. I told myself if I got a chance, I was going to go for it. On the last black I was just thinking, "This is to win the match, not to win the World Championship." My dad had said, "Give it everything, and hopefully you'll become world champion one day." As I'm on the black, I'm thinking, "This one is for him." There was no way in the world I was going to miss it.'

The next challenge was to do it again. Two years later, he did, beating Ding Junhui 18–14. He retained the title in 2017, coming from 10–4 down to defeat Higgins 18–15. A fourth world crown followed in 2021, when he got the better of his boyhood friend Murphy, 18–15. 'When I was that young kid practising at Willie Thorne's, I'd have taken one, never mind four,' he says with a sense of disbelief.

By now, Selby and Vikki had a daughter, Sofia, but unresolved grief was impacting his daily thoughts. In a sport as mentally demanding as snooker, the additional pressure of fighting his feelings led to an inevitable reckoning. It came with a tweet from a service station on the drive back from the 2022 Masters, where he had been beaten in round one: 'Just want to apologise to all my friends and family for letting them down. Mentally not in a good place at moment, had a relapse and trying to bottle it up and put a brave face on is not the way. I promise I will get help and become a better person.'

The dam had broken. Selby had long laboured under the nickname 'The Jester from Leicester' because, despite his hard-man image, he was known as someone who liked a laugh and a joke at tournaments, but this humour had to a degree been a cover for deep-seated pain.

'I knew there was trauma,' he says. 'I was always having dark days a couple of times a week, but I just thought I was having a down day. Then, years later, I saw [heavyweight boxer] Tyson Fury on TV, and I could relate to everything he was saying. I was feeling like that years ago. Having spoken to the doctor, he said I'd been going through it since my dad passed away. I built a wall around myself, tried to shut myself off from everyone and tried to get through it on my own. He explained it was like a Coke bottle: if you shake it, sooner or later it's going to explode.'

Selby sought professional help. The snooker world, where he had found a second family, was overwhelmingly sympathetic, although this did not extend to the far reaches of the internet. Unlike champions of years gone by, Selby and his contemporaries had the often toxic world of social media to tolerate. He had long been the target of trolls after having the temerity to stand up to, indeed to beat, the popular O'Sullivan.

'No one knows what's happening in people's lives. You're expected to go out and put on a show,' he says. 'People are quick to judge in sport, the keyboard warriors on social media. I don't read much stuff about myself. Some people are quite cruel. Everyone gets it. It's the world we live in. I just try and take the positives and not the negatives.'

Self-care is an ongoing process, and Selby has had ups and downs since his initial admission that he was struggling. 'I used to lock myself in the house and not go out,' he says. 'Now, when I have relapses, I still try to do something, get myself out speaking to people. I'm managing it better than I was.'

His game is not to everyone's taste. He has a difficult relationship with O'Sullivan, who labelled him 'The Torturer'. Selby has turned it into a positive. 'I thought he was saying it because I get under his skin,' he says. 'If he's not talking about me, then I'm not a person he fears. Every time he goes into a match against me, he knows he has to work for every chance. I'm not just going to lie down and roll over.'

His achievements and the manner of them win praise from Hendry. 'Ronnie at his best is unplayable, and Selby is the same,' Hendry says. 'When he plays that game where he strangles the life out of you, I couldn't have played against that. I would have to go for everything and hope they went in. I couldn't mix it with him. It's a game I completely admire.'

'I feel I've done more than enough to make my dad proud of me,' says Selby, the kid given no hope of a future who became a man with more achievements than most in his chosen sport. He represents the very ordinariness that has so appealed to the British public and those further afield and helped snooker retain its popularity.

However, there is something eagle-eyed readers may have noticed by this point. Every player mentioned has been male. Where are all the women?

14

GIRLS JUST WANT TO HAVE FUN

Reanne Evans has all the attributes needed to be a star. Naturally confident, grounded and with a bubbly personality, she also has a record of success to rival any other player in modern snooker.

Yet footage of Evans's many triumphs does not form part of the iconography of the sport. It doesn't exist. The women's game was treated for decades almost as an irrelevance. Snooker was invented by the chaps, at a time when class and the patriarchy were not questioned, and old attitudes prevailed for much of the 20th century and well into the 21st. Despite moves to provide a better showcase for female players, they do not enjoy anything close to the profile of their male counterparts.

Born in 1985, at the height of the UK snooker boom, Evans was introduced to the game by her family. 'My two brothers both played,' she says. 'Richard made centuries, but Ryan was more competitive. I followed him round, picked up a cue and went from there.'

As far as Evans was concerned, snooker was a fun game. At a young age she had no reason to believe playing it was not considered the done thing for girls. In fact, many working men's clubs had historically operated a men-only policy. Britain had had a female prime minister for eleven and a half years, but some things had not changed, as Evans discovered one night in Ladywood, Birmingham.

'My brother was playing in the Midlands championship,' she says. 'I went with his girlfriend, but when we got to the door, we were told we couldn't go in the snooker room. I'd never known anything like that before. I was always welcome, so was my mum. My brother is pretty hot-headed, and he was like, "In that case, have the match, because that's my girlfriend and that's my sister, and they follow me everywhere." We waited ten minutes, and then this big Scottish guy who was on the committee said we could come in if we sat in the corner and didn't have a drink. This was all new to me. You didn't need to give my brother any ammunition – he won the match. I thought it was disgraceful. There was a woman serving behind the bar. I couldn't believe it was happening.'

Even as Evans's stock rose through her performances in the West Midlands league, progress was slow. 'A few years later, we went back to the same place for a league match,' she says. 'The team had to put in a letter to see if we could go in there. I was only playing one frame. I was allowed to play it, but then had to leave.'

This experience was not uncommon. To some men, sport was seen as a refuge away from their wives and family life, a place to relax after the stresses of the working day, but snooker has long been popular with women as well, both in terms of spectating and playing. The Women's Billiards Association was formed in 1931, and in 1934 staged the first Women's Professional Snooker Championship. Ruth Harrison, a coal miner's daughter from Durham, defeated Gloucester's Joyce Gardiner 7–6 in the final, winning the last four frames to complete a comeback. The event continued, albeit with a mere handful of entries, although the men's professional championship, dominated by Joe Davis, did not attract many more players, such was the predominance of billiards over snooker at the time. The women's championship moved to Burroughes Hall in Soho Square, the home of cue sports during the 1930s and 1940s, but when war intervened was not staged from 1940 until 1948, when Harrison won the last of her eight titles.

In 1949, Agnes Morris beat Thelma Carpenter 16–15 in the final, before Carpenter beat her 16–7 a year later, but with interest in professional snooker all but dead following Davis's retirement a few years earlier, the women's championship went into the same hibernation as the World Championship.

There was still an amateur circuit, and recreational interest in women's snooker was increasing. All-female teams were established, competing in the Shuttleworth Cup. Valerie Hobson, the well-known British actress, was president of the Women's Billiards Association a few years before she married John Profumo, who was forced to resign as secretary of state for war over a scandal involving his affair with a teenage model, Christine Keeler, who was also in a relationship with a Soviet attaché.

The Profumo Affair was one of the landmark moments of the 1960s, a tale of sex and intrigue, and arguably the point at which the culture of deference towards those in power began to shift. Only three women had ever served in Cabinet before Harold Wilson's Labour Party won the 1964 election, a few months after the scandal blew up. Of Wilson's ministers, Barbara Castle proved among the most popular and effective, and in 1970 she introduced the Equal Pay Act, which prohibited preferential treatment and remuneration for men over women.

Such progressive attitudes were not always reflected in wider culture. The popular *Carry On* films, which ran from 1958 to 1978, included a number of talented comedy actresses but typically presented women as battleaxes (Hattie Jacques), nagging wives (Joan Sims) or sex objects (Barbara Windsor). In fairness, the men were similarly caricatured as lecherous (Sid James), wildly camp (Kenneth Williams) or youthfully naive (Jim Dale). The point being, although legislation was introduced to alter inequities, attitudes to gender roles were hard-wired.

Women's football had become a popular attraction in Britain after the First World War, but the Football Association banned its member clubs from staging all-female matches from 1921 until 1970, stating: 'Complaints having been made as to football being played by women, Council felt impelled to express the strong opinion that the game of football is quite unsuitable for females and should not be encouraged.'[1] It was still many years before women's sport became accepted as mainstream entertainment; as recently as 2011, there was no female representation on the BBC's annual Sports Personality of the Year shortlist.

Women's snooker continued at Soho Square until Burroughes Hall was taken over by Riley's in 1967 and then demolished to make way for offices. As *Pot Black* showcased the best male players, the women's game all but disappeared. However, a chink of light emerged in 1976 when the tobacco brand Embassy became sponsors of the World Championship, also contributing money to a women's event at Middlesbrough Town Hall (the thinking may have been that women smoked just as men did). Vera Selby won the £500 first prize and went on to become a referee and part of the BBC's commentary team for the 1982 World Championship.

Embassy did not renew their sponsorship of the women's event, and it was four more years before it was restaged. Mandy Fisher, a player herself, and frustrated by the lack of opportunities, was instrumental in founding the World Ladies Billiards and Snooker Association (WLBSA) in 1981, building up a circuit and inspiring girls to take the sport seriously. This led to the emergence of snooker's first female star, Allison Fisher (no relation to Mandy), who at the age of seventeen won the first of seven world titles.

Fisher was talented and had personality, and she joined Barry Hearn's Matchroom stable, partnering Steve Davis in mixed-doubles events. Together they won the 1991 World Masters, and she made the first televised century break by a woman at another mixed-doubles tournament in Germany in 1993. By now, Hearn, sensing there could be money in women's snooker, was promoting the WLBSA World Championship, securing television coverage from Sky. The first prize rose from £3,500 in 1989 to £10,000 a year later.

Fisher became a marketable star of the sport, but she was also a more than capable player. Invited into Hearn's Matchroom League event, she defeated three leading male players: Neal Foulds, Mike Hallett and Tony Drago. When, in 1991, the professional game went open to anyone who could afford to pay the entry fees, she took the plunge, but reached a ranking of only 191st.

The 1994 Women's World Championship, played in Delhi, saw the first prize fall back to £7,500. Feeling the opportunity to move the women's game forward had been lost, Fisher quit snooker after winning the title for a seventh time and headed to the US to play nine-ball pool. She became a multi-champion in this very different cue-sports discipline, earning the nickname 'The Duchess of Doom'. In 2009, she was inducted into the Billiards Congress of America Hall of Fame.

Karen Corr, who won three world titles in the 1990s, followed Fisher to the US, leaving Kelly Fisher (no relation to Mandy or Allison) as the leading player as the 21st century approached. Fisher, from Yorkshire, won the world title five times before she also departed for the States, realising there was a more lucrative living to be made on the pool circuit.

Enter Evans, who as a teenager was impressing locally in league matches. At sixteen, she entered the 2002 Women's World Championship, the semi-finals and final of which would be played at the Crucible on spare mornings when there was no action in the professional event. 'I played a league match at Stoke against

Neil Selman, and he gave me the forms to enter the [Women's] World Championship,' she says. 'I had no clue what to expect. I didn't think I was good enough, I didn't know what the standard would be like or whether I would enjoy it. I managed to qualify for the Crucible, beating Lynette Horsburgh on the final black. My mum was having palpitations, bless her. I'd never dreamed of being a snooker player. I didn't understand the meaning of it, but when I got to the Crucible, I felt it. It drew me in, and I thought, "I want this."'

She wanted it so badly that she won it 12 times between 2005 and 2019, including ten in succession. Yet prize money was a few thousand here and a few thousand there, and the finals were not televised, with tournaments played in clubs and receiving little media coverage. The nadir arguably came one year at the Crucible, when the players about to face off in the Women's World Championship final turned up for their morning contest to find that the match balls were locked in a cupboard, with the person who had the key not yet at the venue. Soon, the event was cut adrift and returned to being held in clubs away from the limelight.

That there was a circuit at all was down mainly to the efforts of Mandy Fisher, who kept battling for the women's cause in the face of widespread indifference. 'I wouldn't be here if it wasn't for Mandy, the same as a lot of the players,' Evans says. 'We owe her a lot for what she's done. She dragged it off the floor and got it going. I've got so much respect for her.'

In 2015, a step forward came when the WPBSA, under the chairmanship of Jason Ferguson, took over the running of the women's game. Participation levels increased over the next decade, with 180 players from 25 countries on the World Women's Snooker ranking list. Tournaments have been held in the US, Thailand, Belgium and Australia, as well as in the British heartlands.

In 2024, the Women's World Championship was staged in a major arena in China, receiving live online coverage. 'I walked in and saw that stage and thought, "This is how it should be." They were much better conditions,' says Evans. The title was won by a home-grown player, Bai Yulu, whose emergence, along with Thailand's Mink Nutcharut, suggests that the next generation of female talent will come from Asia.

At least in the 21st century genuine efforts have been made to eradicate the idea that snooker is solely for men. Women had played senior roles behind the scenes for years, in particular Ann Yates, who was WPBSA tournament director for much of the 1980s and 1990s. As the sport entered the new millennium, moves were made to place more women in prominent positions. Michaela Tabb, a pool referee from Dunfermline, was fast-tracked as a snooker official and soon proved her worth, refereeing a number of high-profile matches, including the World Championship finals of 2009 and 2012.

In the same period, another Scottish woman brought her professionalism and good humour to one of snooker's most daunting roles, fronting the many hours of live BBC coverage. Born in St Andrews in 1965, Hazel Irvine grew up obsessed with sport. She had a sticker book for the 1972 Munich Olympics and nursed ambitions to be an Olympian herself, but from a young age also understood the power of television to paint a narrative during major sporting events.

'The faces and voices of those days: Ron Pickering, David Coleman, Frank Bough, Dickie Davies . . . They were absolute titans, and their authority wasn't challenged. They were totemic figures, part of our cultural life,' Irvine says. 'There were rhythms to the sporting year, you knew what was on when, and I was a child of that.'

The teenage Irvine pursued her interest in sports journalism by writing reports on hockey matches for the local newspaper, but the broadcasters she admired were all male. 'There were no female journalists on the telly,' she says. 'You couldn't say, "I wanted to be like her," because there wasn't anyone to be like. Then Sally McNair appeared on *Scotsport* [on STV]. She copped a lot of the flak and nonsense about women on the TV. It was 1978. I was thirteen, and I'd barely seen a woman on the telly.'

After university, Irvine became a production assistant at Radio Clyde before moving to STV in 1987. Aged 22, she was given a chance in front of camera after McNair went on maternity leave. 'I used to do the "other sport" round-up, and one of the earliest desks I did was about Stephen Hendry. Then I did a feature with him, so my start in broadcasting coincided with his formative years in the sport,' she says.

Irvine impressed her bosses to the extent that she co-presented ITV's network coverage of the Seoul 1988 Olympics. She then moved to the BBC, where she became a presenter of *Grandstand*, *Ski Sunday* and sundry Olympic and Commonwealth games. Snooker had long been fronted by David Vine, but he retired in 2000, after which the BBC decided to freshen up its coverage. Jane Hoffen had presented snooker for Sky, but on the national broadcaster it had long been a male preserve.

'It was 2001 when I got the call from Barbara Slater [then the BBC's head of sport],' Irvine says. 'She said, "I think this will be a good fit." She asked me what I knew about snooker, and I said, "I know as much as most people." I watched it every year, but my nuanced appreciation of the game was not up there. My first gig was football, so I walked into a very male environment. I had to earn my stripes, put more work in, think about what questions to ask. I could never get away with asking, "Good game today, yeah?"

I knew I had to be disciplined and do the research. I had a lot of experience. I'd done a lot of Olympic Games and World Cups. I'd had to do the groundwork for a lot of sports, so I knew what would be needed in terms of preparation.'

Irvine says she found the snooker world 'very welcoming', adding, 'I never felt judged. It didn't matter that you hadn't played.' She quickly formed a popular partnership with Steve Davis and John Parrott, former world champions who were still playing but were moving into the media.

'There is no ego with Hazel,' Parrott says. 'We'd help her with the terminology early on, and within a couple of tournaments she'd got the lot. She's always prepared, never misses a trick. She always has a good question to ask. She's made us better.'

Irvine also became genuinely fascinated by snooker. Her first World Championship in the presenter's chair in 2002 saw Peter Ebdon win deciding frames in the semi-finals and final to dramatically become champion. In particular, his last-gasp semi-final victory over Matthew Stevens convinced Irvine of the power of snooker to captivate. 'It was so exciting,' she says. 'I'd never lived a match like that before, like I could reach down and touch what was happening. That was a game-changer for me. Peter potted a key pink towards the end. If he missed it, he was out. I remember thinking, "That's so courageous." It was a proper revelation about how dramatic a sport can be.

'With football, you have a natural rhythm, two halves, and it all lasts 90 minutes. With snooker, they are like chapters, like peeling an onion, revealing the different rhythms of the match. If you compare it to the Olympics, it's like night and day. [In the latter] you are juggling 20 sports in a day, spinning plates. It's an information-fest as you make sense of what's going on, and that's a fantastic challenge – intellectually, a massive challenge to stay on top of it all. I really get a buzz from those events. The luxury of a match that might have four sessions is very rare. Consequently, you have to be better prepared. To be able to continue to inform people when it doesn't look like there's anything else to say is a challenge. There are two players – what do we really know about them? You have to know them as people as much as players.'

Tabb's high profile as a referee opened the door for many other women to become officials, to the extent that it is no longer commented on. Similarly, Irvine's long tenure as the face of the BBC's coverage has led to the likes of Seema Jaswal (BBC), Jill Douglas (ITV) and Rachel Casey (Eurosport) becoming established, trusted fixtures in British living rooms during tournaments.

Yet compared to their male counterparts, there is still a paucity of female players. The historical imbalance in participation levels, rooted partly in prejudice, means far more boys have been introduced to snooker at a young age than girls. As recently as 2019, Rebecca Kenna, at the time third in the women's rankings, was prevented from playing two matches in the Crosshills and District League in Yorkshire because of the men-only policy still operating at some venues. 'To be told you can't play the sport you love because of your gender is ridiculous and it's quite upsetting,' Kenna told the BBC.[2]

In an attempt to raise the profile of the women's game and stress the openness of the World Snooker Tour, beginning in 2021 two places on the professional circuit were awarded to female players each year. A mixed-doubles event was established in 2022, although this lasted only two seasons.

Evans recognises the genuine attempts to increase representation, but women have struggled on the professional tour, and it is hard not to get downhearted. 'When we first got a tour card, I thought it would be brilliant and help develop the women's tour, but it hasn't happened in the way I thought it would,' Evans says. 'Long term, I think the tour cards will damage the women players. We need a professional women's tour, with women playing women regularly on TV or streaming. That's how you'll gain crowds and participation. None of the women on the main tour have shown their potential. I go into tournaments wanting to believe I can win them, to be competitive right to the end, but I go into these matches without any chance of winning the trophy. I'm not being negative, that's just how it is. The only way to make it more positive is having a professional women's tour alongside the main tour, at the same venues. That's the only way, for me, that it can grow to the stature where I think it should be.'

To Evans, the well-meaning ethos that everyone is equal is in fact counterproductive. 'It's all got lost in the idea that there's no difference between male and female, so let's put us all together, but in the long run I think it's hurt us,' she says. 'We want to play better players to improve, but for women's snooker to grow, it has to be separate. I don't mean this horribly, but I think men are more selfish. They are more single-minded. They can focus on one thing, and that's it. They can use snooker as a get-out, whereas a woman's brain is 24/7 doing dances and backflips, thinking about everything. If I was at a tournament, it would be, "Who's got [daughter] Lauren?" You wouldn't ask that of Ronnie. We still have that attitude around.'

For all her frustrations, Evans is rightly proud of her career. She has won more than 70 titles in the women's game, and in 2019 was awarded an MBE in recognition of her achievements. 'It was so surreal,' she says. 'I was like, "I'm from Gornal and I've got an MBE. What's going on?" It's one of the best achievements for a woman in snooker, and sport in general, to be appreciated for what you've done. There are a lot of tears and hard work and dedication which goes into it, and money as well. You think, "Maybe it was all worth it."'

To many, though, snooker remained about the men, or rather, one man in particular, whose career survived numerous torments as he became the greatest of them all.

15

ROCKET MAN

It was the morning of 20 April 2013, the opening day of the World Championship. The sun shone on Sheffield as Saturday shoppers swarmed the city centre. Backstage in the Crucible, Ronnie O'Sullivan received the customary knock on his dressing-room door, a sign that the match would be starting imminently. It was a procedure he had gone through countless times before, but this was different. The adrenalin was coursing more quickly through his body as expectation inside the theatre grew. He was a four-time winner of the world title but still had something to prove.

O'Sullivan had played only one match since the previous year's World Championship. For once, his oft-repeated threats to walk away from the game, or at least take an extended break, had come to fruition. Now, he was back inside the sport's most unforgiving goldfish bowl, more the centre of attention than ever, with everybody wondering if he would rise to the occasion or fall flat on his face.

In the 100-year story of professional snooker, O'Sullivan has enjoyed the longest spell at the very top. For the last 34 years he has been a professional, and for most of that time the best player in the sport. More than that, he has been an endless source of fascination, a unique character capable of sublime brilliance but also confounding resentment towards the sport he has come closer than anyone to mastering.

'If you have a personality like mine, you're never really satisfied, even if you win tournaments,' he says. 'I can be pretty hard on myself if I haven't played to a certain level. I always have pride of performance. If I win the tournament, it's a huge bonus, but I want to play well.'[1]

And played well he has, at least to the eyes of the mere mortals who have watched him. One by one, the records set by Stephen Hendry have fallen to O'Sullivan: most ranking titles, most 'triple crown' majors (World Championship, UK Championship and Masters), most centuries, most maximums. And yet a career of unparalleled achievement has left him a tortured soul, apparently incapable of experiencing the level of fulfilment his record should provide.

It's worth noting that O'Sullivan has not always been a beloved figure. In his early years, many thought him a nuisance, a tearaway, a loose cannon who would quickly flame out and fail to fulfil his potential. The first example of this thinking came at the 1996 World Championship. Still only 20, he came into the tournament without much success that season but defeated Canadian Alain Robidoux 10–3 to make a lightning-fast start. However, the match ended in a storm of controversy, which marked the start of a shift in media attitudes towards O'Sullivan, who had thus far been regarded as a boy-wonder figure.

Robidoux, struggling badly, had become upset that O'Sullivan was playing shots left-handed, something he had done before, but never on such an exalted stage. Robidoux's argument was that this was disrespectful, and with the concluding frame well out of his reach, he made his point by playing on needlessly for snookers, with just the pink and black balls remaining. O'Sullivan's response was to reject easy pots to win the match, meaning eight minutes of farce live on BBC television as the match refused to end.

Both players were at fault, but O'Sullivan received almost all of the criticism. The *Observer* ran an article that began with the leading question: 'Do we, or do we not, like Ronnie O'Sullivan?'[2]

The fuss that ensued after what could easily have been just a routine first-round win nudged O'Sullivan closer in the public mind to Alex Higgins than Jimmy White, who for all his off-table hellraising, was regarded as a gentleman in the arena. Days of headlines took their toll. Under siege, O'Sullivan snapped. Entering the press room with his friend Derek Hill, he was informed by Mike Ganley, the assistant press officer, that Hill's trainers were in breach of the dress code.

O'Sullivan reacted in violent fashion, physically assaulting Ganley by biting him on the lip. This was an ugly incident that could have resulted in criminal prosecution – and did indeed recall the worst excesses of Higgins. A disciplinary panel was hastily convened, with the widespread expectation that O'Sullivan would be thrown out of the tournament. In the event, he was fined £30,000 but allowed to play on.

John Higgins had been waiting to see whether his quarter-final with O'Sullivan would take place, with the tribunal result coming late the night before their match was due to begin. He did not seem affected by the rumpus when he built a 10–6 lead, but O'Sullivan overturned it to win 13–12. He was into the semi-finals and firmly in the eye of a storm. At the press conference, emotion poured from him:

> In the last few days I've been in a daze. The mental pressure has been incredible and I never want to go through it again. It would be wonderful to win the world title for my dad. I love him to bits and I know we will be together one day. I've never felt like this and would just like to thank everyone who has stood by my side. I'm no saint, but I don't pretend to be. My dad's done wrong, and so have I, but I'm trying to make up for it now. I've looked at the press-box and seen it full of

people who want to shout me down, but I'm sick of people trying to make me into the new Alex Higgins of snooker. I'm not like that.[3]

But this was not the end of it. Louise Port, a nineteen-year-old working for BBC Radio, complained about inappropriate sexual comments allegedly made towards her by O'Sullivan. It was more fuel for the media fire. In the space of a week, journalists had gone from describing O'Sullivan as a 'troubled star' to a 'bad boy' to a 'wild man'.

Not for the first time, class played its part. O'Sullivan was no saint, and his behaviour left a lot to be desired, but he was being portrayed almost as a feral member of the underclass rather than a 20-year-old, one who was uneasy in the spotlight and struggling to deal with the pressures of top-level sport and fame. Needless to say, the very journalists who called for him to be banned were in time asking why there weren't more 'characters' in snooker like Ronnie O'Sullivan.

There's no doubt, though, that he was a troubled man at the Crucible in 1996, which for him ended with a semi-final defeat to Peter Ebdon. Physically, he was overweight. He was abusing his body with too much food and alcohol, leading his mother to issue him harsh instructions to sort himself out. He took up running and hit the gym. A year later, he returned to Sheffield transformed. Slimmed down, with a healthy complexion, he appeared before the snooker world looking every inch a star, confirming this status by making his record-breaking maximum. He became known as 'The Rocket', a nickname that suggested explosive excitement.

Still, it took him another four years to become world champion as he battled various addictions and self-destructive demons that pushed him to the edge. At the 2002 World Championship,

O'Sullivan made an unwarranted and unprovoked attack on Hendry before they met in the semi-finals:

> The most satisfying thing for me would be to send him home to Scotland as quickly as possible for a nice summer off. I'll say hello to him because it's hard to ignore someone, but he's not my cup of tea. I know if I do get beat and he comes up and does a moonie in front of me and goes 'nah nah nah', I'll just look at him and say well done and say go back to your sad little life.[4]

He attempted to justify this trash talk by dredging up an old incident where Hendry had had the cue ball replaced – as per the rules and per his prerogative – following a miss out of a snooker by O'Sullivan, but really this was more self-sabotage, perhaps a subconscious desire to alleviate the pressure by creating an excuse for losing. For his part, Hendry hardly needed any more motivation to beat him. He did so, 17–13.

After ten years as a professional, O'Sullivan had won 11 ranking titles. By comparison, Hendry had captured 22 after his first decade on tour. O'Sullivan was winning events but not dominating. His father, watching on from prison, believed he needed more steel in his game, so he got hold of a number for Ray Reardon, who had been largely absent from the scene for several years. Reardon recalled the experience with relish: 'One day, I'm at home, and the phone rings. He says, "It's Ronnie O'Sullivan." I said, "No, you're not Ronnie. I know his voice." He said, "No, I'm his dad." He was in jail, so he'd borrowed a phone to get in touch with me. He said, "Do you think Ronnie should be winning more than he is?" A few months go by, and Ronnie phones me. I said I thought it was a good idea to work together. We met in the Crucible practice room. He put his hand out, and I ignored it and gave him a hug. I said, "You've given me ten years on my life by inviting me here." I knew what he wanted, but I wanted him to tell me. I was looking for information, but Ronnie doesn't give information, he sucks it out of you. He didn't like the defensive side of the game, but you win on defence, it's how you get in. We'd been there a week, and one day he said, "I'm fed up of potting these balls, introduce me to something else." I said, "I have a little [note]book. I'm going to lie in bed tonight and put you in snookers." Next morning, he does his usual practice session, and then he says, "I'm ready." We started with an easy snooker, then another one. I wanted to get inside his mind to see how he read the situation. He began to like it. Another day goes by, and I get him to lay snookers instead of escaping. He struggled a bit at the beginning, but then he loved it. He became better at it than me.'

The partnership immediately paid off. With tactical toughness in his game and a new determination in his heart, O'Sullivan won a second world title in 2004, overwhelming Hendry 17–4 in the semi-finals and Graeme Dott 18–8 in the final. More than the achievement of winning, he seemed to be genuinely enjoying snooker again. The buzz of his junior days was back. Reardon, at the time in his early 70s, was young at heart, similarly eccentric and an obvious surrogate father figure.

The following season, the new, improved, engaged O'Sullivan won three ranking titles of the eight contested and trounced John Higgins 10–3 to win the Masters for the second time, a decade after his first victory in the tournament. By now, his association with Reardon and the consistency it had helped establish was striking fear into opponents, but O'Sullivan's propensity for self-sabotage reared up at the UK Championship later in the year. Playing Mark King, a fierce rival from their days as Essex juniors, he demonstrated his antipathy to his opponent's style of play by wearing a towel over his head while sitting in his chair. The cutaways to O'Sullivan had a surreal, absurd air to them. Reardon had seen enough and departed, but the two remained friends. 'A lot of the things he taught me I've retained – they are imprinted in me,' O'Sullivan says. '50 to 60 per cent of it is stuff that will never, ever leave me. The other 30 to 40 per cent was very advanced stuff, and for a lot of it I would need to have a freshen-up on it. Some of the safety and defensive stuff he blew my mind with.'

There had been signs that O'Sullivan's mental state was still fragile at the 2005 World Championship. He reached the quarter-finals and was coasting when leading Peter Ebdon 8–2, but Ebdon was renowned for a gritty determination more associated with the snooker of old and slowed the match down. At one point, he took five minutes to make a break of 12. Gradually, the layers of O'Sullivan's patience unravelled. His facial expressions revealed his frustration. At one point, he stood on his chair; he even dragged his nails across his forehead, leaving scars. He was in pain, some inflicted by Ebdon and some by himself. He lost 13–11.

'I didn't play that well but I stopped him from playing, which is not an easy thing to do,' Ebdon says, two decades on. 'It got tactical, and I enjoyed that. I was fiercely determined to win.'

Most of the media did not see it that way, nor did many snooker fans, and there was an immediate backlash, even in the age before social media. 'It was mind-blowing,' Ebdon says. 'I got quite upset. There was some hostile questioning. I was on a high after winning, and I was genuinely shocked. Because you don't want to get drawn into playing the other person's game, playing faster than you normally would, you end up playing slower than you normally would. I was using a soft tip at the time, and the problem with it was that I was leaving loads of chalk on the cue ball. If I saw chalk on the white, I had to have it cleaned. I couldn't play the shot knowing that the cue ball was covered with chalk. My pace probably had a lot to do with that. Looking back on it, I'd have liked to have played a bit quicker.'

Opinions remain divided on Ebdon's tactics, but he had done a number on O'Sullivan, proven he could be broken down and exposed his vulnerability. The 2005/6 season was a lean one for O'Sullivan, with only the Premier League trophy to show for it. He was booed at the Grand Prix final in Preston as he made his entrance against Higgins, having said after beating Barry Hawkins in the semis that he would 'rather be at home gardening' than playing in the tournament. With the crowd behind his opponent, he struggled, and Higgins produced an electrifying display, making four centuries in a row and winning 9–2.

Then, at the 2006 UK Championship in York, came one of the low points of O'Sullivan's career. Trailing Hendry 4–1 in their quarter-final, he missed a pot, shook Hendry's hand and walked out. The best-of-17-frame match had been conceded in frame six.

BBC presenter Hazel Irvine remembers the day well. 'We were trying to eat something just after the interval,' she says. 'I remember seeing what had happened, then it was about getting everything under the desk out of sight. We came back to the studio, and I was like, "I don't really know what's going on." The main emotion was confusion. There was clearly something wrong with him but I wasn't sure we could shed a lot of light on it at the time. He was clearly very troubled. You can only report that. You can't solve it. You can't make it better. I felt a great sadness for him.'

As ever with O'Sullivan, reaction was sharply split. Many felt it was an act of petulance, that he had abdicated his professional responsibilities. Others, like Irvine, were simply worried about his mental state and appealed for understanding. O'Sullivan was fined

£20,800 by the WPBSA. He attempted to restore his image by wearing an 'I Love Snooker' T-shirt, but it was not hard to win people over again on the table. Just a few weeks after the walk-out, O'Sullivan won his third Masters title at a raucous Wembley Arena. His opponent, China's Ding Junhui, had been barracked by an unpleasant section of the audience and, trailing 9–3, had himself attempted to concede the match, even though it was first to ten. This time, O'Sullivan showed his best qualities. He spoke to Ding in his dressing room at the interval, persuaded him to continue and, after beating him 10–3, took time to put his arms around him, expressing genuine concern as to his welfare.

Ding speaks of him now with a childlike awe. 'He was my hero. I liked to watch his games as a little boy,' he says. 'He loved to talk to me, have a chat when we would meet. I like that he enjoys watching me play.'

Within the space of a month, between the York walkout and his sportsmanship at Wembley, the snooker world had seen what, in a wider sense, it has witnessed over the course of his whole career: the best and the worst of Ronnie O'Sullivan. His life, his career, felt dependent on both sides of the coin, as if the good days could not come without the bad. In 2008, he made lewd remarks at a press conference in China, earning more opprobrium, and then a few weeks later won a third World Championship. It seemed every time he plumbed the depths, he immediately hit the heights.

Audiences largely adored him, with even those who found his personality hard to admire seduced by his performances in the arena. O'Sullivan at times showed few signs of reciprocation. At the 2010 World Open in Glasgow he potted 15 reds, 15 blacks and yellow to pink, before deciding not to pot the last black for a 147 in protest at what he saw as the low prize for a maximum: £4,000 for the highest break of the tournament rather than a specific bonus, due to the increased regularity of 147s. The referee, Jan Verhaas, virtually ordered him to pot it 'for the fans', and O'Sullivan finally obliged. However, the audacity of such behaviour seemed to make him more popular with spectators. It certainly kept snooker in the headlines.

His career by now was a tightrope walk between stellar performances and self-destructive episodes. O'Sullivan was lacking stability, and it began to tell in his results. He went to the German Masters in Berlin in February 2012 having not won a ranking title since the Shanghai Masters three years earlier. In his opening match, a best-of-nine-frame encounter, he trailed Andrew Higginson 4–0. An early, ignominious exit beckoned, but something had changed in his life and career that would help him win this match, the tournament and many more in the years that followed.

At the previous year's World Championship, O'Sullivan had been introduced to Dr Steve Peters, a sports psychiatrist who has also worked with several British Olympians. They shared a passion for running, and like Reardon, Peters was another older father figure who won O'Sullivan's trust with some straight talking. They discussed O'Sullivan's state of mind in matches, how he often wanted to flee the arena. Peters explained these were perfectly normal emotions. The key was in learning to control them.

Using the tools given to him by Peters, O'Sullivan began to manage his mental state in matches better, digging in when the going was bad. At the Crucible in May 2012, he won a fourth world title but, emotionally shattered by the twin efforts of scaling snooker's ultimate mountain and all the work he had done on his mental state, he felt he needed a break. Journalists had lost count of the number of times he had said he would walk away from snooker, but this time he carried through on his threat, playing just one low-key match but taking no part in the game's major tournaments.

It gave others a chance to claim the spotlight, and they did. Judd Trump emerged as a new threat to the established order, while Neil Robertson and Mark Selby enhanced their reputations as consistent winners. O'Sullivan followed it all from afar. He could not disengage completely. When it came to the Masters in January 2013, he found himself getting in his car and driving to Alexandra Palace to watch the semi-final between Selby and Dott. He had missed being on the circuit, seeing people. Like it or not, he was defined as a snooker player.

Which brings us again to 20 April 2013. O'Sullivan was back at the Crucible, but in what shape? He had practised solidly ahead of the championship but had no matches under his belt. However, this king across the water was prepared to fight to keep his crown. He lost only 16 frames in breezing through the first three rounds, to face Trump in the semi-finals. The generational baton was not yet ready to be passed on. O'Sullivan won 17–11.

In the final, he faced Barry Hawkins, who had broken through that season as a ranking-title winner at the Australian Open. It was a high-quality match. O'Sullivan made six centuries and won 18–12. 'I've been up and down like a whore's drawers,' he told Hazel Irvine afterwards, typically mixing charm, cheek and brutal honesty.

It was a stunning achievement to win the sport's biggest title after a year away. O'Sullivan was now on five world titles, only one behind Steve Davis and two away from Hendry's modern-day record. In 2014, a hat-trick beckoned when he led Selby 10–5 in the final. Selby hung on to win the last two frames of the session and stay in touch, before wresting control on the last day, neutralising O'Sullivan's attacking game with smart match snooker.

Selby's style is not to everyone's taste – O'Sullivan included – but he demonstrated poise and focus in turning the match around to win 18–14.

There is little love lost between the two men, opposites in every sense in terms of background, personality and playing style. 'We're not best pals,' Selby says. 'I have respect for him as a player – he's the greatest to play our game – but I don't know the guy. I've not been in his company or around him for long enough to know him. He's a lot older than me, and I don't know him well enough to know if I'd get on with him.'

The 2014 defeat was scarring for O'Sullivan, who had been the best player for sixteen days, only to lose on the seventeenth, a new and confusing situation for him, especially given the vast contrast in approaches to snooker between him and Selby. At root, watching Selby, he experienced confusion, unable to work out why someone would want to play like that, perhaps unaware that not everyone was able to play like him. Maybe it instilled doubt in his own game. Even though he continued to win tournaments, his Crucible record dropped off dramatically. In 2018, put under pressure by Ali Carter in their second-round match, he shoulder-barged him while returning to his seat. A year later, an amateur qualifier, James Cahill, defeated him in the first round.

His two contemporaries, John Higgins and Mark Williams, had continued to enjoy success. Williams won the world title for a second time in 2003 and, after apparently entering decline, did so again in 2018. Higgins had to wait nine years for his second world title in 2007, but swiftly won it again in 2009 and 2011. From 2017 to 2019, he reached three successive world finals.

O'Sullivan failed to reach a World Championship semi-final for six years following his loss in the 2014 final, but in 2020, he would again face Selby, this time in the semis. However, this was a very different World Championship. The COVID-19 pandemic had largely shut down sport. The championship could not be played in April as usual, but after the Tokyo Olympics were cancelled, a two-week slot on the BBC opened up in August. Barry Hearn, never one to waste a crisis, persuaded them to broadcast snooker's greatest show. There were even spectators there on day one, before the government once again moved the goalposts, leaving the championship to play out in eerie silence. Yet this suited O'Sullivan. Always the player most in demand with media and the public, he discovered an ironic new-found freedom among the restrictions. Social distancing meant nobody could get close to him, leaving the fortnight purely about snooker.

Against Selby, he was 16–14 down. Instead of allowing his opponent to dictate the rest of the match, he loosened up, playing wild hit-and-hope escapes from snookers, which raised eyebrows but did the trick. O'Sullivan won 17–16 and beat Kyren Wilson 18–8 in the final.

Two years later, in 2022, he equalled Hendry's record of seven world titles with an 18–13 defeat of Trump. The match ended with O'Sullivan in floods of tears, holding on to Trump as the emotion poured from him. He had put himself through the mental pain barrier but once again come out as the champion.

The hits kept on coming. In 2023, O'Sullivan became the oldest winner of the UK Championship, 30 years after he had become the youngest. He extended his record in the event to eight titles, a feat he repeated at the Masters a few weeks later. His status as by far the biggest name in snooker was underlined by an Amazon Prime documentary, *The Edge of Everything*, which followed his journey to a seventh world title.

His hellraising days firmly behind him, his greatest passion became running, an activity that afforded him physical and mental well-being. He was also keen to demonstrate his world view, campaigning for both Ed Miliband and Jeremy Corbyn when they were Labour Party leader and, in the 2024 general election, for Faiza Shaheen, who stood in the Chingford and Woodford Green constituency as an independent after being deselected by Labour for tweets criticising Israel.

His natural charisma saw him signed up by Eurosport, where he presented his own programme and did studio punditry during tournaments. He also fronted *American Hustle*, a series for the History Channel, in which he toured the US. He was twice shortlisted for the BBC Sports Personality of the Year award.

So much of the genius of O'Sullivan, and therefore the fascination, is based on the unknowable. 'He's the only person that I would be intrigued to know what pictures he sees when he starts playing, because I think he sees different pictures,' says Steve Davis. 'I think he sees things in a different way to what I remember thinking and seeing. He's the most amazing player.'

Davis agrees that O'Sullivan's behaviour can be as hard to fathom as his superior play. 'I don't think many players can associate with what he says. Whilst we know the game has its pressures, and there's a lot you have to take on board to try and win events, we don't necessarily know what's going through his mind. We know he's a different type of person, and we're all exasperated sometimes when he comes out and says things that seem like they're disrespectful to the game or other players. There's other times when he says he doesn't mind if he loses, and we can't really associate with it. Most times you have an empathy with what someone is saying, but sometimes with him I don't. I'm not the same animal as him, but how can you untangle the strange life he's had?'

Alan McManus has closely examined O'Sullivan's game and the way he switches the momentum in his favour. 'The genius of him is knowing what to do if the chips are down,' he says. 'He's really adaptable within a match, which is really difficult to do. There's structure within the madness. I believe he doesn't know that he has this genius. He knows he's really good, but he doesn't really know just how good he is. I watched him once on the practice table, and I had to turn away – it was like watching Einstein writing down an equation. I was like, "What the blazes is that?" He makes moves that don't exist, you can't plan them. He just has a deep intellect about the game that no one else has. If you're sitting watching him from your chair when he's at the table, there's electricity going on. He makes you feel inadequate. He makes you feel like you've never played before, because you're watching something that's beyond anyone.'

Judd Trump transitioned from fan to rival, at one point seeming likely to inherit the mantle as the game's new star attraction, only for O'Sullivan to stubbornly remain in the spotlight. 'Ronnie's the only person who could disrespect you in his comments, and you'd still want to speak to him at the next tournament,' Trump says. 'He has that aura about him. He's completely different. You have to remember his upbringing compared to everyone else. Anyone who went through what he went through is never going to be normal. That's also what helps him. I don't think he feels pressure the way other people feel it. If he does, he's so good at dealing with it.'

Their epic man-hug at the end of the 2022 world final suggested a warmth between them, which Trump confirms. 'I've always had a reasonably good relationship with him,' he says. 'I'm not best friends with him – I'd struggle to be with the age difference – but he's someone who's taken as much time out for me as anyone else in the game, being able to practise with him and doing exhibitions. That made it more comfortable playing him. You want to be liked by him.'

Hazel Irvine has many times been the person asking the questions of O'Sullivan in the television studio, an experience laced with unpredictability, and even a sense of danger, but she has formed an understanding of the man as much as the player. 'He sets clear parameters as to what is in, or not in, his remit at any given time,' she says. 'He doesn't want to talk generally about what's just happened. It's maybe not good for him to talk about his match, and I understand that. You have to be prepared to give and take. It can be difficult. You never know what will be okay with him on any given day, but I respect that.'

Barry Hearn managed O'Sullivan when he was starting out but having become World Snooker Tour chairman in 2010, became another authority figure. 'Our relationship has changed quite dramatically, sadly,' he says. 'I managed him twice during his career. I wasn't the same big brother as I was for Steve because Ronnie was so influenced and spoilt by his mum and dad. They weren't like Steve, coming from a council house in Plumstead, or me from one in Dagenham. Ronnie lived in a big house in Chigwell. I was always impressed with him in those days because he seemed on the outside to cope with his situation far better than his years. Initially, he was driven by the thought of winning titles and taking the trophy to show his dad, but I think inside, emotionally, he developed a different layer of personality. He became very anti-establishment, very anti-authority, so naturally after a while there wasn't the same bond between us. Matchroom got bigger and bigger. I couldn't spend time managing people. I think there was a little bit of resentment beginning to build up that I was the policeman, and he didn't like that sort of relationship.'

Despite the thawing in their relationship, Hearn recognises O'Sullivan's continued importance to the sport. 'Do I bend the rules for Ronnie? Sometimes. He's a genius, and they aren't the same as the ordinary man,' he says. 'You have to adjust to how you deal with certain people. Ronnie could have been fined every day of his life, but that's not the answer. Sometimes you have to put your arms around someone.'

Hearn, like many others in snooker, has been exasperated by comments made over the years by O'Sullivan. A frequent refrain is that he would not let his own children play snooker. However, several players theorise that such comments are designed to alleviate pressure. Stuart Bingham, a regular practice partner, has seen O'Sullivan's dedication close-up. 'He says he doesn't practise, but he practises harder than anyone else on tour,' Bingham says. 'He must have five or six tables dotted around the area, and he won't be in the same place more than two days on the trot, but he's playing. He picks at every little detail and tries to improve everything. He's always looking at people and will try things he notices. He tries to take pressure off himself. I played him in an exhibition in Bucharest in front of 2,000 people. I said, "I bet you love all this." And he said, "No. Because I've got to perform." He feels that pressure – the one everybody has come to see. He's very clever about what he says. Even when he's not in a tournament he makes sure people are talking about him. If he does lose, he can say he couldn't be bothered. It takes that edge off him.'

Shaun Murphy is less forgiving of O'Sullivan's outbursts, citing a formative incident that left a sour taste in the mouth. 'We fell out when I was young,' he says. 'Ronnie verbally abused me when I was twelve, and I never forgave him. I vividly remember it. I still have immense respect for his levels of play as a snooker player. I watch in awe at the things he's able to do, because I know how hard it is. His ability as a player is completely unmatched.'

For Murphy, O'Sullivan's behaviour has been frustrating to witness. 'He's the biggest needle-mover in the sport, the biggest we've ever seen,' he says. 'That brings you some forgiveness. When the golden goose lays the golden egg, you get treated differently. There's no question over the years that various chairmen have treated him more leniently over his offences because of the attention he brings to snooker, and commercially that's probably correct. But one of the reasons I idolised Steve Davis so much was I was brought up in a world when being the greatest meant a lot more than how good you were at playing snooker, and unfortunately, for all of the good things Ronnie has done in terms of his snooker ability, I think he's done an equal amount of, if not more, damage to the sport from an ambassadorial point of view. I think it's such a shame that he hasn't done for snooker in his ambassadorial position the things that people he says he looks up to – like Roger Federer and Novak Djokovic – have done, that he hasn't taken a leaf out of their book and treated the sport that's given him so much the same level of respect. If he had used his platform for good, he could have single-handedly dragged snooker into a different stratosphere in terms of popularity. He could have made us much more mainstream.'

There are other players who privately echo Murphy's view, but by no means all agree with his assessment. Despite their many intense battles, Ebdon speaks of O'Sullivan with admiration. 'Ronnie has so many gears, he always seems able to find enough,' he says. 'That's such a special talent to have. For a game that's so competitive, it's almost not competitive when he's at his best. If he really wants to win a tournament, he's capable of finding what he needs. The most amazing player.'

John Virgo feels the three-way rivalry between O'Sullivan, Higgins and Williams has brought out the best in each of them, but that O'Sullivan stands the tallest. 'What careers they've had,' he says. 'Maybe they've spurred each other on. They probably look at what each other has done. They are great players and have all left a legacy. Ronnie is the best I've ever seen. The record books will tell you.'

Neil Robertson is in no doubt as to O'Sullivan's status, comparing him to the greats of other sports. 'I don't think anyone will get as good as Ronnie,' he says. 'In terms of talent, he's up there with Lionel Messi, Roger Federer, Michael Jordan, Tiger Woods. He's in that untouchable bracket. He's on his own. It's been a privilege to be able to compete with him when he's been at his best. In ten years' time, I believe the tour will be a lot easier in terms of winning the biggest prizes. This period will always be remembered as *the* period, like in tennis with Federer, [Rafa] Nadal, Djokovic and [Andy] Murray.'

And what of Hendry, for so long considered the greatest of all time, until O'Sullivan took one record after another? 'He's an unbelievable player,' he says. 'The longevity is incredible. I won't lie, it's not easy seeing the records go. You've dedicated your whole life to breaking someone else's records, and all of sudden you see someone doing it to you. Steve Davis has handled that a lot better than I have. I still get pangs of jealousy, thinking I should come back and stop him, which is completely deluded. Funnily enough, when he won the seventh, it took a bit of pressure off, because everyone was talking about whether he would do it. I don't want him to win eight – of course I don't – but I think he will.'

Ultimately, Hendry has had to accept what he can plainly see with his own eyes. 'I'm completely happy to say Ronnie is the greatest,' he says. 'He's taken the game, in terms of winning, of dominating opponents, scoring, to a level which is incredible. Deep down he wants to win the eighth, because then it really is clear-cut.'

How satisfied is O'Sullivan with his many achievements? He has been a source of joy for millions of fans but often gives the impression that he has derived very little himself. It has been an emotional roller coaster, but however scary roller coasters are, the first thing most people want to do at the end of a ride is start a new one. His ambition now is somewhat touching in its simplicity: just to be happy.

'Every year, I put a list down of the tournaments, and after each one I put a smiley face, a neutral face or a miserable face, and thankfully for the last five or six years it's been 90 per cent happy faces,' he says. 'That's not because I've won tournaments, it's because I enjoyed them, have felt ready to play. A lot of the problems for me in the past was when I'd win a tournament, go to the next one and win that, and suddenly I'd won three tournaments on the bounce and I'd feel depressed. I'd be like, "What's the point in doing this?" So I've learned to have gaps in between. There's no point winning tournaments and not being happy. It's about being ready to play. Did I give 100 per cent to every match I played in? And if I have, then it's a smiley face.'

For a character some dismiss as arrogant, O'Sullivan is remarkably reticent about praising himself. Even when he considers all that he has done, he backs away from self-congratulation, underplaying it all and reducing it to basic feelings.

'As I've reached them and gone past them, I look back at the numbers and think, "They're good numbers,"' he says. 'I'd have never believed as a seventeen-year-old, when I won my first UK Championship, that I'd have eight of them, eight Masters as well from 14 finals. I've done pretty decent in Sheffield as well. I've had a great career. If I could win another World Championship, that'd put me out on my own. A lot of people say, "You've gotta win the eighth," but why do I? Seven's all right. I was happy with four. Once I got to four I thought, "That's a good number."'

O'Sullivan's fragile state of mind persists into middle age. Frustrated with how he was playing during the Championship

League in January 2025, he smashed up the cue he had used since 2011 and unceremoniously threw it into a bin in the players' room. He did not compete again until the World Championship three months later, where, despite an obvious rustiness, he made it through to the semi-finals. Again, though, self-sabotage seeped in. O'Sullivan changed the ferrule of his cue from brass to titanium during the match and then back again, leaving him all at sea against a rampant and determined Zhao Xintong, who beat him with a session to spare, 17–7.

Everyone wants to unravel an enigma. Perhaps O'Sullivan's greatest power is that he remains unreachable, equal parts the king of all he surveys and a lost soul. The end of *The Edge of Everything* finds him lying on a bed, contemplating the struggle he has chosen:

> With snooker you have to put up with all that toxic competitiveness. It's so ugly. That's why I have to just do my job, play my game, be happy, content. You can't win. There's no end to it: 'He's winning, he's great, he's amazing, he's the greatest player of all time.' And then he's losing: 'He's slipping, are his days numbered?' I've heard that for 30 years. You're always going to find a problem. And I just go, 'Fuck you. I don't give a fuck.'[5]

16

FOR TOMORROW

In June 2016, the British public voted by a narrow margin to end their membership of the European Union. 'Brexit' will be debated by historians for decades, but it seemed to many like a national identity crisis. What sort of country did we think we were? What sort of country did we want to become?

Snooker had already wrestled with its own existential questions, as the 21st century saw major changes in the way people consumed content. The old days of four television channels were long in the past. Rupert Murdoch's Sky TV had screened a number of tournaments throughout the 1990s but formed a dim view of those running the sport and broadcast its last ranking event in 2004, preferring instead to champion Barry Hearn's Premier League, which included a shot clock to speed up play.

Other innovations designed to cater to those with shrinking attention spans included six-reds snooker, played, as the name suggests, with six reds rather than 15, and power snooker, a glitzy but rather confusing affair in which players saw their points total rocket up if they potted a 'power ball'. These variations failed to seriously threaten the established game, but with sports such as cricket and tennis embracing shorter formats, there was a consensus forming that this was what an increasing number of spectators wanted.

The real problem, though, was snooker's administration, which had long been beset by infighting, mismanagement and ego-driven civil wars. A stream of AGMs and EGMs over the decades led to a merry-go-round of WPBSA chairmen. Rex Williams was replaced by John Virgo, who gave way to John Spencer, who was kicked out in favour of Geoff Foulds, before Williams returned. Mark Wildman replaced Williams. Jason Ferguson replaced Wildman. At one point, former England cricket captain Tony Lewis was chairman. From 2004 to 2009, Sir Rodney Walker headed the board.

Matters had come to a head in 2001, when a consortium led by Ian Doyle's management stable, which included Stephen Hendry and Mark Williams, and backed by City firm Warburg Pincus, announced a rival tour. Months of unpleasantness followed, with players at loggerheads as to the way forward and which side to choose. Crucially, the BBC pledged to remain with the WPBSA, just as they had supported the British Darts Organisation (BDO) after the Professional Darts Corporation established its own rival world championship in 1994.

John Higgins was prominent in siding with the status quo. 'There was a divide between a lot of the players at the time,' he says. 'I was in a rival camp because I didn't get on with Ian Doyle and his stable. I couldn't bring myself to side with them. Maybe, looking back, it would've been better, but I couldn't do it.'

The WPBSA ensured the support of enough players, and therefore its own survival, by signing up a number on 'promotional contracts', whereby they were paid large sums to undertake work outside of tournaments – in reality, a way of buying their support. Plans for the rival tour were dropped. A court case followed in which the WPBSA's monopoly position was questioned, but little changed. The bloodletting could have damaged snooker's credibility with sponsors and broadcasters, but fresh faces were emerging as a new era dawned.

The first new star of the millennium was Paul Hunter, whose angelic good looks and thirst for fun soon made him a natural crowd favourite. Born in Leeds, his father, Alan, introduced him to the game, and he was quickly making waves as a junior, and at just sixteen finished runner-up in the English Amateur Championship.

Early in his professional career, he was reprimanded for a naked streak in Blackpool and fined for a positive test for cannabis, pointing to a Jack the Lad character in the vein of Jimmy White, more mischievous than malicious. At nineteen, he won his first ranking title, the 1998 Welsh Open, but his real breakthrough came three years later at the Masters.

Hunter trailed Irishman Fergal O'Brien 6–2 after the first session but ended up winning 10–9. After the match, he explained to the assembled media that he had retired to his hotel at half-time with his girlfriend, Lyndsey, and 'put Plan B into operation'. It was a throwaway remark, but it ended up as the front-page splash in the *Daily Star*, and a new tabloid snooker hero was born.

With his flowing blond locks, Hunter became known as 'The Beckham of the Baize'. Here was a fine player with some personality, someone who did not take himself too seriously and seemed to enjoy the limelight. His status was further enhanced by two more last-gasp Masters wins. In 2002, he recovered from 5–0 down to beat Mark Williams 10–9. More remarkable was his fightback from 7–2 down to defeat Ronnie O'Sullivan 10–9 in 2004. In between, he came agonisingly close to reaching the World Championship final. He led Ken Doherty 15–9 in their 2003 semi-final but lost 17–16. It felt certain that he would have many more chances to land snooker's biggest title, but fate cruelly intervened.

Just before the 2005 China Open, Hunter was suffering from stomach pains and underwent tests. While in Beijing, he discovered he had cancerous neuroendocrine tumours. He continued to play while undergoing chemotherapy but became very ill. His last match was at the Crucible in 2006. He was clearly in pain, and Neil Robertson beat him 10–5, a match the Australian found a difficult experience.

'It was awful,' Robertson says. 'He was unbelievably courageous to even play. He was struggling so much. Watching at home, you wouldn't have realised how ill he was. When he was stretching over the table, he was in a lot of pain. It's the only time I've played a match where I was emotionless. But you had to play it, and he had to play to get his ranking points.'

Hunter died in October 2006. He was just 27, a golden boy denied his golden future. The BBC's Hazel Irvine saw the effect the tragedy had on those working in the sport. 'It was horrible, dreadful,' she says. 'I've worked in lots of different sports, but I don't think many of us in broadcasting have been so connected to a person as we all were with Paul, because he was one of these amazing, happy-go-lucky people. Snooker genuinely is a family, and the player's family are part of that wider family. Paul was such a life-affirming person. Everyone on the tour felt it very deeply.'

Hunter had entertained on the biggest stages, just as Hendry, the Class of '92 and many others did in the early part of the 2000s, but a dark cloud was descending, or alternatively, it was lifting: tobacco sponsorship, a chief source of revenue since the 1970s, was stubbed out by Tony Blair's Labour government. It would end in 2003, with the World Championship, bankrolled by Embassy since 1976, given an extension until 2005.

That year's event was won in sensational fashion by a qualifier, only the second to triumph at the Crucible. Shaun Murphy's great-uncle Jimmy had been an enthusiastic billiards player, and his father, Tony, played snooker for money at the local golf club. At eight, Murphy wrote to Santa for a small table. 'It escalated pretty quickly,' he says. 'It went from being something that was completely new to the centre of my universe, and to some degree it still is.'

So successful was Murphy as a junior that he was given special dispensation to turn professional a few weeks before turning sixteen, the stipulated age for being allowed on tour, a decision that did not meet with universal approval. 'I had a terrible experience very early on,' he says. 'My first few weeks as a pro were spent at the Plymouth Pavilions for the summer qualifiers of 1998. One pro took it upon himself to invite me for a coffee, which I thought was lovely. I thought he was going to show me the ropes. He took me to a café, we sat down, and he absolutely tore me a new one, saying I had no right to be there, it was a disgrace I was allowed in, some little upstart, who did I think I was, and so on. That was my welcome to the tour.'

Murphy outwardly projected self-confidence and seemed old beyond his years. Maybe some thought he was flash, but his upbringing had been difficult. Badly bullied at school, he was removed at the age of thirteen and educated at home. Money had been tight due to the varying success of his father's business dealings. 'I came from a hard background,' he says. 'We had it very tough. We were almost homeless when I was nine years old. We'd do house clearances and car-boot sales to scratch a few quid together to pay my entry into junior tournaments. Even now, I quite regularly go back and sit in the car outside the houses I grew up in, just to take a couple of minutes to remember what it was like.'

Murphy soon fell off tour and took two years to return. By 2004, he was considering looking for another career, but he reached a semi-final at the British Open and a few months later qualified for the Crucible for the third time. In the first round he beat Scottish player Chris Small, who was struggling with a chronic back condition, before meeting John Higgins, one of the title favourites.

Murphy won 13–8, a result that made the whole snooker world sit up and take notice. He was no longer a cocky kid. This was a player who had matured into a serious prospect.

In the quarter-finals he faced his boyhood idol, Steve Davis. As a child, Murphy had chased Davis down a street in Sheffield for his autograph. As a man, he hammered him 13–4. In the semi-finals he defeated Peter Ebdon 17–12, and so at the age of 22, he took his place in snooker's showpiece match against Matthew Stevens, who had finished runner-up to Williams in 2000.

With Embassy's enforced exit, there was a heightened sense of importance surrounding the occasion. All the former champions had been invited, and so, before the final session, Murphy and Stevens posed with the likes of John Spencer, Ray Reardon, Dennis Taylor . . . men who had put snooker on the map, legends they were eager to emulate.

From 10–6 down overnight, Murphy won 18–16. He had been 150–1 in the pre-tournament betting. Only Stephen Hendry, at 21, had won the title at a younger age. 'I still haven't fully understood it,' Murphy says. 'I remember having a dream in the days after the final about what it would be like to win it. I woke up, went to get a drink from the kitchen and walked past the trophy. Momentarily, I'd forgotten.'

Like many new champions, his life changed overnight. 'I went from complete anonymity to being stopped in the street every day,' he says. 'I wasn't ready for it. You go into bookshops, and the shelves are full of books telling you how to cope with failure. There are none telling you how to cope with success. In my year as champion, if there was an envelope being opened, I was there. I really did try to be what I thought was a good ambassador for the game, but I lost myself somewhere in there.'

Ebdon sympathises. Like Murphy, he felt the weight of

becoming world champion in 2002, an ambition he had long strived to make real but which hung heavy round his neck. 'When you achieve your ultimate goal, it can sometimes leave a big hole,' Ebdon says. 'I didn't enjoy the wins as much as I wanted to.'

Murphy's victory attracted a peak viewing audience of 7.8 million on BBC2, more than that year's FA Cup final or any of the five Test matches that comprised the thrilling England vs Australia Ashes series that summer, televised by Channel 4. It should have given snooker a shot in the arm, but the sport had a financial hole to fill and became obsessed instead with matters of image. It tried various cosmetic changes, such as a tournament where one player wore a red shirt and his opponent a blue one, and experimenting with getting rid of bow ties, which left players looking as if they'd got dressed in a hurry. It was all tinkering around the edges as the circuit began to contract. The number of tournaments dwindled, and players began to fear for their futures. They needed someone with experience of the worlds of sport and commerce to rescue them. First-hand knowledge of the snooker circuit would be a plus. In reality, there was only ever one candidate. Enter, or rather re-enter, Barry Hearn.

Since stepping back from snooker, he had seen his Matchroom empire grow through lucrative promotions in boxing and darts, which Hearn helped revitalise when he took over the running of the PDC in 2001, building it up into a multimillion-pound circuit. 'Snooker was almost where the BDO was with darts when they came to me,' Hearn says. 'You can look at it two ways. One is that I'm a cynical, hard-headed businessman that saw an opportunity. That's part of it. But the other side is that I believe when you feel you owe people something, that you have to pay your dues. I'm a money man. "Benevolent despot" is the term that suits me because I do want to push the game forward, but I want to do it in a way that creates a sustainable business behind it. When they came to me and said, "Would you oppose Sir Rodney?" I said, "You'll have to get rid of him first, because then I'll know you're for real." And they actually did it. I couldn't believe it.'

Walker was voted out as WPBSA chairman, and Hearn took the reins, but he knew the old way of doing things had to change. He wanted full control if he was to devote himself to transforming snooker's fortunes. 'I said, "Give me a few months, and I'll consider where snooker is and what we should be doing,"' he says. '"I'll write you a report, and then I've paid my debt to a sport which changed my life." By the time I'd finished the report, I could see so much opportunity, so the last line of the report said, quite simply, "I should own this sport." That triggered a big division in the game. Which way do you want to go?'

It came down to a vote in Sheffield, with players asked to choose between the Hearn plan and an alternative proposal headed by businessman John Davison and supported by Lee Doyle, son of Ian. 'They called an EGM, with only the top 64 having a vote, so you needed 33 votes,' Hearn says. 'I had nowhere near that because Doyle managed at least 14 players and worked his socks off to get the rest. He brought John Davison in. Three weeks before the vote, Davison came up with a plan, which was better than mine in terms of quick money, but he wasn't capable of implementing the changes that were needed. Players don't think that way, though, and he was promising more money. I suggested he stepped away and I'd give him 15 per cent of World Snooker, with me doing all the work to make it a success. It quite appealed to him, but it was a bribe really. I was eliminating him from the game to leave myself with a clear field. But Doyle talked him into not doing that because he thought he had the votes already to win.'

Here, Hearn's charisma and business record proved to be

decisive factors. 'I said, "We should have a debate in front of the players,"' he says. 'I think Doyle told Davison not to go because they already had the votes, and also I'd kill him, because I'm good at public speaking. On the day, there was an empty chair. I was invited to say a few words. So I stood up and said, "You guys have come here today. You've paid your airfares, your train fares, your petrol money out of your own pocket to listen to two people telling you about the future of this sport. One of them is here. The other one is an empty chair. If you want to be treated like a cunt, vote for the empty chair. If not, vote for me." And I sat down. Five or six players changed their vote and we won.'

It was a narrow victory, 35–29, but paved the way for lasting change. New tournaments were added to the calendar. Hearn brought ITV back into the fold and expanded into new territories. Prize money began rising. From £3.5 million when he took over in 2010, it was at £20 million in 2025.

Ebdon had been one of the biggest opponents of the proposed Hearn revolution, but he now admits he was wrong. 'Barry coming in was the best thing that ever happened to the game,' Ebdon says. 'I was just a players' man and I tried to do my best for them. I didn't agree with giving away control of the association. Hindsight is a wonderful thing, and I think Barry has been unbelievable for snooker and everything else he's ever got involved in. He's a supreme businessman. He's transformed the lives of so many players through the opportunities he's given them. Looking back, it was something that needed to happen.'

Britain itself was by now experiencing a novelty in the form of a coalition government, the first since the wartime ministry of the 1940s, after New Labour's years of power were ended in 2010. The Conservatives under David Cameron were the largest party but needed the support of Nick Clegg's Liberal Democrats to govern. In snooker, there was similarly a new sense of pulling together for the common good.

After years of stagnation, it was now a fresh, exciting era, and into it emerged a remarkable talent. Judd Trump was a boyhood prodigy from Bristol, introduced to snooker by his father, Steve, a lorry driver who gave up his weekends to take his son to junior competitions around the UK. Blessed with innate ability, at eight years of age Trump won the Bristol league's division four individual title, and at nine and ten respectively the division three and two titles.

Still only ten, he reached the finals of the national Under-15 and Under-13 championships in the year 2000, played over a weekend in Gateshead. Coming into the event he had not lost a league match for 30 months. In the Under-15 final, Trump defeated James Croxton, a fourteen-year-old, 5–3 to become the youngest-ever winner of a national title.

Trump remembers first playing on a snooker table at the age of five. 'There was a club my dad used to go to called Snooker City in Bristol. I'm pretty sure I potted the first ball I ever went for, and he was a bit shocked,' he says. 'Every couple of weeks I'd be in the paper for winning tournaments. My dad used to take me everywhere. He was driving a lorry every day, and then he'd get up at 7 a.m. at the weekend and drive two hours to Leicester or wherever the tournament was. He'd never moan. I'd hopefully win and take all the prize money.'

Trump was a typically shy boy who, in snooker, found a world in which he could fully immerse himself. He loved playing, but his rapid rise had its challenges. At thirteen, he won the Pontins Open event in Prestatyn, beating former world number five Mike Hallett in the final. The bottle of champagne that came with the trophy was of no interest to him as he celebrated on the swings.

'There were times in the junior days, when we were at Pontins, when I'd have to go to bed a lot earlier than some of the other kids,' he says. 'At the time, you're kind of, "Why me?" My dad knew the talent was there and what he had to do to look after me and keep me away from the other kids, who were more easily led astray, playing on fruit machines all night in the arcade. At the time, I remember hating it, but looking back it massively helped my success.'

Trump turned professional at sixteen with a fair amount of hype, which he found difficult to ignore, but he was soon dealt a reality check. 'I remember watching it on TV and thinking they weren't that good,' he says. 'It was only the top names I had any respect for. The lower-ranked players I thought I'd breeze through. The first tournament, I was 2–2 with Fergal [O'Brien], and he won 5–2. That was the first time I thought, "These other players are actually decent." There were six tournaments and a Masters qualifier, so one-sixth of the season was already gone. Then Ding [Junhui] beat me 9–2 in the UK Championship, and I realised he was a completely different level.'

With few tournaments to play in, it was hard to get any momentum, but in 2009 he won the Championship League, a behind-closed-doors event for top players, before breaking through in style two years later, winning the China Open in Beijing, before a run to the World Championship final, firmly putting him on the radar as a new sporting star. His attacking flair, youth and adventurous shot-making made him a natural crowd favourite. Ed Miliband, the Labour Party leader, even tweeted his approval.

John Higgins beat him 18–15 in their Crucible final, but a new force had clearly arrived. 'I was struggling with my own expectations. I thought I should easily be delivering by then, but something clicked in China. There was something about that week, like a weight had been lifted off my shoulders,' he says. 'I went into the World Championship firmly believing I was going to win it. I just didn't think I'd miss. I wasn't scared of anyone. I've never been so relaxed in my life.'

Trump won the 2011 UK Championship and various other tournaments, but by late 2018, aged 29, was feeling he was not quite fulfilling his potential. Part of the problem was the age gap between him and the other leading players. With little besides snooker in common, he felt isolated. His younger brother, Jack, had been a promising player himself, winning the English national under-15 and under-13 titles, but did not pursue a professional career and became a greenkeeper at a Bristol golf club. He agreed to accompany Trump on tour, acting as a cornerman, helping to organise his schedule and being a source of inspiration, and if necessary, telling his brother some home truths.

'I struggled in China and other events because I was always on my own,' Trump says. 'I was doing so much better than people my age and I don't particularly mix with the older players because I don't think I have too much in common with them, so by the time I was getting to the last 16 in China I didn't really want to be there any more. It was very, very lonely. I didn't have the enthusiasm of even leaving my room and going to practise. It was holding me back. When Jack came on board, the intensity of the practice went up, and within a month I felt like a different player.'

He won the first event under their new set-up, beating Ronnie O'Sullivan 9–7 to win the Northern Ireland Open. Two months later, in January 2019, he outplayed O'Sullivan 10–4 to win the Masters. Later that season, he triumphed at the Crucible, becoming world champion with arguably the finest-ever display in a final as he made a record seven centuries in defeating Higgins 18–9.

'I had so much belief in myself,' Trump says. 'I knew I was

playing too well not to win, but John's record against me helped. I couldn't take my foot off the gas because I knew how many times he'd come back against me. There are a handful of times where you'll have a purple patch and everything is going in, but to do it in a world final, I don't think there's many players that have played as well after the first session for the whole rest of the game. It was pretty much faultless snooker. I was able to enjoy it because everything was so natural to me.'

Trump was world champion and became world number one. The following season, he won a record six ranking titles. The floodgates had well and truly opened. One of the first players to embrace the new world of social media, he was a perfect talisman for the changed times, but the old guard stubbornly refused to yield. In 2022, he reached the semi-finals of the World Championship to face Williams. O'Sullivan met Higgins in the other semi. The Class of '92 were still producing high-quality performances, and O'Sullivan remained the sport's biggest name. In the final, he beat Trump 18–13.

For all his successes, Trump's failure to add further World Championship trophies to his CV has left some questioning his status. In the new millennium, the World, UK and Masters titles – the 'triple crown' – became established as the sport's majors, in line with tennis grand slams, although historically this was not always the case. They were all broadcast by the BBC, which retained an elevated position in the broadcasting landscape through its free-to-air coverage. By 2025, Trump had won five of these titles, compared to O'Sullivan's 23. However, many other big, prestigious tournaments came to be added to the calendar. In 2024, Trump won the Saudi Arabia Masters, which carried the same first prize as the World Championship: £500,000.

'There's expectation because of the other events I've won, but people forget how hard it is to win,' Trump says of the World Championship. 'There's such a fine line from getting to the final and winning it. I've been in three finals, which is a pretty good achievement. I've only lost to Ronnie and John. Other players have had slightly easier draws. When I lost to John, I was young and naive, and when I lost to Ronnie, I had nothing left in that first session. I was probably the better player in that tournament, but I didn't have the momentum after the match with Mark Williams. He drained me; the amount of emotion that came out of that semi-final completely ruined me the first day of the final.

'For me, the goal was to win it once. I'd be slightly annoyed if I didn't win it again, but I'm not really that bothered. I know in my own mind how much success I've had in the game. Just because people don't consider it as good because of the TV channel it's on doesn't really mean that much to me. I'm not caught up in the records. I can only do my best. When my career ends, I'll know I gave it my absolute all. It wasn't through a lack of trying.'

Neil Robertson, with whom Trump has enjoyed an outstanding rivalry, has sympathy. Among their many high-quality matches was the 2019 Champion of Champions final, in which they compiled eight centuries between them. Robertson denied Trump a second UK Championship victory by beating him 10–9 on the last pink in the 2020 final. The Australian is keen to fight Trump's corner when it comes to discussion of which trophies he has captured.

'You don't get to choose the tournaments you play well in,' says Robertson. 'I find it crazy when Judd's criticised. I admire him. He really wants to focus on winning ranking titles. He wants to be number one for titles. He's great for the game, a really good ambassador for the sport. He plays properly. He plays to try and win. Some of the others are hard to break down when they're trying to stop you from playing, like a football team that sits in their own box and just defends. Judd's very aggressive, so you're never fully relaxed in your chair. I enjoy the excitement of that.'

Murphy, like Trump and Robertson, has completed the triple crown but recognises that they lag behind the likes of O'Sullivan and Hendry in the pantheon of all-time greats. He believes Trump has helped raise standards to such a degree that he is now a victim of them.

'It's a predicament I understand only too well because I'm in the same boat,' Murphy says. 'If he's anything like me, any time one of those majors rolls round, he'll give a pint of blood to get one over the line. Can Judd win more of them? Of course. The problem is, when you have a shining light like Judd Trump forcing everyone else to improve, you almost become a victim of your own success because you've made everyone get better. They all work harder to catch you up.'

Trump was the latest in a long line of ordinary guys made good. In 2024, another, Kyren Wilson, became world champion. His father, Rob, had multiple sclerosis, while his mother, Sonya, had been diagnosed with breast cancer. His wife, Sophie, suffered a silent stroke brought on by her epilepsy. This very human backdrop made his achievement all the more remarkable but at the same time relatable. Like Trump, like the other players with their names etched on the famous silver trophy, Wilson was someone who had found their place in the world through this slightly eccentric but skilful game that continued to enthral audiences.

With so many competing attractions, how has snooker survived the changing times and retained its appeal? 'It's not simple, but it's not complex like some sports,' says the BBC's Hazel Irvine. 'There's something compelling about the drama, and the essence of the sport is its quietness. With all of the shouting and the screaming and the bawling from every sport and every device, there's something charming about quietness and drama and engagement and absorption of tension. In every other sport there's someone shouting their mouth off. There's very little sport that is staged over such a chunk of time that allows you to absorb yourself in one thing at one time. Our lives are so ephemeral and so complex now, yet there's a simplicity to snooker, even though it's really difficult to play. And there's the personalities and the presentation of them, the feeling you are welcomed into this world and you don't have to be tribal about your allegiances. Thus, there is a purity about the sport that I think very few others have. There's something enduring about that.'

Snooker still had to embrace the modern world. As the 2020s dawned, Hearn secured lucrative online streaming contracts with Rigour in China and Eurosport in the UK and Europe. The World Snooker Tour poured its energies into a digital strategy, using social media platforms to spread the word to every corner of the globe. Professionals emerged from countries where snooker would once have been anonymous, such as Latvia, Switzerland, Ukraine, Malaysia and Iran. The global audience for the sport grew to an estimated 500 million.

Snooker even survived a pandemic. In 2020, many major sporting events were cancelled due to COVID-19, which saw much of the world locked down in an effort to prevent the spread of the virus. In this worrying, confusing time, Hearn saw an opportunity. Working with the government, his team devised a plan to stage a snooker event behind closed doors in Milton Keynes, broadcast on ITV. The public, stuck at home, were missing televised sport.

Strict protocols involving testing, a bubble environment, one-way systems and social distancing were enforced, and on 1 June 2020, the Championship League became the first sporting event staged in the UK since the lockdowns had begun three months earlier. With the Tokyo Olympics postponed, Hearn realised the BBC had two weeks' worth of empty schedules in the August slot cleared for the Games. Again under strict rules, the World Championship was moved to the summer, and snooker fans were able to witness O'Sullivan winning his sixth world title.

Players got used to Milton Keynes over the next year, as it was where most tournaments were held, even non-UK events such as the German Masters. It gave them a chance to earn a living and snooker fans something to watch from afar, until vaccines meant it was safer for crowds to return.

'It changed people's perceptions of what was possible but also made us appreciate what we had,' says Irvine. 'The 2021 [World] Championship was an important moment for all sport. It was the first time crowds had been allowed back in at any indoor venue in this country. We were paving the way, showing what was possible, and snooker should be congratulated for that.'

The COVID pandemic was another external problem to be dealt with, and snooker did. It had been buffeted by the winds of change for decades and somehow came up with solutions. Through it all, the Crucible's place in the bigger picture began to be questioned. A theatre in Sheffield that can seat only 980 people felt to some an anachronistic venue for the sport's biggest event, which could surely sell many thousands more tickets. Yet talk of moving the event to China never came to anything. Saudi Arabia has become the latest cash-rich location cited as a possible future home for the tournament.

Money talks, but memories nourish the soul. In the fight for snooker's future direction, the various protagonists could learn much from the past, from a century in which this humble game mushroomed from obscurity to international prominence, rooting itself deeply in the hearts of millions.

In 2017, Dennis Taylor appeared on the BBC's reality series *The Real Marigold Hotel*, in which a group of celebrities travelled to India. It was 60 years since he had first glimpsed a snooker table as a boy in Coalisland. As part of the programme, he was invited to visit the Ooty Club, where the rules of snooker were established in the nineteenth century.

Taylor, a national celebrity because of a game that began life in this former British Army outpost, found it a moving experience. 'The billiard room is just the same as it was back then,' he says. 'They have cues that are nearly 100 years old. They let me play on the table, and it was quite emotional. I thought back to where I started. Now, I was standing in the place where the rules of snooker were written. It was an incredible experience. Amazing.

'Just to think, if I hadn't looked through that door and seen the coloured balls on the green table, I'd probably be working in the town where I was born. Yet I have all these experiences and memories, my whole life, because of snooker.'

BIBLIOGRAPHY

Burn, Gordon, *Pocket Money* (Faber and Faber, 1986)
Cooper, Brendan, *Deep Pockets* (Hachette UK, 2023)
Davis, Fred, *Talking Snooker* (A&C Publishers, 1979)
Davis, Steve, *Interesting* (Ebury Press, 2015)
Doherty, Ken, *Life in the Frame* (John Blake, 2010)
Dott, Graeme, *Frame of Mind* (John Blake, 2011)
Everton, Clive, *Black Farce and Cue Ball Wizards* (Mainstream, 2012)
—— *The Embassy Book of World Snooker* (Bloomsbury, 1993)
—— *A History of Billiards* (English Billiards, 2012)
Gadsby, Paul, and Luke Williams, *Masters of the Baize* (Mainstream, 2005)
George, Colin, and Tedd George, *Stirring Up Sheffield* (Wordville, 2021)
Griffiths, Terry, *Griff* (Michael Joseph, 1989)
Hearn, Barry, *My Life* (Hodder & Stoughton, 2023)
Hendry, Stephen, *Me and the Table* (John Blake, 2018)
Higgins, Alex, *From the Eye of the Hurricane: My Story* (Headline, 2007)
James, Clive, *Glued to the Box* (Jonathan Cape, 1983)
O'Sullivan, Ronnie, *Ronnie* (Orion, 2004)
—— *Running* (Orion, 2014)
Parrott, John, *Right on Cue* (Robson Books, 1991)
Rafferty, Jean, *The Cruel Game* (Elm Tree Books, 1983)
Reardon, Ray, *Ray Reardon* (David & Charles, 1982)
Spencer, John, *Out of the Blue and Into the Black* (Parrs Wood Press, 2005)
Taylor, Dennis, *Frame by Frame: My Own Story* (MacDonald, Queen Anne, 1985)
Thorburn, Cliff, *Playing for Keeps* (Partridge Press, 1987)
Trelford, Donald, *Snookered* (Faber and Faber, 1986)
Virgo, John, *Say Goodnight, JV: My Autobiography* (John Blake, 2017)
White, Jimmy, *Behind the White Ball* (Hutchinson, 1998)
—— *Second Wind* (Trinity Mirror, 2015)

NOTES

CHAPTER 1
1 Clive Everton, *A History of Billiards*, 2012.
2 'How Snooker Started', *Snooker Scene*, September 2019.
3 *The Embassy Book of World Snooker*, 1993.
4 'How Snooker Started', *Snooker Scene*, September 2019.

CHAPTER 2
1 *The Story of a Champion*, BBC TV, 1976.
2 Clive Everton, 'Early Championships in the Age of Joe', *Snooker Scene*, September 2019.
3 *The Story of a Champion*, BBC TV, 1976.
4 Ibid.
5 Fred Davis, *Talking Snooker*, 1979.
6 Ibid.

CHAPTER 3
1 John Spencer, *Out of the Blue and Into the Black*, 2005.

CHAPTER 5
1 Alex Higgins, *From the Eye of the Hurricane*, 2007.
2 Ibid.
3 Robert Chalmers, 'Higgins Fights Back', *Observer*, 20 February 1994.
4 Ibid.
5 Clive Everton, 'Alex the Bad, Sad Villain of the Green Baize', *Sunday Times*, 1 April 1990.

CHAPTER 6
1 Crucible *Fanfare*, *The Stage*, 18 November 1971.
2 Colin George and Tedd George, *Stirring Up Sheffield*, 2021.
3 Ibid.
4 'Two Theatres in One', *The Stage*, 11 November 1971.

NOTES

5 Mike Watterson, 'The First Crucible', *Snooker Scene*, February 2016.
6 Ibid.
7 John Spencer, *Out of the Blue and into the Black*, 2005.
8 Terry Griffiths, *Griff*, 1988.
9 Ibid.
10 Ibid.
11 Ibid.
12 David Hendon, 'Terry Griffiths: 30 Years on from Glory', *Snooker Scene*, April 2009.
13 Clive James, *Glued to the Box*, 1983.

CHAPTER 7
1 Cathy Booth, 'Snooker's Sex Appeal Lures Women Viewers to British TV', UPI, 7 June 1983.
2 Byron Rogers, 'Screen: A Bad Year for Channel Trawling, *Sunday Times*, 21 December 1986.
3 'Grade Breaks with Snooker', Dublin *Evening Herald*, 16 May 1988.
4 Ian Edwards, 'Giving Air to Unorthodox Views', *The Times*, 26 February 1987.

CHAPTER 8
1 Bernard Levin, 'When Only the Ultimate Will Do: The Pursuit of Excellence', *The Times*, 13 October 1986.

CHAPTER 9
1 Jimmy White, *Second Wind*, 2014.
2 Ibid.

CHAPTER 10
1 John Goodbody, 'TV Trimming Its Most Popular Sport', *The Times*, 13 February 1990.
2 Anne Spackman, 'Shaping Sport's Future', *Sunday Times*, 19 January 1986.
3 Clive Everton, 'O'Sullivan a Big Tip for the Future', *Guardian*, 26 August 1992.
4 Ronnie O'Sullivan, *Ronnie*, 2003.
5 Clive Everton, 'The Trials of Cue-Ball Wizard without

Form – Ronnie O'Sullivan Begins His Final Attempt to Become the Youngest World Champion at the Crucible Tonight', *Guardian*, 20 April 1996.
6 *Snooker Scene*, January 1995.

CHAPTER 12
1 Clive Everton, *Black Farce and Cue Ball Wizards*, 2007.
2 Steve Acteson, 'Department Welcomes Drug Ban by Governing Body', *The Times*, 9 January 1988.
3 Clive Everton, *Black Farce and Cue Ball Wizards*, 2007.
4 Nick Harris, 'Why Higgins Should Start His 30th World Championship with No Stain on His Name', 24 April 2024. sportingintelligence832.substack.com.
5 Ibid.
6 https://wpbsa.com/governance/disciplinary.
7 https://wpbsa.com/wp-content/uploads/230606-WPBSA-v-Snooker-Players-Final-Decision.pdf
8 Ibid.
9 Ibid.

CHAPTER 14
1 Suzanne Wrack, 'How the FA Banned Women's Football in 1921 and Tried to Justify It', *Guardian*, 13 June 2022.
2 'Rebecca Kenna Quits Snooker League Over "Men-Only" Rule', BBC website, 26 March 2019.

CHAPTER 15
1 Television interview with the author at the 2024 Saudi Arabia Masters.
2 Kevin Mitchell, 'Jokers Who Drive Us Wild', *Observer*, 21 April 1996.
3 Tony Stenson, 'Even Ron's Dad Says: You're Out of Order, Son! It's Ebdon Next for Shamed Star', *Daily Mirror*, 2 May 1996.
4 Dan Rookwood, 'Ronnie Gives Hendry a Rocket', *Guardian*, 2 May 2002.
5 *The Edge of Everything*, Studio 99, 2023.

INDEX

Ainsworth, Peter 11–12, 13, 15
Asian Open 172–3, 177
Attenborough, David 36
Australia 38, 39–40, 42, 90, 102, 158, 167, 168, 169, 170–171, 221
  World Championship in 44–5, 79, 171
Australian Open 172, 207, 238

BA&CC (Billiards Association and Council Control) 27, 30–31, 43
BBC 26, 27, 46, 61, 63, 64, 84, 90, 93–4, 97–8, 150, 151, 261
  and female commentators 222–5
  see also Grandstand; Pot Black; and see World Championship, 1979 – present
BBC radio 21, 32–3
Belfast (UK) 56, 58, 221
Belgium 171, 172, 175
Benson & Hedges (sponsors) 43–4, 95
Big Break (BBC programme) 150
billiard halls 12, 26, 34, 48, 49, 51, 53, 197
Billiard Player (magazine) 10, 19
billiards 6–8, 11, 12, 13, 14, 15, 16, 17, 20, 43, 48, 55, 106, 217
Billiards Association 14, 17–18, 27, 30–31, 43
Billiards and Snooker (magazine) 35, 43
Bingham, Stuart 178, 205–8, 244
Birmingham (UK) 16, 18, 37, 39, 40, 57, 144, 216–17
Blackburn (UK) 68, 105–6, 119
Blackpool (UK) 25, 26, 70, 78, 124, 145, 146, 251
Bolton (UK) 58, 59, 160
Bradford (UK) 108, 196–7, 200
Brecel, Luca 175–6
British Legion club (Selly Park, Birmingham) 57, 59
British Open 66, 130, 149, 164, 174, 253
Burroughes Hall (London) 17, 18, 217, 219
Canada 40, 106, 158–64, 171

Chamberlain, Neville 8–12, 13
Championship League 175, 259, 264–5
Channel 4 93, 103, 112, 255
Charlton, Eddie 38, 40, 42–3, 44, 82, 110, 143, 160, 167
Chas & Dave 98
China 102, 151–2, 175, 176–80, 193–4, 208, 222, 236, 264, 265
China Open 177–8, 211, 251, 259, 260
Class of '92 143–4, 145–6, 149, 151, 155–7, 189, 239, 245–6, 252, 261
class and snooker 13–14, 15, 26, 49–50, 87, 179, 216, 231
COVID-19 pandemic 193, 240, 264–5
Crucible Theatre (Sheffield) 73, 74–8, 79–80
  and Women's World Championship 220, 221
  see also World Championship, 1979 – present

Davis, Fred 24, 25–6, 27, 28, 35, 36–7, 42, 50, 53, 77, 105, 183
  and brother 21–3, 25, 80
  myopia of 21–2
  and World Championship 79–80, 95
Davis, Joe 16–25, 26, 27–8, 33, 36, 42, 43, 50, 57, 76, 77, 105, 159–160, 183
  and brother 21–3, 25, 80
  dominance of 20–21, 24, 25, 217, 218
  professional titles 18–20, 21, 23
Davis, Steve 5, 41, 52–3, 63, 88–92, 102–3, 107, 143, 149, 151–2, 156, 166, 172, 182, 199, 203, 204, 219, 224, 254
  and Alex Higgins 60–61, 72, 186
  dedication/professionalism of 88–9, 92, 124, 245
  and Hearn *see under* Hearn, Barry
  impact of 204
  and O'Sullivan 140, 147, 241
  and politics 100

271

and popular culture 98–9
temperament of 188, 196
and White 133, 134, 171
World Championship defeat (1985) 109–21
World Championship wins 1, 91, 100, 104, 122–3, 139, 162
Devonshire Regiment 6, 8, 10, 13
Ding Junhai 176–180, 195, 213, 236, 259
Doherty, Ken 70–71, 136, 147, 148, 149, 151, 164–5, 176, 178, 183, 251
Donaldson, Walter 25–6, 27, 28
Dott, Graeme 169, 185, 208, 233, 238
Doyle, Ian 69–70, 123–4, 144, 148–9, 157, 250, 256
Drago, Tony 172, 174, 220
drugs/drug testing 65, 66, 110, 128–9, 154, 162–3, 164, 182–3, 189, 251
Dubai 148–9, 172

East, Trevor 62, 93, 97, 110, 111, 112, 116
Ebdon, Peter 83, 126, 135, 149, 155, 176, 178, 224, 231, 234–5, 245, 254–5, 257
Edge of Everything, The (2023 documentary) 240, 248
Edmonds, Ray 30–31, 94
Embassy (sponsors) 45, 73, 75, 83–4, 95, 219, 252
English Amateur Championship 14, 17, 34–5, 81, 206, 251
European Open 130, 171–2, 192, 203
Eurosport 2, 174–5, 186, 200, 225, 241, 264
Evans, Reanne 216–17, 220–221, 222, 225–7
Everton, Clive 19, 26, 28, 29, 34, 43–4, 54, 78, 82, 91, 94
  on Alex Higgins 46, 58, 60, 69
  on origins/development of snooker 6, 7, 12
  on O'Sullivan 137, 147
  on Reardon 42, 46

Field, The (magazine) 9–10, 12, 13–14
Fisher, Allison 219–220
football 93, 101, 108–9, 150, 180, 182, 203, 219, 223, 224

Foulds, Geoff 89, 184, 250
Foulds, Neal 52, 90, 96–7, 102, 107, 127–8, 133–4, 172, 220
Frame of the Day (BBC programme) 81
Francisco, Peter 158, 183–4
Francisco, Silvino 109, 110, 158, 163, 172, 173, 183–4

gambling 8, 13, 49, 50, 51, 52, 53, 89, 191
  see also match-fixing
Germany 164, 174, 188, 220, 237
Give Us a Break (BBC comedy drama) 97
Glendenning, Raymond 26, 36
Grand Prix 66, 107–8, 124–5, 141, 149, 169, 185, 189, 235
Grandstand 28, 29, 43, 46, 81, 84, 223
Griffiths, Terry 62, 63, 64, 66, 77, 80–85, 91, 92, 96, 98, 104, 107, 110, 129, 143, 160, 161, 172, 173, 184, 198–9
Gross, Ron 52, 58

Hallett, Mike 66, 130, 173, 198, 220, 258
Hearn, Barry 48, 49–50, 51, 53, 86–7, 109, 144, 172, 182, 206, 240, 243–4, 249
  and Steve Davis 88–9, 91–2, 99, 100, 102, 104, 111, 116–17, 119–120, 243
  and women's snooker 219, 220
  as WPBSA chairman 255–7, 264
  see also Matchroom Sports
Hendry, Stephen 1, 66, 67, 72, 123–7, 136–7, 143, 156, 166, 177, 207, 211, 223
  on Ding 178–180
  and Doyle 123–4, 148–9, 250
  impact of 125–6, 134–5, 151, 156
  and John Higgins 144–5
  and Mark Williams 151–3
  mentality of 124, 126, 127, 133, 135–6, 137, 188
  and O'Sullivan 147, 149, 229, 232, 233, 235, 246
  and Steve Davis 124, 125, 130
  and White 129, 130–133, 134, 136, 138
  as youngest world champion 69, 129–130, 254

INDEX

Higgins, Alex 1, 42, 45, 56, 57–73, 77, 82, 90, 98, 129–130, 143, 161
   and 1972 World Championship 58–9, 60, 73, 80, 106
   and 1982 World Championship 63–6, 70, 95, 119
   and alcohol/drugs 46, 57, 62, 65, 66, 67, 68, 70, 182
   erratic behaviour of 62, 63, 66–7, 68–70, 71, 72, 100–101, 181–2, 230
   fans of 57, 58, 61
   illness/death of 57, 71, 72
   impact of 57, 59–60, 70, 72, 164
   and Steve Davis 60–61, 72
   technical prowess of 58, 60, 61, 64, 72
Higgins, John 139–140, 141, 148–9, 150, 151–3, 166, 167, 177, 212, 253–4
   dedication of 144, 146
   and match-fixing 185–9
   and O'Sullivan 141, 149, 155, 230, 233, 235, 239, 245
   see also Class of '92
Hunter, Paul 137, 250–252

India 6, 8, 10, 50, 266
International Open 149, 172
Ireland 151, 164–5
Irish Masters 66, 67, 68, 137, 183
Irvine, Hazel 222–5, 235, 238, 243, 252, 263–4, 265
ITV 2, 27, 29, 62, 92, 93, 94, 97, 99, 103, 109, 223, 225, 257, 264

James, Steve 68, 130, 203
Jameson International 94–5, 107
Johnson, Joe 49, 62, 122, 128, 140, 143, 186–201
Junior Pot Black (BBC2 programme) 37, 202

Karnehm, Jack 94, 107, 161
Knowles, Tony 70, 95, 96, 98, 110, 181, 182, 198, 199
Kray twins 50–51, 147

Lee, Stephen 189–190, 191
Li Hang 192, 194
life pool 8, 13
Lindrum, Horace 21, 23, 27, 161
Liverpool (UK) 18, 201, 203, 204
London (UK) 43, 44, 50–52, 90, 165
Lowe, Ted 36, 38, 94, 99, 102, 114, 115, 116
Lucania chain 48, 50, 51, 86, 88
Lucania National (tournament) 88–9

McManus, Alan 54, 125–6, 132, 133, 139, 147, 241–2
Mahmood, Mazher 185–6, 187–8, 189
Manchester (UK) 20, 42, 43, 46, 66
Mans, Perrie 79, 80, 82, 158
Mary, Queen of Scots 7
Masters
   1979 80, 158
   1980s 61, 65, 125, 129, 162, 184
   1990s 125, 130, 143, 147, 152
   2000 – present 167, 169, 179, 192, 212, 233, 236, 251, 260
match-fixing 30–31, 167, 183–9, 190, 191, 192–4
Matchroom Sports 86, 92–3, 98, 101, 119, 146, 173, 219, 255
maximum breaks 27, 154, 159–160, 161, 162, 174, 201, 236–7
Meadowcroft, Jim 63, 94, 115
Meo, Tony 92, 98, 143
Mercantile Classic 100, 109, 131, 143, 167
Mountjoy, Doug 63, 91, 141–2, 161, 173, 206
Murphy, Shaun 54–5, 134–5, 207–8, 210, 213, 244–5, 252–5, 263

News of the World tournament 27, 28

Olympic Games 44, 179, 182, 222, 223, 224, 240, 265
origins/development of snooker 6–15
   and billiards 6–8, 11, 12, 13, 14, 15
   and British Army 6, 8, 10, 13
   and Chamberlain 8–12, 13
   and class 13–14, 15

and codified rules 12, 13, 14
name of 8–10
and Ooty Club (India) 10, 11, 50, 266
and pyramids/life pool/black pool/snooker pool 8, 12, 13, 14
O'Sullivan, Ronnie 1, 127, 137, 140–141, 145–8, 154–5, 175, 194, 207, 228–48, 251, 260, 261
and audiences 235, 236, 237
dominance of 228–9
fastest maximum break (1997) 154, 231
and father 146–7, 148, 165, 232
fines received 230, 235–6
genius of 61, 241–2, 243–4, 245–6
impact of 244–5
and mental health 154–5, 183, 231, 234, 235, 237–8, 240, 247–8
playing style of 156, 233, 240
and press 229–31
and Reardon 232–3, 234, 237
and Selby 211, 212, 214–15
see also Class of '92

Parrott, John 37, 41, 126–7, 130, 133, 149, 172, 201–4, 224
pool 55–6, 158–9, 220
Pot Black (BBC2 programme) 36–8, 44, 57, 76, 79, 82, 88, 101, 150, 219
impact of 37, 39, 47, 51, 53, 106, 164
Junior 37, 202
Premier League 235, 249
Preston (UK) 78, 106, 143, 147, 235
prize money 19, 91, 102, 104, 106, 180, 257, 261
Pulman, John 20–21, 28, 36–7, 39, 41, 59, 94
pyramids 8, 13, 15

Question of Sport, A (BBC programme) 93–4, 151, 204

Rea, Jackie 28, 37, 58
Reardon, Ray 24–5, 32–5, 36–7, 39–43, 71–2, 76, 143, 164, 254
and O'Sullivan 232–3, 234, 237

and World Championship 24, 39, 42–3, 44–7, 64–5, 79–80, 82, 110
referees 45–6, 70, 78, 114, 211
female 219, 222, 225
Robertson, Neil 156, 167–71, 173, 176, 185, 212, 238, 246, 252, 262–3
Robidoux, Alain 164, 166, 229
Romford (UK) 50, 53, 88, 89, 91, 205
rules of snooker 12, 13, 14
variations in 28, 180, 249

Saudi Arabia 180, 261, 265
Scottish Open 137, 175, 189, 211
Selby, Mark 168, 175–6, 179, 208–15, 238–240
Sheffield (UK) 58, 179, 192, 254, 256
see also Crucible Theatre
Sky 174, 220, 223, 249
snooker audience 57, 58, 61, 90, 92, 95, 96, 235, 236, 237
snooker balls 12, 28, 49, 180
snooker clubs 48–56, 70, 81, 104, 106, 125, 128, 139–140, 164–5, 201–2, 209
and class 49–50
and crime 50–51
decline in 55–6
and gambling 49, 50, 51, 52, 53
Lucania chain 48, 50, 51
'Snooker Loopy' (Chas & Dave song, 1986) 98
snooker plus 28
snooker pool 12, 14
Snooker Scene (magazine) 43, 75
snooker tables 46, 104, 123, 197, 200
social/political change 29–30, 38–9, 85, 97–100, 108–9, 113, 122, 149–50, 190–191, 218, 249, 257–8
South Africa 42, 107, 158, 171
Spencer, John 34–7, 39–40, 41, 42, 44–5, 58, 59, 78, 79, 94, 143, 160, 254
and World Championship 80, 82, 204
as WPBSA chairman 68, 184, 250
sponsors/sponsorship 43–4, 73, 75, 79, 93, 95, 99, 191, 219, 252
Sports Resolutions 190, 192, 193

INDEX

Stevens, Kirk 95, 98, 110, 128, 129, 143, 162–3, 164, 183
Stevens, Matthew 137, 153, 224, 254
Sunday Times 30, 69, 99, 102–3

Tabb, Michaela 222, 225
tabloid press 181–2, 185–9, 229–31, 234, 251
Taylor, Dennis 5, 37–8, 42, 82, 90, 95, 105–21, 143, 198, 204, 254
  and 1985 World Championship 5, 108–21, 196, 205
  and Alex Higgins 1, 67–8, 69, 106
  and the Crucible 76, 77–8
  custom-made spectacles of 106–7
  TV career of 94, 98, 184, 266
television 1–2, 21, 26, 27, 36, 38–9, 46–7, 76, 83, 111–12, 139
  and female commentators 222–5
  and match-fixing 30–31
  and snooker-based comedy 97–8
  viewing figures 5, 90, 92, 97, 109, 120, 131, 255, 264
  see also BBC; Eurosport; Sky
Thailand 102, 146, 172–3, 176, 221
Thatcher, Margaret 1, 38, 85, 87, 99, 100, 108, 122, 216
Thorburn, Cliff 63, 72–3, 76, 77, 78, 90, 102, 107, 110, 117, 143, 158–62, 163, 164, 176, 183, 201
Thorne, Willie 63, 98, 109, 124, 143, 149, 182, 206, 209
Thurston's Hall (London) 18, 22, 23, 25, 36
triple crown 229, 261, 263
Trump, Judd 156–7, 188, 207, 238, 240, 242, 258–63

UK Championship
  1970s 78, 79, 80, 84
  1980 60, 65, 90, 91
  1981 123, 198
  1983/1984 66
  1985 109
  1986 66–7
  1988 141
  1989 125
  1991 69, 130, 131, 204
  1993 147–8
  1994 148
  1998 152
  1999 136, 152
  2005 233–4
  2006 179, 235–6
  2008 185
  2010 188
  2011 260
  2012 212
  2021 175, 192
  2023 240
United States (US) 7, 220, 221

Vine, David 82, 93–4, 117, 124, 132, 223
Virgo, John 15, 41–2, 48–9, 59–60, 77, 80, 84, 96, 101–2, 118, 121, 133, 245–6
  TV career of 94, 150–151
  as WPBSA chairman 71, 101, 250

Wattana, James 137, 173–4
Watterson, Mark 41, 64, 75, 76–7, 79
Watterson, Mike 41, 73, 74–5, 76–7, 78–9, 84, 184
Welsh Amateur Championship 33, 35, 81
Welsh Open 70, 143, 149, 166, 188, 189, 212, 251
Werbeniuk, Bill 163–4
White, Jimmy 63–4, 95, 98, 102, 127–9, 139, 141, 169, 171, 172, 204
  and drugs 128–9, 183
  and Hendry 129, 130–133, 134, 136, 138
  and match-fixing 184
  popularity of 131, 132, 133–4, 230
Wildman, Mark 29, 55, 94, 127, 250
Williams, John 45–6, 70, 114, 115, 116
Williams, Mark 47, 133, 137, 152–4, 167, 175, 177, 188, 195, 250, 251
  and 1999 World Championship 152–3
  childhood/early career of 141–2, 143
  temperament of 153–4, 156
  see also Class of '92
Williams, Rex 21, 28, 29, 31, 37, 59, 80, 94, 141, 249–250

Wilson, Kyren 263
WLBSA (World Ladies Billiards and Snooker Association) 219, 220
women players 216–27
Women's Billiards Association 217, 218
Women's World Championship 220–221, 222
working men's clubs 52–3, 88, 216–17
World Amateur Championship 146, 165
World Championship
  first (1926) 18–19
  1930s 20, 21–2
  1940s 22–4, 25–6
  1950s 27–8
  1960s 29, 35–6, 106, 158
  1970 39
  1971 39–40
  1972 57, 58–9, 60, 80, 106
  1973 42–3, 160
  1975 44–5, 171
  1976 45–6, 73
  1977 73, 76–7, 78, 160
  1978 79–80, 158, 160
  1979 77, 81–2, 83, 90, 160
  1980 61, 63, 90–91, 102, 160–161
  1981 91
  1982 63–6, 70, 95, 119
  1983 66, 161, 162
  1984 129, 139
  1985 5, 109–21, 196
  1986 124, 196, 198–9
  1989 67, 68–9, 102, 104, 203
  1990 127, 129, 143
  1991 203–4
  1992 130–131
  1993 131
  1994 70–71, 131–2
  1995 132, 135, 184
  1996 126, 135, 229–230, 231
  1997 135–6, 154, 166–7
  1998 136, 151, 167
  1999 137–8
  2000 152–3, 207
  2001 154–5, 183
  2002 224, 232
  2003 167, 190, 239, 251, 252
  2004 233
  2005 54, 234–5, 252, 253–5
  2006 252
  2007 212, 239
  2008 236
  2010 169–170, 185
  2011 188, 239, 259–260, 261, 262
  2012 237
  2013 228, 238
  2014 212–13, 238–9
  2015 207–8
  2016 179, 213
  2018 239
  2019 260–261
  2020 239–240, 265
  2022 156, 240, 261
  2023 175–6
  2025 194–5, 248
  Women's 220–221
World Ladies Billiards and Snooker Association *see* WLBSA
World Masters 144, 219
World Snooker Tour 86, 191, 192, 193–4, 225, 256, 264
World Team Cup 67–8, 78, 164, 172
World Under-21 Championship 144, 165, 169, 176
WPBSA (World Professional Billiards and Snooker Association) 2, 31, 60, 66, 68, 71, 79, 101, 102, 145, 171, 172, 174, 181, 236, 249–250
  challenge to monopoly of 250
  and Hearn 255–7, 264, 265
  and match-fixing 184, 185, 188, 193
  and women's snooker 221, 222

Yan Bingtao 192–3, 194
Yates, Phil 53–4, 59, 67, 82, 89–90, 103, 127, 137, 141, 145, 154, 171–2, 173, 212

Zhao Xintong 192–3, 194–5, 248

www.ingramcontent.com/pod-product-compliance
Lightning Source LLC
Chambersburg PA
CBHW050341230426
43663CB00010B/1938